Dedications and Acknowledgements

I dedicate this book to my daughter, Caroline; my parents, Bob and Trudy; and my sister, Kay. Without their support, I could not do what I love.

I would like to thank the faculty and staff of the William E. Laupus Health Sciences Library at East Carolina University for giving me the support to undertake this project. I also would like to thank my co-author, Stacy Magedanz, for agreeing to write for this project—she is a great colleague and librarian. Thank you also to all of my English teachers, from the 1st grade through college, who taught me everything I know. Teachers of all kinds from elementary school to the university do indeed shape the future of the world. And for my friends and family, I thank you for being there for me.

–Jeffrey Coghill

To my mother, the English teacher, who taught me to love both reading and writing.

–Stacy Magedanz

CliffsStudySolver™
English Grammar

By Jeffrey Coghill and Stacy Magedanz

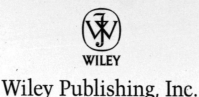

WILEY

Wiley Publishing, Inc.

Published by:
Wiley Publishing, Inc.
909 Third Avenue
New York, NY 10022
www.wiley.com

Copyright © 2003 Wiley Publishing, Inc. New York, New York

Published by Wiley Publishing, Inc., New York, NY
Published simultaneously in Canada

Library of Congress Control Number: 2003049739

ISBN: 0-7645-3766-0

Printed in the United States of America

10 9 8 7 6 5 4 3

1B/RQ/QW/QT/IN

About the Authors

Currently a medical librarian at East Carolina University in Greenville, NC, **Jeffrey Coghill** grew up an Army brat and graduated from Heidelberg American High School in Heidelberg, Germany. He went on to earn his B.A. in English from Methodist College in 1983, his M.A. in English from Western Carolina University in 1986; and his M.L.I.S. in library studies from the University of Alabama in 1997. He resides in Greenville, NC, with his lovely teenage daughter, Caroline, and his West Highland White Terrier, Alfie, a.k.a. "Alfred, Lord Tennyson."

Stacy Magedanz is currently a Reference Librarian at California State University, San Bernardino. One of her first jobs in high school was as a proofreader for her local newspaper. She earned Bachelor's and Master's degrees in English from the University of Nebraska-Lincoln, where she helped edit academic manuscripts while in graduate school. She spent two years as an editor and proofreader in the Office of the Reporter of Decisions of Nebraska Supreme Court and Court of Appeals before earning a Master's degree in Library Science from the University of Missouri-Columbia.

Jeffrey and Stacy were former librarians and colleagues at McNeese State University in Lake Charles, LA.

Publisher's Acknowledgments

Editorial

Project Editor: Suzanne Snyder

Acquisitions Editor: Greg Tubach

Copy Editor: Katie Robinson

Technical Editors: Tim Ryan and Jeannine Freudenberger

Editorial Assistant: Blair Pottenger

Composition

Project Coordinator: Ryan Steffen

Indexer: Tom Dinse

Proofreader: Mary Lagu

Wiley Publishing, Inc. Composition Services

Table of Contents

Study Guide Checklist

❑ 1. Take the Pretest, which will test your initial understanding of this workbook's subject matter.

❑ 2. Use the answer sections of the Pretest to guide you to the chapters and chapter sections you need to review.

❑ 3. Familiarize yourself with the content of the chapters you need to review.

❑ 4. Take the self tests provided in the chapters, including the Chapter Problems and Supplemental Chapter Problems located at the end of each chapter.

❑ 5. If, upon checking your answers to the Chapter Problems and Supplemental Chapter Problems, you find you have some errors, go back to the specific section(s) of the chapter and review the section(s) again.

❑ 6. Take the Customized Full-Length Exam, which tests your overall knowledge of English grammar. The Customized Full-Length Exam presents various levels of difficulty with directions on which questions to answer.

❑ 7. Review chapter sections as directed in the Customized Full-Length Exam.

❑ 8. Explore the Glossary and Abbreviations appendix.

Introduction

The grammar of a language is the set of rules that govern its structure. Grammar determines how words are arranged to form meaningful units. Every language has its own distinctive grammar, and people who speak a language from early childhood onward intuitively understand its structure in much greater detail than could ever be explained in one book. So why do people study grammar?

To understand the study of English grammar, it is helpful to know something about its history. Relatively few English grammar books existed until the eighteenth century, when the intellectual spirit of the Enlightenment prompted numerous writers to "scientifically" examine the English language. Unfortunately for future generations of students, instead of looking at what English actually does, most of these writers focused on what they thought English ought to do. With this idealized vision in mind, they set out to improve, perfect, and defend English. They based many of their rules about English grammar on the patterns of other languages that they considered to be perfect models—especially Latin and Greek—which had for centuries been the languages of science and learning in Europe. In some cases, they simply invented rules that appear to have been based on nothing but personal preference. These rules spread and were accepted as authoritative, regardless of whether they reflected how most people used the language. This was the rise of *prescriptive* grammar, which tells how English should be, rather than how it actually is. Prescriptive grammar is still alive and well. More than one self-appointed grammar expert has made a career out of lamenting the decline of the English language and criticizing other people's grammar "mistakes."

The modern science of linguistics, which studies the structure and function of language, has little use for the ideas of prescriptive grammar. Linguists focus on *descriptive* grammar, which simply describes how a language works and attempts to explain why. Descriptive grammar acknowledges that different types of language usage exist, but does not consider one kind of usage better or worse than any other kind.

So when we talk about grammar, we are really talking about two different things. On the one hand, grammar represents the deep structures of a language, the rules that govern how words fit together and how they do not. On the other hand, grammar also represents socially determined ideas about what is "correct." Most grammar handbooks include a mix of these two types of grammar. Grammar handbooks teach about basic grammatical structures, but they also pass on ideas about what is considered an acceptable use of language for a well-educated person. This book is no different.

Languages are much like living creatures; they are not always neat and logical, and they grow and change over time. Words acquire new meanings, and old words die out. A grammar usage that is acceptable in one century might be totally unacceptable in the next. Ideas about acceptable usage also vary among English-speaking countries; for example, an expression that sounds perfectly normal to an American might sound bizarre to an Australian. As languages grow and change, grammar rules also change. However, prescriptive grammar rules tend to become frozen in time, repeated by editors and teachers from year to year, even when the rules do not reflect the current practice of the majority of English writers and speakers.

In this book, we have tried to point out some of these old and outdated rules. We have tried to distinguish between rules that have to do with pure grammar—the structure of English itself—and rules that really state preferences about style. We have also tried to distinguish between formal, written English (where the rules are more strict) and the more informal, spoken variety of English (where the rules of conversational give and take are much looser).

Most people work with a variety of language styles (and sometimes a variety of languages) throughout their daily lives. English usage varies by geographic area, by ethnic or national group, or even by age group. A teenager from New York and an elderly farmer from Nebraska probably use quite different styles of language when they speak to their friends. Being able to recognize and correctly use the appropriate style of language for a particular situation is a real and highly valuable skill.

Students who are native speakers of English rarely think about the structure of the language they use. For these students, becoming aware of the patterns of their language can help them think in new ways about how they express themselves. The ability to write and speak in clear, simple, and engaging language can be learned, but not without examining the mechanics of English. Understanding grammar rules can help writers and speakers use language in a way that will make their ideas heard and help them communicate with the largest possible audience. Sophisticated writers and speakers also know when to break the standard rules to give their expression special impact. Understanding some basic grammar principles is also an enormous help to English speakers attempting to learn other languages whose grammatical structures might be radically different from English.

Students approaching English as a foreign language need a basic framework to help them learn it. English is such a rich language that no one could teach—or learn—all its marvelous variations. Studying basic English grammar provides a starting point for these students, one that will serve them well in many situations.

We, as teachers, editors, writers, and speakers of English, see great value in the study of grammar. We hope that the readers of this book will find it valuable as well.

Jeffrey Coghill and Stacy Magedanz

Pretest

Directions: Questions 1-1 through 1-10

Give the plural forms of the following nouns.

1-1. Analysis

1-2. Building

1-3. Porch

1-4. Reference

1-5. Cross

1-6. Absence

1-7. Speaker

1-8. Page

1-9. Man

1-10. Erratum

Directions: Questions 1-11 through 1-20

In the following sentences, give the possessive form of each word indicated.

1-11. _____ (Seattle) lights were beautiful at night.

1-12. _____ (Bob) and _____ (Tom) radio show is excellent.

1-13. The _____ (Evans) house was painted just this week.

1-14. My _____ (mother) and _____ (father) trip was cancelled because of bad weather.

1-15. _____ (Sandra) and _____ (Maureen) computers are not online today.

1-16. _____ (Joe), _____ (Matthew), and _____ (David) new telephones are in the warehouse.

1-17. My _____ (sister) new washing machine and dryer were delivered over the weekend.

1-18. By the sound of the last bell, the _____ (teacher) patience has worn thin.

1-19. A dog that belonged to the _____ (Davis) was found safe.

1-20. For now, _____ (Janice) work was halted to begin another project.

Directions: *Questions 1-21 through 1-25*

Use **a, an, the,** or no article to fill in the blanks.

1-21. _____ song was 15 minutes long.

1-22. His sweater was _____ herringbone pattern.

1-23. The platter was _____ imperfect shape.

1-24. She was paid $20 _____ hour as a tutor.

1-25. Jim was _____ useful and _____ purposeful person.

Answers: *Questions 1-1 through 1-10*

1-1. Analyses

1-2. Buildings

1-3. Porches

1-4. References

1-5. Crosses

1-6. Absences

1-7. Speakers

1-8. Pages

1-9. Men

1-10. Errata

If you missed 3 or more of the preceding 10 questions, study *plural nouns, p. 36.*

Answers: *Questions 1-11 through 1-20*

1-11. Seattle's lights were beautiful at night.

1-12. Bob and **Tom's** radio show is excellent.

1-13. The **Evans'** house was painted just this week.

1-14. My **mother** and **father's** trip was cancelled because of bad weather.

1-15. Sandra's and **Maureen's** computers are not online today.

1-16. Joe's, Matthew's, and **David's** new telephones are in the warehouse.

1-17. My **sister's** new washing machine and dryer were delivered over the weekend.

1-18. By the sound of the last bell, the **teacher's** patience has worn thin.

1-19. A dog that belonged to the **Davises** was found safe.

1-20. For now, **Janice's** work was halted to begin another project.

If you missed 3 or more of the preceding 10 questions, study *showing possession with nouns, p. 38.*

Answers: *Questions 1-21 through 1-25*

1-21. **The** song was 15 minutes long.

1-22. His sweater was **a** herringbone pattern.

1-23. The platter was **an** imperfect shape.

1-24. She was paid $20 **an** hour as a tutor.

1-25. Jim was **a** useful and (no article) purposeful person.

If you missed 2 or more of the preceding 5 questions, study *articles, p. 41.*

Directions: *Questions 2-1 through 2-5*

Select the correct option.

2-1. It was **she/her** on the phone.

2-2. The task fell to Sarah and **I/me.**

2-3. They/them will bring the ladder for **he/him.**

2-4. **We/us** chess players started our own club.

2-5. Michael and **I/me** met **he/him** and his sister.

Directions: *Questions 2-6 through 2-10*

Supply the missing words in the following sentences.

2-6. The man _____ gave you the bicycle is my uncle.

2-7. Those files _____ Mr. Miranda wanted are on my desk.

2-8. The candidate _____ you interviewed for the paper won the election.

2-9. The family _____ house burned down received community support.

2-10. I enjoyed the movie _____ you were watching on TV.

Directions: *Questions 2-11 through 2-13*

Select the sentence choice that contains no errors.

2-11. A. I like them cookies.
　　　B. I like that cookies.
　　　C. I like those cookies.

2-12. A. This new policy takes effect Monday.
　　　B. These new policy takes effect Monday.
　　　C. That new policies take effect Monday.

2-13. A. Which shoes are yours? This are mine.
　　　B. Which shoes are yours? Those are mine.
　　　C. Which shoes are yours? That are mine.

Directions: *Questions 2-14 through 2-18*

Supply the missing words in the following sentences, or select the correct option.

2-14. The flute belongs to Mrs. Chen. The flute is _____.

2-15. The dog belongs to me. The dog is _____.

2-16. The car belongs to us. The car is _____.

2-17. I know your/you're going to like him.

2-18. I did my part, now they must do theirs/their's.

Directions: *Questions 2-19 through 2-23*

Select the correct option.

2-19. Tim hurt **he/him/himself** lifting that box.

2-20. The boss gave **we/us/ourselves** the day off.

2-21. Chris **and I/me/myself** were asked to participate.

2-22. I don't have time; please do it **you/yourself.**

2-23. When the package arrives, please call Lu or **I/me/myself**.

Directions: *Questions 2-24 through 2-27*

Supply the correct form of the verb *to be* to agree with the subject.

2-24. Everyone _____ coming to the party.

2-25. Some _____ going, but others _____ not.

2-26. The few who came _____ not disappointed.

2-27. Nobody _____ asking my opinion.

Directions: *Questions 2-28 through 2-32*

Insert the correct word: **which, what, who, whom,** or **whose.**

2-28. _____ office is yours?

2-29. _____ idea was it to close the store early?

2-30. _____ is the solution to this problem?

2-31. _____ will the contract be given to?

2-32. _____ is working with Susan?

Answers: Questions 2-1 through 2-5

2-1. She

2-2. Me

2-3. They, him

2-4 We

2-5. I, him

If you missed 2 or more of the preceding 5 questions, study *personal pronouns, p. 51.*

Answers: *Questions 2-6 through 2-10*

2-6. Who

2-7. That or which

2-8. Whom

2-9. Whose

2-10. That or which

If you missed 2 or more of the preceding 5 questions, study *relative pronouns, p. 57.*

Answers: *Questions 2-11 through 2-13*

2-11. C

2-12. A

2-13. B

If you missed 2 or more of the preceding 3 questions, study *demonstrative pronouns, p. 60.*

Answers: *Questions 2-14 through 2-18*

2-14. Hers

2-15. Mine

2-16. Ours

2-17. You're

2-18. Theirs

If you missed 2 or more of the preceding 5 questions, study *possessive pronouns, p. 63.*

Answers: *Questions 2-19 through 2-23*

2-19. Himself

2-20. Us

2-21. I

2-22. Yourself

2-23. Me

If you missed 2 or more of the preceding 5 questions, study *reflexive and intensive pronouns, p. 65.*

Answers: *Questions 2-24 through 2-27*

2-24. Is

2-25. Are, are

2-26. Were

2-27. Is

If you missed 2 or more of the preceding 4 questions, study *indefinite pronouns, p. 67*.

Answers: *Questions 2-28 through 2-32*

2-28. Which

2-29. Whose

2-30. What

2-31. Whom

2-32. Who

If you missed 2 or more of the preceding 5 questions, study *interrogative pronouns, p. 70*.

Directions: *Questions 3-1 through 3-5*

Underline any direct objects and double underline any indirect objects.

3-1. She gave me her address.

3-2. The game was exciting to watch.

3-3. No one except me knew her name.

3-4. Gino asked us to go with him.

3-5. I called him a liar.

Directions: *Questions 3-6 through 3-10*

Supply the correct form of the verb indicated.

3-6. Every day, Carmela (walk) her children to school.

3-7. I (live) in Oregon for 10 years. Before that, I (live) in Canada.

3-8. By the time I arrive, everyone (eat) all the cake already.

3-9. I cannot help you right now. I (cook) dinner.

3-10. She called while I (shower).

Directions: *Questions 3-11 through 3-15*

Change the verbs in the following sentences from active to passive voice.

3-11. Margo is taking the dog for a walk.

3-12. Throughout history, influenza has claimed many lives.

3-13. George Washington Carver invented many products based on peanuts.

3-14. City regulations prohibit parking next to fire hydrants.

3-15. The detective will arrest the thief.

Directions: *Questions 3-16 through 3-20*

Supply the correct form of the verb indicated.

3-16. _____ the process beginning with step one. (repeat)

3-17. Kamilah _____ English in her spare time. (study)

3-18. The board proposed that the resolution _____ tabled. (be)

3-19. If she _____ available, she would tell you the same thing. (be)

3-20. _____ carefully to the next song. (listen)

Directions: *Questions 3-21 through 3-25*

Underline the verb in each sentence.

3-21. The plane took off on schedule.

3-22. I am looking forward to seeing New York City.

3-23. Turn the light off, please.

3-24. The police had given up hope of finding the missing boy.

3-25. Our car broke down outside of town.

Directions: *Questions 3-26 through 3-30*

Choose the correct option in the following sentences.

3-26. Next week, we **will/would** study modal auxiliaries.

3-27. We **should/might** not feed the wild bear.

3-28. If I **can/could** go, I will see you at the game.

3-29. She **can/may** touch her nose with her tongue.

3-30. I **may/would** be happy if I had something to eat right now.

Directions: *Questions 3-31 through 3-33*

Supply the correct form of the verb indicated.

3-31. _____ and _____ are her favorite activities. (sew, garden)

3-32. _____ wild mushrooms is never a good idea. (eat)

3-33. Please avoid _____ this memo to anyone else. (show)

Directions: *Questions 3-34 through 3-36*

Supply the correct form of the verb indicated.

3-34. We expect _____ the proposal by tomorrow. (finish)

3-35. The owners of the restaurant plan _____ the business. (expand)

3-36. His dream was _____ to New York and become an actor. (go)

Directions: *Questions 3-37 through 3-40*

Supply the correct form of the verb indicated.

3-37. I keep hearing a _____ sound in my ears. (ring)

3-38. _____ dizzy, she had to sit down. (feel)

3-39. Although _____ and _____, the book was still valuable. (tear, stain)

3-40. The mail had arrived, _____ good news from home. (bring)

Answers: *Questions 3-1 through 3-5 (Note: Boldface stands for the double underline asked for in the instructions for this section.)*

3-1. She gave **me** her address.

3-2. No direct or indirect object.

3-3. No one except me knew her name.

3-4. Gino asked **us** <u>to go</u> with him.

3-5. I called <u>him</u> a liar.

If you missed 2 or more of the preceding 5 questions, study *transitive and intransitive verbs: direct objects, p. 79,* and *indirect objects, p. 81.*

Answers: *Questions 3-6 through 3-10*

3-6. Walks

3-7. Have lived, lived

3-8. Will have eaten

3-9. Am cooking

3-10. Was showering

If you missed 2 or more of the preceding 5 questions, study *verb tenses, p. 84.*

Answers: *Questions 3-11 through 3-15*

3-11. The dog was being taken for a walk by Margo.

3-12. Throughout history, many lives have been claimed by influenza.

3-13. Many products based on peanuts were invented by George Washington Carver.

3-14. Parking next to fire hydrants is prohibited by city regulations.

3-15. The thief will be arrested by the detective.

If you missed 2 or more of the preceding 5 questions, study *voice, p. 107.*

Answers: *Questions 3-16 through 3-20*

3-16. Repeat

3-17. Studies

3-18. Be

3-19. Were

3-20. Listen

If you missed 2 or more of the preceding 5 questions, study *mood, p. 111.*

Answers: *Questions 3-21 through 3-25*

3-21. The plane <u>took off</u> on schedule.

3-22. I am <u>looking forward to</u> seeing New York City.

3-23. <u>Turn</u> the light <u>off</u>, please.

3-24. The police <u>had given up</u> hope of finding the missing boy.

3-25. Our car <u>broke down</u> outside of town.

If you missed 2 or more of the preceding 5 questions, study *phrasal verbs, p. 113.*

Answers: *Questions 3-26 through 3-30*

3-26. Will

3-27. Should

3-28. Can

3-29. Can

3-30. Would

If you missed 2 or more of the preceding 5 questions, study *modal auxiliaries, p. 116.*

Answers: *Questions 3-31 through 3-33*

3-31. Sewing, gardening

3-32. Eating

3-33. Showing

If you missed any questions between 31 and 33, study *gerunds, p. 120.*

Answers: *Questions 3-34 through 3-36*

3-34. To finish

3-35. To expand

3-36. To go

If you missed any questions between 34 and 36, study *infinitives, p. 122.*

Answers: *Questions 3-37 through 3-40*

3-37. Ringing

3-38. Feeling

3-39. Torn, stained

3-40. Bringing

If you missed 2 or more of the preceding 4 questions, study *participles, p. 124.*

Directions: *Questions 4-1 through 4-5*

Supply the missing coordinating or correlative conjunctions in the following sentences.

4-1. Monty _____ Richard are on the basketball team.

4-2. Use glue _____ tape to fix the torn poster.

4-3. After winning the race, I was tired _____ happy.

4-4. _____ Marie _____ Karen is the manager on duty.

4-5. They donated _____ coats and scarves, _____ gloves and hats.

Directions: *Questions 4-6 through 4-10*

Supply the missing subordinating conjunction or conjunctive adverbs in the following sentences.

4-6. We went for a walk _____ it was cold and windy.

4-7. Wait here _____ I get my coat.

4-8. She will meet us _____ her meeting is over.

4-9. The plan is good; _____ we lack the resources to carry it out.

4-10. You must revise this paper; _____ you will fail the course.

Answers: *Questions 4-1 through 4-5*

4-1. And

4-2. Or

4-3. But

4-4. Either, or

4-5. Not only, but also

If you missed any questions between 1 and 3, study *coordinating conjunctions, p. 135*. If you missed any questions between 4 and 5, study *correlative conjunctions, p. 137*.

Answers: *Questions 4-6 through 4-10*

4-6. Even though

4-7. While

4-8. After (or when)

4-9. However (or unfortunately)

4-10. Otherwise

If you missed any questions between 6 and 8, study *subordinating conjunctions, p. 138*. If you missed any questions between 9 and 10, study *conjunctive adverbs, p. 143*.

Directions: *Questions 5-1 through 5-10*

In the following sentences, underline the preposition or compound preposition.

5-1. Without a good second baseman, our team always lost.

5-2. Contrary to directions, it took an hour to finish the project.

5-3. She entered the interstate via the entrance ramp.

5-4. The lifeguard warned that beneath the surface there was an undertow today.

5-5. With my inheritance, I bought a new truck.

5-6. She admitted it was, among other things, an oversight.

5-7. An aircraft landed on the tarmac after midnight.

5-8. It was a squirrel that caused the power outage.

5-9. I came aboard the ship at a nearby port.

5-10. Their mascot was next to an elephant.

Directions: *Questions 5-11 through 5-35*

Underline the prepositional phrases in the following sentences.

5-11. The party was declared over by 12 p.m.

5-12. Because we waited so long, the waiter brought us an order of hors d'oeuvres free.

5-13. In addition to being a few minutes late, we were disorganized.

5-14. The field was called out of bounds by the referee.

5-15. Upon my return to Greenville, I will resume my normal schedule.

5-16. Jim went to Gainesville by way of I-75.

5-17. Gail drove toward the brightly lit gas station.

5-18. Within a few minutes, the group was ushered into the foyer.

5-19. Beneath the steps lurked a stray cat.

5-20. Contrary to popular belief, Robert was still a candidate for office.

5-21. I like to be around intelligent people.

5-22. Instead of leaving quickly, we lingered for another hour.

5-23. The boat floated alongside the pier all day.

5-24. The ball floated like a cork on the surface of the water.

5-25. In spite of a huge turnout, the concert was trouble free.

5-26. The concert sparked few incidents, apart from a few cases of lost concertgoers.

5-27. Throughout the night, workers came and went hurriedly.

5-28. A sign was put on the door in case anyone showed up.

5-29. Alfie was calm amid all the chaos.

5-30. We finished the course along with several others.

5-31. The orders were given out as per the instructions.

5-32. The cars were placed in front of the garage.

5-33. Tyler went into the ski lodge.

5-34. Our belongings were placed upon the roof for safekeeping.

5-35. They arrived via the U.S. highway that ran nearby.

Answers: *Questions 5-1 through 5-10*

5-1. <u>Without</u> a good second baseman, our team always lost.

5-2. <u>Contrary to</u> directions it took an hour to finish the project.

5-3. She entered the interstate <u>via</u> the entrance ramp.

5-4. The lifeguard warned that <u>beneath</u> the surface there was an undertow today.

5-5. <u>With</u> my inheritance I bought a new truck.

5-6. She admitted it was, <u>among</u> other things, an oversight.

5-7. An aircraft landed <u>on</u> the tarmac after midnight.

5-8. It was a squirrel that caused the power outage.

5-9. I came <u>aboard</u> the ship at a <u>nearby</u> port.

5-10. Their mascot was <u>next to</u> an elephant.

If you missed 2 or more of the preceding 10 questions, study *prepositions and compound prepositions, p. 151.*

Answers: *Questions 5-11 through 5-35*

5-11. The party was declared <u>over by 12 p.m.</u>

5-12. <u>Because we waited so long</u>, the waiter brought us an order <u>of hors d'oeuvres</u> free.

5-13. <u>In addition to being a few minutes late</u>, we were disorganized.

5-14. The field was called <u>out of bounds</u> <u>by the referee</u>.

5-15. <u>Upon my return</u> <u>to Greenville</u>, I will resume my normal schedule.

5-16. Jim went <u>to Gainesville</u> <u>by way</u> <u>of I-75</u>.

5-17. Gail drove <u>toward the brightly lit gas station</u>.

5-18. <u>Within a few minutes</u>, the group was ushered <u>into the foyer</u>.

5-19. <u>Beneath the steps</u> lurked a stray cat.

5-20. <u>Contrary to popular belief</u>, Robert was still a candidate <u>for office</u>.

5-21. I like to be <u>around intelligent people</u>.

5-22. <u>Instead of leaving quickly</u>, we lingered <u>for another hour</u>.

5-23. The boat floated <u>alongside the pier</u> all day.

5-24. The ball floated <u>like a cork</u> <u>on the surface</u> <u>of the water</u>.

5-25. <u>In spite of a huge turnout</u>, the concert was trouble free.

5-26. The concert sparked few incidents, <u>apart from a few cases</u> <u>of lost concertgoers</u>.

5-27. <u>Throughout the night</u>, workers came and went hurriedly.

5-28. A sign was put <u>on the door</u> <u>in case anyone</u> showed up.

5-29. Alfie was calm <u>amid all the chaos</u>.

5-30. We finished the course <u>along with several others</u>.

5-31. The orders were given out as <u>per the instructions</u>.

5-32. The cars were placed <u>in front</u> <u>of the garage</u>.

5-33. Tyler went <u>into the ski lodge</u>.

5-34. Our belongings were placed <u>upon the roof</u> <u>for safekeeping</u>.

5-35. They arrived <u>via the U.S. highway</u> that ran nearby.

If you missed 2 or more of the preceding 25 questions, study *prepositional phrases, p. 154.*

Directions: *Questions 6-1 through 6-5*

Underline the adjectives in the following sentences.

6-1. The green car flashed by our position.

6-2. The ocean has warm currents a few miles offshore.

6-3. Our ideal evening out is dinner and a movie.

6-4. They were flagrantly violating the law.

6-5. Karen is purposeful in her studies.

Directions: *Questions 6-6 through 6-10*

Underline the adverbs and explain their function in the following sentences.

6-6. Earl is rarely late for work.

6-7. On Tuesday, the new computer system will arrive.

6-8. The vase used to be placed there on the mantel.

6-9. The document was delivered speedily to its destination.

6-10. I sent my report to my boss monthly without fail.

Directions: *Questions 6-11 through 6-15*

Find the correct form of the adjectives or adverbs in the following sentences.

6-11. Becky is feeling good/better/well than she has in a few days.

6-12. The fun/funnier/funniest/more funny/most funnier thing happened to me on the way to work yesterday.

6-13. The good/better/best things in life are free.

6-14. Jeremiah said the recent bout with the flu was badly/worse/the worst he had ever had.

6-15. His teachers said he was articulate and intelligent/more intelligent/the most intelligent.

Directions: *Questions 6-16 through 6-20*

Find the adverbs in the following sentences.

6-16. I seriously considered the offer.

6-17. She rarely comes by the office in the morning.

6-18. The bicycle moved close to us quickly and smoothly.

6-19. We rode our scooters home leisurely from the park.

6-20. Our group has been shopping today.

Directions: *Questions 6-21 through 6-25*

Find the adjective or adverbial phrases in the following sentences and indicate each.

6-21. We moved carefully through the hedgerows.

6-22. Sam and Dave behaved as if they were rock stars.

6-23. They did not complete the assignment because the groups had been slow.

6-24. The cat was in the house.

6-25. She was happy with the plans.

Directions: *Questions 6-26 through 6-30*

In the following sentences, choose the correct comparatives and superlatives.

6-26. He was **funny/funnier/the funniest** person in our class.

6-27. She did **badly/worse/the worst** than she thought on the test.

6-28. We had gone **far/farther/the farthest** than we had anticipated.

6-29. Charles was **old/older/the oldest** brother in the family.

6-30. The parade was **large/larger/the largest** in parade history.

Directions: *Questions 6-31 through 6-35*

Correct the dangling and misplaced modifiers in the following sentences.

6-31. With the truck coming down the street, the car was in the way.

6-32. While running out for an errand, my car did not start.

6-33. I noticed the flat tire on my bike while outside.

6-34. When sitting down at the bar, a beer was waiting for us.

6-35. To do well at golf, a good set of golf clubs are necessary.

Answers: *Questions 6-1 through 6-5*

6-1. The <u>green</u> car flashed by our position.

6-2. The ocean has <u>warm</u> currents a <u>few</u> miles offshore.

6-3. Our <u>ideal</u> evening out is dinner and a movie.

6-4. They were flagrantly violating the law. (no adjectives)

6-5. Karen is <u>purposeful</u> in her studies.

If you missed 2 or more of the preceding 5 questions, study *adjectives, p. 161.*

Answers: *Questions 6-6 through 6-10*

6-6. Earl is <u>rarely</u> late for work. (the adverb *rarely* indicates the frequency of Earl's lateness)

6-7. <u>On Tuesday</u>, the new computer system will arrive. (the adverb *On Tuesday* indicates the time when some event is to happen)

6-8. The vase used to be placed <u>there</u> on the mantel. (the adverb *there* indicates the place where the vase was usually found)

6-9. The document was delivered <u>speedily</u> to its destination. (the adverb *speedily* indicates the manner in which a document was delivered)

6-10. I sent my report to my boss <u>monthly</u> without fail. (the adverb *monthly* modifies the verb *sent* and indicates that the report is given at a regularly scheduled time)

If you missed 2 or more of the preceding 5 questions, study *adverbs at work, p. 163.*

Answers: *Questions 6-11 through 6-15*

6-11. Becky is feeling <u>better</u> than she has in a few days. (comparative degree)

6-12. The <u>funniest</u> thing happened to me on the way to work yesterday. (superlative degree)

6-13. The <u>best</u> things in life are free. (superlative degree)

6-14. Jeremiah said the recent bout with the flu was the <u>worst</u> he had ever had. (superlative degree)

6-15. His teachers said he was articulate and intelligent. (if someone is positive in one instance, they are positive in another: *articulate* (positive case) = *intelligent* (positive case); the comparison should agree in number and case)

If you missed 2 or more of the preceding 5 questions, study *comparatives and superlatives, p. 170.*

Answers: *Questions 6-16 through 6-20*

6-16. I <u>seriously</u> considered the offer.

6-17. She <u>rarely</u> comes by the office in the morning.

6-18. The bicycle moved close to us <u>quickly and smoothly</u>.

6-19. We rode our scooters home <u>leisurely</u> from the park.

6-20. Our group has been shopping <u>today</u>.

If you missed 2 or more of the preceding 5 questions, study *adverbs, p. 163.*

Answers: *Questions 6-21 through 6-25*

6-21. We moved carefully <u>through the hedgerows</u>. (Adjective phrase)

6-22. Sam and Dave behaved <u>as if they were rock stars</u>. (Adverbial phrase)

6-23. They did not complete the assignment <u>because the groups</u> had been slow. (Adjective phrase)

6-24. The cat was <u>in the house</u>. (Adjective phrase)

6-25. She was happy <u>with the plans</u>. (Adjective phrase)

If you missed 2 or more of the preceding 5 questions, study *adjective and adverbial phrases, p. 168.*

Answers: *Questions 6-26 through 6-30*

6-26. He was **the funniest** person in our class.

6-27. She did **worse** than she thought on the test.

6-28. We had gone **farther** than we had anticipated.

6-29. Charles was **the oldest** brother in the family.

6-30. The parade was **the largest** in parade history.

If you missed 2 or more of the preceding 5 questions, study *comparatives and superlatives, p. 170.*

Answers: *Questions 6-31 through 6-35*

6-31. The car was in the way with the truck coming down the street.

6-32. While I was running out for an errand, my car did not start.

6-33. While outside, I noticed the flat tire on my bike.

6-34. When we sat down at the bar, we noticed a beer was waiting for us.

6-35. A good set of golf clubs are necessary to do well at golf.

If you missed 2 or more of the preceding 5 questions, study *misplaced modifiers and dangling participles, p. 175.*

Directions: *Questions 7-1 through 7-5*

Underline the complete subjects in the following sentences.

7-1. There were three sandwiches on the table.

7-2. Carrying your own backpack is required on the hike.

7-3. Lizards and birds have similar characteristics.

7-4. It is unfortunate that the skate park closed.

7-5. The soft, chewy brownies were irresistible.

Directions: *Questions 7-6 through 7-10*

Underline the complete predicates in the following sentences.

7-6. Jeffery enjoys reading and writing poetry.

7-7. The lamp broke.

7-8. He has dreadlocks that reach to his waist.

7-9. Either Tim or Henry will lead the practice.

7-10. The books fell off the shelf during the earthquake.

Directions: *Questions 7-11 through 7-13*

Underline any direct objects and double underline any indirect objects.

7-11. Roman gladiators fought lions.

7-12. We took my mother to the airport.

7-13. Dan bought Lily a corsage.

Directions: *Questions 7-14 through 7-17*

Underline the noun phrase, adjective phrase, or prepositional phrase in each sentence.

7-14. Preparing for a marathon is strenuous.

7-15. The painting hangs on the wall in the bedroom.

7-16. Dodging the raindrops, everyone ran inside.

7-17. The beehive, dripping honey, attracted a bear.

Directions: *Questions 7-18 through 7-21*

Are the underlined sections phrases or clauses?

7-18. <u>His ears ringing</u>, he moved away from the amplifier.

7-19. The sweater <u>that I knitted</u> did not fit him.

7-20. <u>The snow fell</u>, and <u>the fire crackled</u>.

7-21. <u>The trees lining the road</u> are willows.

Directions: *Questions 7-22 through 7-24*

Are the underlined clauses dependent or independent?

7-22. Mr. Hillis, <u>whom you met yesterday</u>, is a florist.

7-23. <u>The curtain fell</u>, and <u>the play was over</u>.

7-24. She is a good basketball player <u>even though she is not very tall</u>.

Directions: *Questions 7-25 through 7-28*

Are the following sentences simple, compound, complex, or compound-complex?

7-25. The chair broke when I fell on it.

7-26. While I tried to keep up, the phone rang nonstop, and customers kept coming in.

7-27. I did not want to miss the test, but I was too sick to go to school.

7-28. Dogs and cats make good companions and help relieve loneliness.

Directions: *Questions 7-29 through 7-33*

Change each sentence into the type indicated.

7-29. It is raining. (interrogative)

7-30. He went to the gym. (interrogative)

7-31. Are you going to the store? (declarative)

7-32. Did you call your mother? (imperative)

7-33. Are you wearing a raincoat? (imperative)

Directions: *Questions 7-34 through 7-36*

Change the following sentences from active to passive, or from passive to active.

7-34. The wind tipped over the garbage can.

7-35. Bees carry pollen.

7-36. Speeding is prohibited by state law.

Directions: *Questions 7-37 through 7-42*

Which sentence has no errors?

7-37. A. She speaks several languages. Including French, Chinese, and English.
　　　　B. She speaks several languages; including French, Chinese, and English.
　　　　C. She speaks several languages, including French, Chinese, and English.

7-38. A. James builds furniture he learned woodworking from a cabinet maker.

B. James builds furniture. He learned woodworking from a cabinet maker.

7-39. A. Saffron is an expensive spice, it flavors many Mediterranean dishes.

B. Saffron is an expensive spice; it flavors many Mediterranean dishes.

7-40. A. Dominating the landscape, Mount Fuji is visible from many miles away.

B. Dominating the landscape, you will see Mount Fuji from many miles away.

7-41. A. Either Ted or Paul has the keys to the supply room.

B. Either Ted or Paul have the keys to the supply room.

7-42. A. We have drive, ability, and we can get the support we need.

B. We have drive, ability, and the support we need.

Answers: *Questions 7-1 through 7-5*

7-1. There were three sandwiches on the table.

7-2. Carrying your own backpack is required on the hike.

7-3. Lizards and birds have similar characteristics.

7-4. It is unfortunate that the skate park closed.

7-5. The soft, chewy brownies were irresistible.

If you missed 2 or more of the preceding 5 questions, study *subjects, p. 184.*

Answers: *Questions 7-6 through 7-10*

7-6. Jeffery enjoys reading and writing poetry.

7-7. The lamp broke.

7-8. He has dreadlocks that reach to his waist.

7-9. Either Tim or Henry will lead the practice.

7-10. The books fell off the shelf during the earthquake.

If you missed 2 or more of the preceding 5 questions, study *predicates, p. 188.*

Answers: *Questions 7-11 through 7-13 (Note: Boldface stands for the double underline asked for in the instructions for this section.)*

7-11. Roman gladiators fought <u>lions</u>.

7-12. We took <u>my mother</u> to the airport.

7-13. Dan bought **Lily** <u>a corsage</u>.

If you missed 2 or more of the preceding 3 questions, study *objects, p. 190.*

Answers: *Questions 7-14 through 7-17*

7-14. <u>Preparing for a marathon</u> is strenuous.

7-15. The painting hangs <u>on the wall in the bedroom</u>.

7-16. <u>Dodging the raindrops,</u> everyone ran inside.

7-17. The beehive, <u>dripping honey,</u> attracted a bear.

If you missed 2 or more of the preceding 4 questions, study *phrases, p. 192.*

Answers: *Questions 7-18 through 7-21*

7-18. Phrase

7-19. Clause

7-20. Clauses (both)

7-21. Phrase

If you missed 2 or more of the preceding 4 questions, study clauses, p. 195.

Answers: *Questions 7-22 through 7-24*

7-22. Dependent

7-23. Independent (both)

7-24. Dependent

If you missed any of the preceding 3 questions, study *clauses, p. 195.*

Answers: *Questions 7-25 through 7-28*

7-25. Complex

7-26. Compound complex

7-27. Compound

7-28. Simple

If you missed 2 or more of the preceding 4 questions, study *sentence types: compound and complex, p. 200.*

Answers: *Questions 7-29 through 7-33*

7-29. Is it raining?

7-30. Did he go to the gym?

7-31. You are going to the store.

7-32. Call your mother.

7-33. Wear a raincoat.

If you missed 2 or more of the preceding 5 questions, study *sentence types: declarative, imperative,* and *interrogative moods, p. 202.*

Answers: *Questions 7-34 through 7-36*

7-34. The garbage can was tipped over by the wind.

7-35. Pollen is carried by bees.

7-36. State law prohibits speeding.

If you missed 2 or more of the preceding 3 questions, study *sentence types: passive and active voice, p. 204.*

Answers: *Questions 7-37 through 7-42*

7-37. C

7-38. B

7-39. B

7-40. A

7-41. A

7-42. B

If you missed 2 or more of the preceding 6 questions, study *common pitfall: frequently encountered sentence problems, p. 205.*

Directions: *Questions 8-1 through 8-31*

Punctuate and capitalize the following sentences.

8-1. The raiders scored first

8-2. Col johnson is the battalion commander

8-3. In the first place we were the first ones on the slopes that morning

8-4. No you cannot have another piece of candy

8-5. Caroline and sometimes Kristin are first in line to go to the water park

8-6. We could not help seeing that there were green blue and yellow colors

8-7. I used to live near 7400 Ramsey Street Fayetteville North Carolina

8-8. Dear Mr Jackson

8-9. The American Heart Association raised some 28679000 for research last year

8-10. She asked me where are you headed to today

8-11. In the nick of time we had our car back on the road nevertheless we got to the lodge later than we had expected

8-12. For now there were enough snowmobiles for us to ride in tandem pairs yet because we had some inexperienced riders the trip into the park was slow and methodical

8-13. For his thesis jeff wrote about several poets from the british romantic period Wordsworth the creator of the movement Coleridge the master of british romantic poetry and Blake one of the best practitioners of the art of poetic writing

8-14. Dear Mr vice president

8-15. Luke 2 14

8-16. Did you get the notes from class today

8-17. How could it happen she asked

8-18. Fantastic

8-19. Kims house was unharmed by the storm

8-20. The lewis dog hid from the neighbors who tried to catch him

8-21. The mens coats were removed from the cloakroom

8-22. The inspector generals decision was considered final and irrevocable

8-23. Tim graduated from high school in 80.

8-24. Its time for the group to begin its work.

8-25. Toms and Tims cars had to be repaired in the front driveway

8-26. The decision was final according to the FCC

8-27. For quite some time, Bill waited and later asked me what on earth are we going to do with one hundred dozen doughnuts

8-28. Which song do you like better Rock Around the Clock or Chantilly Lace

8-29. One of the main characters in the novel said It is better to have us here on the scene than down at the station

8-30. Sparta was a major city state in the mediterranean sea area

8-31. For how long did the situation have to go on for what reason did we stop our forward progress

Directions: *Questions 8-32 through 8-45*

Use capitalization and punctuation in the proper places in the following sentences.

8-32. sam adams will be the professor for this class.

8-33. The candidates came from california and oregon.

8-34. I saw soft drink advertising from pepsi and auto advertising from dodge.

8-35. When I traveled to europe, especially in france and germany, I was amazed at the number of people who spoke english.

8-36. The magna carta was signed in england in 1215.

8-37. When I go to washington dc I hope to visit the air and space museum at the smithsonian institute.

8-38. O for the love of mike, exclaimed the surprised teacher.

8-39. I want to one day be the commissioner of either the nfl or mlb.

8-40. He was a proud son of the south.

8-41. She was adamant about pressing her point when are we going to get this project started

8-42. Because of the visit by the royal family the local crowd expressed a great deal of pro british sentiment.

8-43. mars is sometimes referred to as the red planet.

8-44. Chaucers Canterbury Tales are among the most famous medieval poems.

8-45. After years of having americans in their midst, the natives had become throughly americanized.

Directions: *Questions 8-46 through 8-65*

Correctly use abbreviations, acronyms, or numerals in the following sentences; also correct the punctuation and capitalization.

8-46. The court case of jackson v nelson was heard today in judge harry comptons court.

8-47. dr marvin harris md was the leading pediatrician in greenville.

8-48. there were one hundred seventy seven miles from raleigh to asheville

8-49. gen allen johnson gave a speech about service to our country to students at grove park high school.

8-50. 2 new cars were brought to the car lot on memorial drive.

8-51. I bought a new vcr and dvd player at the electronics store.

8-52. Homer was a greek epic poet of the 8 century bc who wrote the iliad and the odyssey.

8-53. The flight was due to leave at 8 pm, est.

8-54. The ncaa made a ruling on working student athletes last week.

8-55. ve day is may 8 1945.

8-56. At the meeting, 87 members were present.

8-57. There were 34000 students at the university.

8-58. 15 million dollars were spent on the new arena.

8-59. One of the most famous speeches from shakespeares plays comes from hamlet, act 3, scene 1, lines 55 through 88.

8-60. Channel six has the best reception without cable tv.

8-61. The first astronauts walked on the moon on July 30 1969 from the lunar module eagle and the spacecraft apollo 11.

8-62. moby dick is a difficult novel for many high school students.

8-63. Use figure 5 to find the answer to the problems in questions two through seven.

8-64. The chemical symbol for lead is Pb and comes from the Latin plumbum, which was the lead weight used to determine straight lines in building.

8-65. Homo erectus is referred to in the new world encyclopedia as an branch of homo sapiens, now extinct.

Answers: *Questions 8-1 through 8-31*

8-1. The Raiders scored first.

8-2. Col. Johnson is the battalion commander.

8-3. In the first place, we were the first ones on the slopes that morning.

8-4. No, you cannot have another piece of candy.

8-5. Caroline, and sometimes Kristin, are first in line to go to the water park.

8-6. We could not help seeing that there were green, blue, and yellow colors.

8-7. I used to live near 7400 Ramsey Street, Fayetteville, North Carolina.

8-8. Dear Mr. Jackson,

8-9. The American Heart Association raised some $28,679,000 for research last year.

8-10. She asked me, "Where are you headed to today?"

8-11. In the nick of time, we had our car back on the road; nevertheless, we got to the lodge later than we had expected.

8-12. For now there were enough snowmobiles for us to ride in tandem pairs; yet, because we had some inexperienced riders, the trip into the park was slow and methodical.

8-13. For his thesis Jeff wrote about several poets from the British Romantic period, Wordsworth, the creator of the movement; Coleridge, the master of British Romantic poetry; and Blake, one of the best practitioners of the art of poetic writing.

8-14. Dear Mr. Vice President:

8-15. Luke 2:14

8-16. Did you get the notes from class today?

8-17. "How could it happen?" she asked.

8-18. Fantastic!

8-19. Kim's house was unharmed by the storm.

8-20. The Lewis' dog hid from the neighbors who tried to catch him.

8-21. The men's coats were removed from the cloakroom.

8-22. The Inspector General's decision was considered final and irrevocable.

8-23. Tim graduated from high school in '80.

8-24. It's time for the group to begin its work.

8-25. Tom's and Tim's cars had to be repaired in the front driveway.

8-26. The decision was final according to the F.C.C.

OR

The decision was final according to the FCC.

8-27. For quite some time, Bill waited and later asked me, "What on earth are we going to do with one hundred dozen doughnuts?"

8-28. Which song do you like better, "Rock Around the Clock" or "Chantilly Lace"?

8-29. One of the main characters in the novel said, "It is better to have us here on the scene than down at the station."

8-30. Sparta was a major city-state in the Mediterranean Sea area.

8-31. For how long did the situation have to go on? For what reason did we stop our forward progress?

If you missed more than 12 of the preceding 31 questions, study *Chapter 8: Punctuation, Capitalization, and Other Issues, pp. 227–270.*

Answers: *Questions 8-32 through 8-45*

8-32. Sam Adams will be the professor for this class.

8-33. The candidates came from California and Oregon.

8-34. I saw soft drink advertising from Pepsi and auto advertising from Dodge.

8-35. When I traveled to Europe, especially in France and Germany, I was amazed at the number of people who spoke English.

8-36. The Magna Carta was signed in England in 1215.

8-37. When I go to Washington, DC, I hope to visit the Air and Space Museum at the Smithsonian Institute.

8-38. "O, for the love of Mike!" exclaimed the surprised teacher.

8-39. I want to one day be the commissioner of either the NFL or MLB.

8-40. He was a proud son of the South.

8-41. She was adamant about pressing her point, "When are we going to get this project started?"

8-42. Because of the visit by the royal family, the local crowd expressed a great deal of pro-British sentiment.

8-43. Mars is sometimes referred to as the Red Planet.

8-44. Chaucer's *Canterbury Tales* are among the most famous medieval poems.

8-45. After years of having Americans in their midst, the natives had become thoroughly Americanized.

If you missed more than 6 of the preceding 14 questions, study *Chapter 8: Punctuation, Capitalization, and Other Issues, pp. 227–270.*

Answers: *Questions 8-46 through 8-65*

8-46. The court case of *Jackson v. Nelson* was heard today in Judge Harry Compton's court.

8-47. Dr. Marvin Harris was the leading pediatrician in Greenville.

OR

Marvin Harris, M.D. was the leading pediatrician in Greenville.

8-48. There are one hundred seventy seven miles from Raleigh to Asheville.

OR

There are 177 miles from Raleigh to Asheville.

8-49. Gen. Allen Johnson gave a speech about service to our country to students at Grove Park High School.

8-50. Two new cars were brought to the car lot on Memorial Drive.

8-51. I bought a new VCR and DVD player at the electronics store.

8-52. Homer was a Greek epic poet of the 8th century B.C. who wrote the *Iliad* and the *Odyssey*.

OR

Homer was a Greek epic poet of the 8th century B.C. who wrote the Iliad and the Odyssey.

8-53. The flight was due to leave at 8 p.m., EST.

8-54. The NCAA made a ruling on working student athletes last week.

8-55. VE Day is May 8, 1945.

OR

V-E Day is May 8, 1945.

8-56. At the meeting, eighty-seven members were present.

8-57. There were 34,000 students at the university.

8-58. Fifteen million dollars were spent on the new arena.

8-59. One of the most famous speeches from Shakespeare's plays comes from *Hamlet,* Act 3, Scene 1, lines 55 through 88.

OR

One of the most famous speeches from Shakespeare's plays comes from *Hamlet,* Act 3, Scene 1, ll. 55–88.

8-60. Channel 6 has the best reception without cable TV.

8-61. The first astronauts walked on the moon on July 30, 1969, from the lunar module *Eagle* and the spacecraft *Apollo 11*.

OR

The first astronauts walked on the moon on July 30, 1969, from the lunar module <u>Eagle</u> and the spacecraft <u>Apollo 11</u>.

8-62. *Moby-Dick* is a difficult novel for many high school students.

OR

<u>Moby-Dick</u> is a difficult novel for many high school students.

8-63. Use *Figure 5* to find the answer to the problems in questions two through seven.

8-64. The chemical symbol for lead is *Pb* and comes from the Latin *plumbum*, which was the lead weight used to determine straight lines in building.

8-65. *Homo erectus* is referred to in the *New World Encyclopedia* as a branch of *homo sapiens*, now extinct.

If you missed more than 7 of the preceding 20 questions, study *Chapter 8: Punctuation, Capitalization, and Other Issues, pp. 227–270.*

Chapter 1
Nouns and Articles

Nouns make up the basic elements of the English language. Together with verbs, nouns form the basic components of nearly all sentence structures. Nouns have traditionally been known as persons, places, or things; but they can be other things as well. The following examples show the noun types and how they are typically used in sentences.

❑ **Persons**

John F. Kennedy was president during the Cuban Missile Crisis.

Melville received advice from *Hawthorne* while writing his novel.

❑ **Places**

Chicago is one of my favorite cities to visit.

Argentina is a country of wondrous beauty.

Louisiana ranks as one of the top states to visit in the country.

❑ **Things**

A *car* is necessary to get around town.

Football is a great sport.

Baseball has been very good to me.

❑ **Activities**

Horseback riding is popular the world over. (*Riding* is considered a gerund [see gerunds, p. 120]. *Horseback riding* is the noun in this sentence.)

He took *writing* to a new level.

Jeff enjoys *flying* airplanes.

❑ **Collections**

Congress is now in session.

A *committee* was appointed to resolve the differences.

We participated in a *team* exercise.

❑ **Concepts**

Liberty is the basis of all freedoms.

Equality was at the forefront of our discussions.

Freedom is not free.

❑ **Conditions**

Democracy is the basis of our government.

Monarchy is the rule of a country by a king or queen.

Socialism focuses on social ownership, not private ownership, of industry.

❑ **Events**

The *Civil War* was fought between 1861 and 1865.

The *birthday party* went very well.

Everyone went to the *concert* and had a good time.

❑ **Groups**

The *VFW* had their meeting on Tuesday night.

The *American Medical Association* released a statement to the news media.

I attended a conference of the *American Library Association*.

❑ **Qualities**

Even at age fifty-six, he could be *childlike* in his *enthusiasm*.

Articles are a unique type of adjective. Amazingly, there are only three articles used in the English language: **the, a,** and **an.** Without these articles, references to everyday, mundane objects would be difficult.

Types of Nouns

Proper nouns name specific persons or concepts. There are instances when nouns are used in a nonspecific way, when not referring to formal or proper nouns. Collective nouns refer to groups of collected nouns. These collective groupings demonstrate that nouns can be both singular or plural depending on use. The goal is to develop a better understanding of nouns and how they are used in sentences.

Proper Nouns

Nouns that name a specific person, place, thing, particular event, or group are called **proper nouns** and are always capitalized. If the noun is nonspecific, that is, the noun refers to a general idea and not a specific person, place, or thing, it is usually not a proper noun, so it is not capitalized.

Specific	*Nonspecific*
Linda Pearson	A woman
World War II	A war
French class	A class
The Great Depression	An era
The American Bar Association	The association
The Alan Parsons Project	The band

Collective Nouns

Nouns that refer to a specific group of persons or things are called **collective nouns;** see the list that follows.

group	club	team	committee	congress
jury	swarm	herd	flock	legislature
class	school	couple	city	congregation

Collective nouns are usually singular, except when referring to the individual members of a group.

> *Singular:* The **committee agrees** with the recommendation. (In this sentence, the reference is to the committee as a whole, not the committee's individual members.)
>
> *Individual members:* The **committee members agree** with the recommendation. (In this sentence, we are referring to all the individual members of the group, not the committee as a whole.)

Also, some collective nouns are considered both singular and plural, depending on their use in a sentence. For instance:

> *Singular:* The **jury is** deliberating.
>
> *Individual members:* The **jury** took **their seats.**

Companies take a singular verb.

> **Kraft Foods** manufactures more than eighty types of cheese.

Musical groups, on the other hand, take a plural verb.

> The Police **are releasing** a new greatest hits CD.
> The Wallflowers **are playing** at the concert hall tonight.

Count versus Noncount Nouns

Count nouns are nouns that represent individual countable items and cannot be seen as a mass or group. Count nouns have both singular and plural forms; their plural is usually formed by adding **–s** or **–es** to the end of the singular form. A few examples of count nouns include: an *atom,* two *atoms;* a *book,* two *books;* a *watch;* two *watches;* and a *child,* two *children.*

Noncount nouns represent abstract concepts, a collection, a group, or a mass and do not have an individual state of being. Many only have a singular form. Some of these nouns include:

> advice
> furniture
> fun
> grammar
> happiness
> junk
> mail
> news
> traffic
> engineering

Note that these nouns do not form plurals. Instead, articles, prepositions, and other modifiers are used to indicate an amount. For instance:

I need a single piece of **advice.**

I would like some **advice.**

I would like all the **advice** you have.

Noncount nouns take the singular demonstrative pronouns *this* and *that*; they never take the plural pronouns *these* and *those*.

Incorrect: Thank you for those advice.

Correct: Thank you for that advice.

Some words are both count and noncount, depending on their usage and the particular definition of the word you are using. Following are a few examples.

Noncount: Last night I ate **fish.** (It is incorrect to say "fishes" in this context.)

Count: There are seven species of fishes in this lake. (When speaking of specific species, **fish** takes the plural **fishes,** making it a count noun.)

Noncount: The windows have twelve panes of **glass.** (When referring to the material **glass,** no plural is used.)

Count: I washed all the **glasses** after the party. (When referring to something you drink out of, **glass** can take the plural form **glasses.**)

Noncount: Tracy has the **experience** needed for the job. (When referring to the abstract concept of experience, it does not take a plural.)

Count: Tracy has had many great **experiences** as a camp counselor. (When referring to specific incidents, **experience** can take the plural form **experiences.**)

Plural Nouns

The usual construction of plural nouns from singular nouns is to add **–s** or **–es** to the end of a word.

Singular	Plural
bird	birds
dog	dogs
cat	cats
glass	glasses
house	houses
kindness	kindnesses (add **–es** to words that end in **–s.**)

How do you know when to add **–s** or **–es?** If a noun ends in any ending but an **–s** or **–ss,** add **–es** to the end of that word to form the plural. Also, If a word ends in **ch, sh, x,** or **z,** add **–es** to the end of the noun:

Singular	Plural
lunch	lunches (add **-es**)
countess	countesses (add **-es**)
lens	lenses (add **-es**)
fish	fishes (add **-es**)
fox	foxes (add **-es**)
buzz	buzzes (add **-es**)

If a word ends in **–y,** change the **y** to **i** and then add **–es** to create the plural, as shown below.

Singular	Plural
baby	babies
sky	skies
library	libraries

Please note the irregular plural nouns, shown in the following table.

Singular irregular nouns	Plural irregular nouns
child	children
foot	feet
goose	geese
man	men
moose	moose
mouse	mice
ox	oxen
woman	women

Hyphenated nouns are pluralized by adding **–s** to the noun. In the examples below, **law** is also a noun. If a word is most likely to be multiplied, it takes the plural; thus, it is not that there is one **mother** and many **laws,** but many **mothers.** (For use of possession with plurals, see showing possession with nouns, p. 38.)

Singular irregular nouns	Plural irregular nouns
mother-in-law	mothers-in-law
father-in-law	fathers-in-law
sister-in-law	sisters-in-law
brother-in-law	brothers-in-law

For words that are derived from foreign languages, watch the singular and plural for proper use. If a Latin word, for instance, ends in **–um,** it will change to **–a**; a word ending in **–us** will change to **–i.**

Singular Latin word	Plural Latin word
alumna	alumnae (female)
alumnus	alumni (male) (gender neutral, informal: alum)
datum	data
erratum	errata
medium	media
memorandum	memoranda or memorandums
phenomenon	phenomena
stimulus	stimuli

Exceptions exist, of course. Consult a dictionary for the proper use of singular and plural Latin-derived nouns.

Showing Possession with Nouns

Showing possession with nouns demonstrates ownership of an object or idea. Possession can also demonstrate a close relationship between two ideas or concepts. Simply add **'s** to a noun for possession.

> John's car, Susan's cat, Caroline's pencil

The exception to this rule is when plural nouns end in **–s** or **–z.** In these cases, the apostrophe can be used alone (apostrophes, p. 239).

> Paris's lights, OR Paris' lights
> Jesus's teachings, OR Jesus' teachings
> Reeves's dog, OR Reeves' dog
> Charles's book, OR Charles' book

For a detailed discussion about possessive pronouns, please refer to possessive pronouns, p. 63.

Unusual Constructions

If a possessive noun sounds awkward, it might be necessary to change the word order or reword the phrase for better effect. In such an instance, an **of** construction can be used for clarity.

Awkward	Better
The page's top	The top of the page
Keats's poems	The poems of Keats
Emma's characters	The characters of Austen's *Emma*

Joint Ownership

When showing possession for compound constructions, the placement of the **apostrophe-s ('s)** indicates who owns or possesses an object. If the **'s** is in the wrong place, the meaning can change accordingly (apostrophes, p. 239).

> The **Sergeant Major's desk** is covered in Army decorations. (In this case, the singular Sergeant Major has an ornate desk.)
>
> The **Sergeants Major's desk** is covered in Army decorations. (In this case, the plural Sergeants Major share an ornate desk.)
>
> *A word of caution:* You can become entangled in possession and plural possession if both are used simultaneously. The plural of *Sergeant Major* should either be *Sergeants Major* (probably most accurate) or *Sergeant Majors*. The plural possessive would then be either *Sergeants Major's* (probably most accurate) or *Sergeants's Major* (although this seems really awkward). The awkwardness of these possessive forms is a good reason to recast the sentence using the construction *of the Sergeants Major*. Regardless of your use, make sure you are consistent.

The following examples show possession by joint ownership.

> My mother and father's house
>
> My brother and sister's treehouse

To show ownership of two or more objects by two or more different entities, designate ownership by each.

> Chuck's and Terry's gym bags
>
> My mother's and father's houses
>
> Tom's and Sue's tennis rackets
>
> Sue's, Vince's, and Cal's golf clubs

Example Problems

In the following sentences, give the possessive case of the noun in parentheses.

1. _____ (Charles) boat was in the water at the dock.

   Answer: Charles's boat was in the water at the dock.

2. We found _____ (Mike) bookbag in the gym.

   Answer: We found Mike's bookbag in the gym. Just add the –**'s** to the person's name.

3. My next-door _____ (neighbor) dog escaped from the house.

   Answer: My next-door neighbor's dog escaped from the house. Just add the –**'s** to the word neighbor.

4.   _____ (John) and _____ (Sarah) barbeque was the highlight of the summer.

Answer: John and Sarah's barbeque was the highlight of the summer. We are showing joint ownership in this sentence. Since the barbeque was hosted by this couple, we need only to show possession after the second person mentioned.

5.   The _____ (men) teams rode separate buses.

Answer: The men's teams rode separate buses. In this sentence, we see the plural of *man* as *men* and possession of the plural by the *men's teams*.

Work Problems

In the following sentences, give the possessive case of the noun in parentheses.

1.   Most _____ (men) teams are very good.

2.   _____ (Monet) paintings are beautiful to see.

3.   The _____ (children) shoe department was at the back of the store.

4.   _____ (Jeff) shirt will need ironing.

5.   _____ (Joe) and _____ (Shannon) house was a great place to have a party.

6.   The _____ (America Cup) was won by the United States.

Worked Solutions

1.   Most men's teams are very good. (In this sentence, **men's** is correct because we are referring to plural of man and the plural possessive of men's teams.)

2.   Monet's paintings are beautiful to see. (In this sentence, **Monet's** is correct because the paintings belonged to [or were possessed by] Monet.)

3.   The children's shoe department was at the back of the store. (Here, since there is more than one department, we have the word **children's** in possession of the shoes.)

4.   Jeff's shirt will need ironing. (In this sentence, since Jeff owns the shirt, we show possession by adding the –**'s** construction to show ownership.)

5.   Joe and Shannon's house was a great place to have a party. (It's **Joe** and **Shannon's** because we are showing joint ownership. Also, since the couple owns one house together, we only need to show ownership by one part of the couple, not both of them individually.)

6.   The America's Cup was won by the United States. (It's **America's Cup** because the proper name for the cup is the America's Cup and the ownership is demonstrated by the first winner of the cup. Also, the America's Cup was first won in 1851 by the sailing ship *America* against the competition of 16 British ships. The *America* won, hence the name.)

Noun-Verb Agreement

Nouns and verbs must agree in number. A singular noun must be used with a singular verb.

> My **sister is** an auditor. (Single noun **sister** agrees with single verb **is.**)
>
> The **car is parked** at the used car lot. (Single noun **car** agrees with single verb **is parked.**)

Likewise, a plural noun must be used with a plural verb for there to be agreement (subjects, p. 184; lack of agreement, p. 214).

> My **sisters are** accountants. (Plural noun **sisters** agrees with plural verb **are.**)
>
> The **cars are parked** at the used car lot. (Plural noun **cars** agrees with plural verb **are parked.**)

This topic is covered more fully in Chapter 7, where the reader will find a detailed discussion and example problems to cover subject-verb agreement.

Articles

Articles are a unique type of adjective. Only three articles are used in English: **the, a,** and **an.** Articles always precede any other adjectives modifying the noun.

Indefinite Articles

A is called the **indefinite article. A** refers to an unspecified or unknown thing. It can also indicate a single thing or one out of many. **A** never refers to plural nouns.

> Is that car **a** 1969 Mustang?
>
> My sister wants to be **a** doctor.
>
> I need to buy **a** cookie sheet.
>
> *But:* I need to buy two cookie sheets.

You should also repeat the **a** when you are talking about two separate things.

> I need to buy a cookie sheet and a jelly roll pan.

If the indefinite article precedes a noun or adjective that begins with a vowel sound, English uses the form **an** for ease of pronunciation

> **An** exam book
>
> **An** angry man.

The test for whether to use **a** or **an** is not whether the noun begins with a vowel (*a, e, i, o,* and *u*), but whether it begins with a vowel **sound** or consonant **sound** when pronounced. Words beginning with the letter *y,* sometimes considered a vowel, take **a** rather than **an.**

> **An** honest mistake (Honest begins with a vowel sound: *on-est.*)
>
> **A** CIA agent (CIA begins with a consonant sound: *see-eye-ay.*)
>
> **An** FBI agent (FBI begins with vowel sound: *eff-bee-eye.*)
>
> **A** yellow scarf, **a** yard, **a** yodeling contest (Yellow begins with a consonant sound: *y-uh.* So does yard and yodeling.)

A UFO, **a** university (UFO and university begin with a consonant sound: *you*; also known as the hard u sound.)

An unidentified flying object, **an** uncomplicated procedure (Nearly all un-words begin with the vowel sound: *uh-n*.)

Noun begins with a consonant sound	*Noun begins with a vowel sound*
a bird	an abacus
a car	an error
a lemon	an issue
a telephone	an order

Gray Area: Articles and the Letter H

The letter H has a varied construction when there is a distinction between a hard h sound and a silent h sound. It used to be correct to say "an historical novel," but the contemporary way is given in the table that follows.

Hard sound	*Silent sound*
a historical novel	an herb
a hickory nut	an honest person
a horse	an honor

Definite Articles

The is called the **definite article. The** refers to a specific or already known thing. It can refer to singular or plural nouns:

> **The** three cars parked across **the** street belong to my neighbor.
> **The** dog chased **the** cat up **the** tree.
> **The** kittens are playing with **the** ball of string.

A/an is often used for the first mention of a thing, and **the** thereafter:

> My father gave me **a** watch. **The** watch belonged to my grandfather.
> **A** coat hung in the closet. **The** coat was torn and stained.

In some cases, nouns do not use articles. In general observations or statements of universal fact, no articles are needed:

> Elephants are mammals.
> Milk is high in calcium.
> *But:* **The** calcium found in dairy products is easily absorbed. (A specific type of calcium.)

Articles are one of the least logical aspects of English. Why is it correct to say "read Chapter 2" but "read **the** second chapter," or "I have **a** cold" but "I have **the** flu"? A few general guidelines follow:

❑ Most proper nouns do not need articles. (Major exceptions are names of rivers, oceans, and certain famous sites or geographical features: **the** Rocky Mountains, **the** Empire State Building, **the** Pacific Ocean.)

❑ Most noncount or collective nouns do not need articles unless they are being used in a specific sense: "I like cheese." (no article), but "**The** cheese they make in Wisconsin is my favorite." (collective nouns, p. 35; count versus noncount nouns, p. 35)

❑ If referring to something indefinite and singular, use **a/an.**

❑ If referring to something indefinite and plural, do not use an article.

❑ If referring to something definite, whether singular or plural, use **the.**

Gray Area: British versus American Article Usage

There are some differences between British and American English and these differences yield some different constructions in certain cases.

British	American
going to hospital	going to **the** hospital
he is in hospital	he is in **the** hospital
she is going to university	she is going to **a** university

This is not to say that the British always leave out articles—that would not be true. The particular cases cited above, however, apply.

Example Problems

Fill in the blanks with **a, an, the,** or no article.

1. I bought _____ new skirt and _____ new pair of jeans. _____ skirt is blue, but _____ jeans are black.

   Answer: **a, a, the, the.** In the first sentence, both items are being mentioned for the first time, and not much is known about them. They are both singular, so the indefinite article **a** is appropriate. In the second sentence, the items being talked about are known, and something specific is being said about them, so the definite article **the** is appropriate.

2. Sergei drives _____ yellow Beetle. He collects _____ cars. He traded _____ old Chevette for _____ Beetle.

   Answer: **a, no article, an, the.** In the first sentence, the reference is to one car, so **a** is appropriate. The second sentence does not need an article because it is making a general statement. In the third sentence, one Chevette is being described; **an** is used because the next word starts with a vowel sound (**old**). Finally, for the second mention of the Beetle, use **the** because it is a specific Beetle being named.

Work Problems

Fill in the blanks with **a, an, the,** or no article.

1. My friend Aaron is _____ farmer. He grows _____ strawberries and blackberries.

2. Aaron's farm is in _____ California. He has _____ antique farmhouse located in _____ valley.

3. _____ farmhouse was in bad shape when he found it. You would not believe all _____ work he had to do to fix it up.

4. Fortunately, most people like _____ strawberries, so he makes _____ good money.

5. He is not _____ rich man, but _____ money he makes keeps him comfortable.

Worked Solutions

1. **A, no article.**

   The indefinite article is often used with names of professions. No article is needed in the second sentence because the nouns are indefinite and plural.

2. **No article, an, a.**

   No article is needed with **California** because most proper nouns do not take articles. The indefinite article is appropriate with **antique farmhouse** because Aaron has only one, and this is first time it has been mentioned. Use **an** with **antique farmhouse** because it begins with a vowel sound. The indefinite article is appropriate with **valley** because it is not specific, and presumably he lives in only one valley.

3. **The, the.**

   The definite article is used with **farmhouse** because it is a specific farmhouse that is being talked about. Use the definite article with **work** also because it is a specific incident of work (**the** work that Aaron did on his house).

4. **No article, no article.**

   No article in needed with **strawberries** because the statement is a general observation. No article is needed with **money** because it is not a countable noun (to say, "I have two moneys" would be incorrect), and it is not being used it in a specific sense.

5. **A, the.**

   The indefinite article is appropriate with **man** because Aaron is only one out of many men who are not rich. In contrast to sentence 4, **money** here has been specifically identified (the money Aaron makes as a farmer), so it needs a definite article, even though it is a noncount noun.

Chapter Problems

Problems

Give the plural form of the following nouns.

1.   addendum

2.   ax

3.   rabbit

4.   goose

5.   enemy

6.   moose

7.   deer

8.   secretary

9.   symphony

10. license

In the following sentences, state the possessive case for each noun in parentheses.

11. My _____ (mother-in-law) car stalled on the way home.

12. The _____ (Claus) cat ran away from the house.

13. There was a meeting of the _____ (Governor) Task Force at noon.

14. Several _____ (states) Commissioners of Insurance met to discuss national policy.

15. At the university, the _____ (women) teams are national champions.

16. There are _____ (Stacy) and _____ (Mark) car keys.

17. We found _____ (Jane) and _____ (Barbara) cars in the parking lot.

18. Master Sergeant _____ (Jackson) office was immaculate.

19. _____ (Mozart) concertos are among the best music in the world.

20. The _____ (county) flooding problems were made worse by the storm.

Insert **a, an, the,** or no article in the spaces below.

21. We considered it _____ honor to get _____ award.

22. _____ commissioner made _____ ruling on the issue.

23. She found _____ food as good as her mother's cooking at _____ local restaurant.

24. _____ lawyer approached the bench.

25. The loan was for _____ indefinite period of time.

Answers and Solutions

1. addenda

2. axes

3. rabbits

4. geese

5. enemies

6. moose

7. deer

8. secretaries

9. symphonies

10. licenses

11. My mother-in-law's car stalled on the way home. (Since the car belongs to the mother-in-law, possession is shown at the end of **law.**)

12. The Claus's cat ran away from the house. (Be aware that the correct version can be either the Claus' or the Claus's cat because the word Claus ends with an **–s.**)

13. There was a meeting of the Governor's Task Force at noon. (The Task Force works for the Governor; possession is added to **Governor.**)

14. Several states' Commissioners of Insurance met to discuss national policy. (In this sentence, the states show possession of the office of the commissioner of insurance. The word **Commissioners** is plural because more than one commissioner met to discuss the policy.)

15. At the university, the women's teams are national champions. (In this sentence, the women's teams own the championships.)

16. There are Stacy and Mark's car keys. (In this sentence, Stacy and Mark have joint ownership of the car's keys.)

17. We found Jane's and Barbara's cars in the parking lot. (This sentence shows that Jane and Barbara each had a car. It is not joint ownership in this case.)

18. Master Sergeant Jackson's office was immaculate. (The office belonged to Master Sergeant Jackson. Show ownership after Jackson.)

19. Mozart's concertos are among the best music in the world. (This sentence shows that Mozart owned [wrote or composed is a better description] the concertos.)

20. The county's flooding problems were made worse by the storm. (The flooding problems belonged to the county. Thus, the county has ownership of the flooding issue.)

21. We considered it **an** honor to get **an** award. OR We considered it **an** honor to get **the** award. (In this sentence, **honor,** since it begins with a vowel sound, gets **an.** The word **award** can be designated either **an award** or **the award** depending on your meaning.)

22. **The** commissioner made **a** ruling on the issue. (The word *commissioner* begins with a consonant. The word **ruling** begins with a consonant and receives the article **a.**)

23. She found (no article) food as good as her mother's cooking at **a** local restaurant. (No article is needed before the word **food.** The word **local** begins with a consonant and takes the article **a.**)

24. **The** or **A** lawyer approached the bench. (The word **lawyer** can be designated either **the lawyer** or **a lawyer.**)

25. The loan was for **an** indefinite period of time. (The word **indefinite** begins with a vowel sound, thus it receives the article **an.**)

Supplemental Chapter Problems

Problems

Find the plural form of the following nouns.

1. roof

2. neurosis

3. desk

4. loaf

5. pencil

6. knife

7. sophomore

8. fish

9. mouse

10. psychosis

In the following sentences, show the possessive form of each noun in parentheses.

11. A _____ (person) compliment is good to hear once in a while.

12. There was a problem with my _____ (father-in-law) phone.

13. _____ (Sam) and _____ (Dave) bus did not last the duration of the tour.

14. Neither _____ (Olga) nor _____ (Nadia) suitcases arrived with their late flight.

15. My _____ (daughter-in-law) first child was born Monday, March 20th.

16. _____ (Elaine) and my car had to be repaired yesterday.

17. _____ (Eileen) and _____ (Van) computers had to be rebooted.

18. The book you refer to came from the _____ (library) collection.

19. _____ (Joe Jackson, Jr.) song played incessantly on the radio.

20. The _____ (babies) toys were strewn everywhere.

Insert **a, an, the,** or no article in the spaces below.

21. He had ____ truck and ____ fishing boat ready to go.

22. ____ ranger told us to park in ____ boat ramp area.

23. She had been cured of _____ cancer.

24. We painted the room ____ off-white color.

25. She had on ____ green uniform.

Answers

1. roofs

2. neuroses

3. desks

4. loaves

5. pencils

6. knives

7. sophomores

8. fishes

9. mice

10. psychoses

11. A **person's** compliment is good to hear once in a while. (showing possession with nouns, p. 38)

12. There was a problem with my **father-in-law's** phone. (showing possession with nouns, p. 38)

13. **Sam and Dave's** bus did not last the duration of the tour. (showing possession with nouns, p. 38)

14. Neither **Olga's nor Nadia's** suitcases arrived with their late flight. (showing possession with nouns, p. 38)

15. My **daughter-in-law's** first child was born Monday, March 20th. (showing possession with nouns, p. 38)

16. **Elaine's** and my car had to be repaired yesterday. (showing possession with nouns, p. 38)

17. **Eileen's and Van's** computers had to be rebooted. (showing possession with nouns, p. 38)

18. The book you refer to came from the **library's** collection. (showing possession with nouns, p. 38)

19. **Joe Jackson, Jr.'s** song played incessantly on the radio. (showing possession with nouns, p. 38)

20. The **babies'** toys were strewn everywhere. (showing possession with nouns, p. 38)

21. He had **a** truck and **a** fishing boat ready to go. (articles, p. 41)

22. **The** ranger told us to park in **the** boat ramp area. (articles, p. 41)

23. She had been cured of (no article) cancer. (articles, p. 41)

24. We painted the room **an** off-white color. (articles, p. 41)

25. She had on **a** green uniform. (articles, p. 41)

Chapter 2
Pronouns

A **pronoun** takes the place of a noun. Like nouns, pronouns can refer to people, places, things, ideas, or abstractions. If a noun includes other words such as articles or modifiers, the pronoun takes the place of all those words closely associated with the noun.

Maria went shopping.
She went shopping.

Mrs. Yamato's children found **the lost dog.**
They found **it.**

There are several varieties of pronouns, which this chapter will review:

❑ **Personal** (I, she, them, we, and so on)

❑ **Relative** (that, who, whom, which)

❑ **Demonstrative** (this, these, that, those)

❑ **Possessive** (mine, yours, his)

❑ **Reflexive** and **Intensive** (myself, himself, themselves, and so on)

❑ **Reciprocal** (each other, one another)

❑ **Indefinite** (someone, anybody, one, each, all, and so on)

❑ **Interrogative** (who, whose, which)

Personal Pronouns

Personal pronouns generally take the place of nouns that refer to people, although the third-person neutral pronoun **it** usually refers to things or animals. Personal pronouns can have two cases: **nominative** or **objective.** Nominative case is used when the pronoun is the **subject** of a verb (subjects, p. 184) or is a **subject complement,** a noun or pronoun that follows a form of the verb *to be* and describes or explains the subject of the verb (predicates, p. 188). Objective case is used when the pronoun is the object of a verb or a preposition.

The following table shows nominative and objective case forms of personal pronouns, both singular and plural.

Nominative singular/plural	Objective singular/plural
I / we	me / us
you / you	you / you
he, she, it / they	him, her, it / them

Some examples of nominative personal pronouns include:

She was an excellent dancer.

If **you** want to go on the field trip, then **you** need to tell Mrs. Martin.

Are **they** prepared to do the job?

Some examples of objective personal pronouns include:

The teacher gave **us** a new project.

I asked **them** to help **me** paint the house.

The doctor told **him** to get more exercise.

Common Pitfall: Multiple Pronouns and What Case to Use

Many people become confused about which case to use when more than one pronoun is involved (example: she and I, him and me). Many students, believing that nominative pronouns sound more "correct," are reluctant to use objective pronouns in such situations. Try splitting the sentence into two parts to determine the correct case for the pronoun.

She/Her and **I/me** went shopping.

She went shopping. I went shopping.

Her went shopping. Me went shopping.

She and **I** went shopping. (**She** and **I** are the subjects of the verb **went;** therefore they must be in the nominative case.)

Miguel went to the movies with **he/him** and **I/me.**

Miguel went with he. Miguel went with I.

Miguel went with him. Miguel went with me.

Miguel went to the movies with **him** and **me.** (**Him** and **me** are the objects of the preposition **with;** therefore they must be in the objective case.)

Common Pitfall: "We" and "Us" as Appositives

The personal pronouns **we** and **us** are sometimes used as **appositives,** which restate or explain a noun in the sentence.

We sophomores will host the school banquet on Saturday.

Sometimes the weather is kind to **us** farmers.

In informal, spoken English, the objective **us** is commonly used as the appositive, but in formal writing, **we** and **us** must still be in the proper case when they are used as appositives.

> *Use:* **We** girls are going skiing next weekend.
> *Not:* **Us** girls are going skiing next weekend. (**Girls** is the subject of the sentence, so its appositive must be in the nominative case.)

Notice that unlike noun appositives, pronoun appositives are not set off by commas.

Common Pitfall: Pronouns as Complements (or "It is I!")

When a personal pronoun acts as a subject complement (following a form of the verb "to be"), it should be in the nominative case (predicates, p. 188). However, in spoken English and in some informal writing, the objective form of the pronoun is used instead.

> Who is there? It's **me!**
> That is **them** over there.

In formal writing, be sure to use the nominative case.

> Who is there? It is **I!**
> That is **they** over there.

Example Problems

For each sentence, select the correct case for the pronoun.

1. **We/us** selected a finalist from among the candidates.

   Answer: **we. We** is the subject of the verb **selected.**

2. **They/them** called **she/her** into the meeting.

   Answers: **they** and **her. They** is the subject of the verb **called. Her** is the object of the same verb.

3. The situation created problems for **she/her** and **I/me.**

   Answers: **her** and **me.** Both pronouns are the objects of the preposition **for.**

4. Antonio will meet Sarah and **I/me** at the club.

   Answer: **me. Me** is the object of the verb **meet.**

Work Problems

For each sentence, determine whether the pronoun is an object or a subject and supply the correct case.

1. **They/them** were unsure whether it had been **she/her** who made the donation.

2. If you see **she/her,** tell **she/her** that Martin and **I/me** will be late.

3. **I/me** gave **they/them** the message from **she/her.**

4. **We/us** beginners need more help from you.

5. Min and **she/her** have been friends for many years.

6. It was **I/me** in the disguise.

7. Will **they/them** tell **we/us** when **they/them** want **we/us** to begin?

8. Give this box to **he/him.**

9. My professor asked me to do some work for **he/him** and his wife.

10. **She/her** asked **we/us** if **we/us** could be quieter.

Worked Solutions

1. **They, she. They** is the subject of the verb **were** (subjects, p. 184); **she** is a subject complement following a past tense form of the verb "to be" (predicates, p. 188).

2. **Her, her, I.** The first **her** is the object of the verb **see,** and the second **her** is the object of the verb **tell** (objects, p. 190). **I** is a compound subject (with **Martin**) of the verb **will be** (subjects, p. 184).

3. **I, them, her. I** is the subject of the verb **gave, them** is the object of the verb **gave,** and **her** is the object of the preposition **from.** (prepositions and compound prepositions, p. 151.)

4. **We. We** is an appositive to **beginners,** the subject of the verb **need. (You,** which does not change case, is the object of the preposition **from.)** (prepositions and compound prepositions, p. 151.)

5. **She. She** is a compound subject, with **Min,** of the verb **have been** (subjects, p. 184).

6. **I. I** is a subject complement (predicates, p. 188). (In informal usage, **me** would be acceptable.)

7. **They, us, they, us. They** is the subject of the verb **tell; us** the object of the verb **tell. They** is the subject of the verb **want; us** is the object of the verb **want.**

8. **Him. Him** is the object of the preposition **to.**

9. **Him. Him** is the object of the preposition **for.**

10. **She, us, we. She** is the subject of the verb **asked; us** is the object of the verb **asked. We** is the subject of the verb **could be.**

Agreement of Pronouns with Antecedents

The noun that a pronoun replaces is called the **antecedent** of the pronoun. Pronouns must **agree** with their antecedents in number, person, and gender. In the examples that follow, the antecedents are underlined and the pronouns are italicized.

> I loaned <u>Janet</u> my <u>textbook</u> so that *she* could copy the homework exercises from *it*.
>
> The proper noun <u>Janet</u> is the antecedent of the pronoun *she*. The noun <u>textbook</u> is the antecedent of the pronoun *it*.

For compound antecedents joined by **and,** the pronoun should be plural.

> I left <u>my backpack and my laptop</u> on the table, but now *they* are not there.

For compound antecedents joined by **or** or **nor,** the pronoun should be singular.

> <u>Michelle or Amanda</u> will drive *her* car.

If the antecedents joined by **or** or **nor** are different in number or gender, the pronoun should agree with the nearest antecedent.

> Before we can proceed, <u>Ms. Ralph or Mr. Kong</u> must give *his* approval.
> The Mitchell twins or Jessica will bring *her* CD player.

However, sentences of this kind are awkward sounding and potentially unclear. They should be rephrased whenever possible.

> Before we can proceed, we must get approval from Ms. Ralph or Mr. Kong.
> Either Jessica will bring her CD player, or the Mitchell twins will bring theirs.

If a pronoun and its antecedent become separated by other nouns, it may not be possible to correctly identify the antecedent (unclear antecedents, p. 213).

> Steve gave Diego a ride to the game so that **he** could talk to **him**.

What are the antecedents of **he** and **him**? Either pronoun could refer to either man. To make the meaning clear, rewrite the sentence.

> Steve gave Diego a ride to the game because Steve wanted to talk to **him**.
> *OR:* Steve gave Diego a ride to the game so the two of **them** could talk.

In the first sentence, the unclear pronoun **he** has been replaced by **Steve**, so **him** can only refer to Diego. In the second sentence, **them** can only refer to the pair of men.

Example Problems

For each sentence, identify any pronouns and their antecedents.

1. The children asked their teacher if they could stay outside, but he told them to come in for class. *Pronouns:* **they, them.** *Antecedent:* **children.** *Pronoun:* **he.** *Antecedent:* **teacher.**

The two plural pronouns, **they** and **them,** refer to the same antecedent, children, but one pronoun is a subject and one is an object. (The possessive pronoun **their** also refers to the children.) The singular pronoun **he** refers to the singular noun **teacher.** (It can be assumed from the context that this teacher is male.)

2. Starting a new business was difficult, but the Singletons were always sure they could do it. *Pronoun:* **they.** *Antecedent:* **the Singletons.** *Pronoun:* **it.** *Antecedent:* **starting a new business.**

    The plural pronoun **they** refers to the entire family, the Singletons. The singular pronoun **it** replaces the noun phrase **starting a new business,** which is one act, even though it requires several words to express the idea.

3. My son encouraged me to go back to college when he enrolled for his Master's degree so that we could study together. *Pronoun:* **me.** *Antecedent:* (none). *Pronoun:* **he.** *Antecedent:* **my son.** *Pronoun:* **we.** *Antecedent:* **my son and me.**

    The personal pronoun **me** does not have a direct antecedent; it simply refers to the speaker. **My son** requires the singular male pronoun **he,** but the speaker and the speaker's son together become **we.**

Work Problems

For each sentence, supply the correct pronouns for the underlined antecedent(s).

1. If <u>Julie</u> comes, tell _____ that I need to see _____ right away.

2. <u>Terry and his brother</u> are both tall, but _____ are not as tall as Mike.

3. I bought a <u>music box</u>, but _____ broke when my sister dropped _____.

4. <u>The homeowner and the contractor</u> signed a document in which_____agreed on the price for the construction work.

5. <u>Larry or Jane</u> will have to lend me _____ phone because I did not bring mine.

Worked Solutions

1. **Her, her** (**Julie** requires a singular, female pronoun.)

2. **They** (**Terry and his brother** requires a plural, third-person pronoun.)

3. **It, it** (**Music box** is a thing, requiring a neutral, third-person singular pronoun.)

4. **They** (**The homeowner and the contractor** requires a plural, third-person pronoun.)

5. **Her** (For this compound subject joined by *or,* the closest antecedent is **Jane,** requiring a singular, female pronoun. However, sentences using mixed antecedents are very awkward and should be avoided whenever possible.)

Relative Pronouns

A **relative** pronoun introduces a subordinate clause that explains or describes a noun (clauses, p. 195). This type of subordinate clause is called a **relative clause**. Relative pronouns are **who, whom, whose, which,** and **that.** Usually the relative pronoun immediately follows its noun antecedent. In the following examples, the noun is underlined and the relative clause is in brackets.

> This is the <u>necklace</u> [**that** my grandmother gave me].
> Where is the <u>man</u> [**whom** you saw]?
> A <u>director</u> [**whose** films were being honored] made an appearance at the film festival.

The relative pronouns **who** and **whom** refer to people. **Whose,** indicating possession, can refer to people, animals, or things. **Which** generally refers to things other than people, and **that** can refer to anything.

> *Correct:* The children **whom** you saw were going to the museum.
> *Correct:* The children **that** you saw were going to the museum.
> *Incorrect:* The children **which** you saw were going to the museum.

The relative pronouns **that, which,** and **who/whom** can be omitted from a relative clause, but only if they do not form the subject of the relative clause.

> *Correct:* The man [**whom** you met yesterday] is my business partner.
> *Correct:* The man [you met yesterday] is my business partner.

You is the subject of the clause, so **whom** can be omitted.

> *Correct:* The man [**who** introduced himself to you] is my business partner.
> *Incorrect:* The man [introduced himself to you] is my business partner.

Who is the subject of the clause, so it cannot be omitted.

> *Correct:* The man [**whose** card I gave you] is my business partner.
> *Incorrect:* The man [card I gave you] is my business partner.

Whose can never be omitted from a relative clause.

Closely related to relative pronouns are **relative adverbs,** which can also introduce relative clauses. Common relative adverbs are **when, why, how,** and **where** (adverbs, p. 163). Unlike relative pronouns, relative adverbs can never be the subject of a clause. Adverbs are modifiers, and modifiers cannot act as subjects.

> The lot **where** I park my car has no shade. (**Where** introduces the relative clause "I park my car." The subject of the clause is **I.**)
> The day **when** we first met was rainy and cold. (**When** introduces the relative clause "we first met." The subject of the clause is **we.** It would also be acceptable to omit **when:** "The day we first met. . . ")

Gray Area: Restrictive "That" versus Nonrestrictive "Which"

An old grammar rule says that the relative pronoun **that** can introduce only restrictive relative clauses and the relative pronoun **which** can introduce only nonrestrictive relative clauses. A

restrictive clause introduces information essential to the sentence and is not set off by commas. A **nonrestrictive clause** introduces supplementary information and is always set off by commas. (See restrictive and nonrestrictive elements, p. 211.) For example:

The watch **that belonged to my grandfather** needs repair. (restrictive)

The watch**, which was made in Germany,** used to chime on the hour. (nonrestrictive)

While this rule might be useful as a memory aid, it does not necessarily reflect current practice. In reality, there is nothing grammatically incorrect about using **which** to introduce a restrictive clause:

The watch *which* **belonged to my grandfather** needs repair. (restrictive)

The choice between **which** or **that** for restrictive clauses is strictly a matter of style, and many writers and speakers would find no difference between the two. However, some teachers and editors still prefer to use **which** for nonrestrictive clauses only, so students should be aware of this rule.

One rule that is grammatically sound: **that** cannot introduce a nonrestrictive clause. In any case, **who, whom, whoever,** or **whomever** are appropriate choices when the clause refers to a person.

Common Pitfall: "Who" versus "Whom"

In spoken English and in some informal writing, **whom** is rarely used, but in formal writing, you must determine whether to use **who** (nominative) or **whom** (objective) when introducing a relative clause. (clauses, p. 195.) To help you recognize whether the pronoun is being used as a subject or an object within the relative clause, try rephrasing the clause as a sentence and substituting a different pronoun for **who/whom**.

I met the artist [**who/whom** painted this picture].

Rephrased: **The artist** painted this picture. OR: **She** painted this picture.

Correct: I met the artist [**who** painted this picture]. (In this relative clause, **the artist/she** is the subject of the verb **painted**; therefore, the nominative case is required.)

He is the kind of person [**who/whom** I admire].

Rephrased: I admire **him.**

Correct: He is the kind of person **whom** I admire. (In this relative clause, **him** is the object of the verb **admire**; therefore, the objective case is required.)

Remember that the key question is how the pronoun functions with the clause. Do not be confused by other words that appear before the pronoun.

Give the package to [**whoever** is working at the front desk].

Because the pronoun follows the preposition **to** (prepositions and compound prepositions, p. 151), some students might reason that the pronoun is the object of the preposition, and therefore use **whomever.** But because **whoever** is the subject of the clause, it must be in nominative case. (**Whoever** is not the object of the preposition in the this case; the entire clause is the object of the preposition.) Compare this sentence:

Give the package to [**whomever** you find at the front desk].

In this relative clause, **whomever** is the direct object of the verb **find** (objects, p. 190), so it must be in objective case. (Rephrased, it would be "you find him at the front desk.")

Example Problems

For each sentence, choose the correct relative pronoun.

1. The movie is about a boy **who/whom** wants to become a dancer.

    Answer: **who. Who** is the subject of the verb **wants.** (*Rephrased:* The boy wants to become a dancer; he wants to become a dancer.)

2. Did you like the tamales **which/that/who(m)** I made?

    Answer: either **which** or **that. Who(m)** is incorrect because it can refer only to people.

3. Have you met the manager **who/whom** Mr. Hernandez hired?

    Answer: **whom. Whom** is the object of the verb **hired.** (*Rephrased:* Mr. Hernandez hired the manager; Mr. Hernandez hired him.)

Work Problems

For each sentence, supply the correct relative pronoun.

1. Michelle likes the ring _____ she saw in the store window.

2. The boy _____ arm was broken is wearing a bright purple cast.

3. The trees _____ grow in this forest are more than 400 years old.

4. The dancers _____ passed the audition performed onstage.

5. The piano teacher _____ you recommended is not taking new students.

Can the relative pronoun be omitted from these sentences? Yes or no:

6. The salesperson whom you spoke to no longer works there.

7. The assembly instructions that came with the bicycle are difficult to understand.

8. I would like to meet the architect who designed this building.

9. The storms which struck the area caused extensive damage.

10. The advice that she gave me turned out to be useful.

Worked Solutions

1. **That** or **which** (relative pronouns referring to things)

2. **Whose** (relative pronoun indicating possession)

3. **That** or **which** (relative pronouns referring to things)

4. **Who** (subject of the verb **passed; that** would also be correct, but not **which** because it cannot refer to people)

5. **Whom** (object of the verb **recommended; that** would also be correct, but not **which** because it cannot refer to people)

6. **Yes,** because **whom** is the object of the relative clause.

7. **No,** because **that** is the subject of the relative clause.

8. **No,** because **who** is the subject of the relative clause.

9. **No,** because **which** is the subject of the relative clause.

10. **Yes,** because **that** is the object of the relative clause.

Demonstrative Pronouns

Demonstrative pronouns point out (or "demonstrate") a noun antecedent.

> **This** is my favorite song.
> **That** was a day to remember.

The table that follows shows the two demonstrative pronouns in singular and plural forms.

Singular	Plural
this	these
that	those

This often indicates something nearer to the speaker, while **that** indicates something farther away. **This** and **that** are also used in contrast to each other.

> **This** is my notebook, but **that** is Trina's notebook.

The antecedent of a demonstrative pronoun is often omitted or may be implied from the context.

> Which earrings do you like best? **These** are nice, but I think **those** are the prettiest.
> I wish you would not do **that.**

When using demonstrative pronouns in your writing, make sure that the antecedents are clear. Demonstrative pronouns can easily become vague and meaningless (common sentence problems: lack of agreement, p. 214).

> We are going to a movie after we finish our homework. That will be fun. (What will be fun? Going to a movie, or finishing our homework?)

This/these and **that/those** can also be used as demonstrative adjectives, to modify nouns (adjectives, p. 161).

Demonstrative adjective:

> **This** car belongs to Trina. (**This** modifies the noun **car.**)

Demonstrative pronoun:

> **This** is Trina's car, not mine. (**This,** acting as the subject of the sentence, stands in for the noun **car.**)

Common Pitfall: "This Kind," "Those Sorts"

The common English expressions **that kind, those sorts, this sort,** and so on, often cause problems related to agreement. First, the adjective and any nouns associated with it must all be singular or all be plural.

> *Incorrect:* Those kind of things . . .
> *Correct:* This kind of thing . . .
> *Correct:* Those kinds of things . . .
>
> *Incorrect:* Those sort of thing . . .
> *Correct:* That sort of thing . . .
> *Correct:* Those sorts of things . . .

Second, the verb following the expression must agree in number.

> *Singular:* That kind of thing **does** not interest me.
> *Plural:* Those kinds of things **do** not interest me.

Example Problems

Select the correct demonstrative pronoun or adjective.

1. With **this/these** problems solved, the rest of the project was easy.

   Answer: **these.** (It modifies the plural noun **problems.**)

2. Do you want to take **that/those** bag, or **this/these?**

   Answer: **that, this.** (Both refer to the singular noun **bag.**)

3. **That/those** sort of behavior will not accomplish anything.

   Answer: **that.** (**Sort** is singular; it agrees with the singular noun **behavior.**)

Work Problems

Supply the correct demonstrative pronoun or adjective.

1. How do you turn _____ machine on?

2. _____ car has low mileage, but _____ one is less expensive.

3. _____ are the sweetest oranges I ever tasted.

4. Many of _____ people had never met each other before.

5. Are _____ the right tools for the job?

6. If you take _____ road, watch out for the potholes.

7. Which photograph should we use for the brochure, _____ or _____?

Chose the correct construction.

8. I always wanted to have **that kind/those kinds** of dog.

9. **This sort/Those sorts** of problems usually **solve/solves** themselves.

10. If you find **that kind/those kinds** of hat, please buy me one.

Worked Solutions

1. **This** or **that** (singular, modifying **machine**)

2. **This, that,** or **That, this** (singular, modifying **car;** used in contrast to each other)

3. **These** or **those** (plural, referring to **oranges**)

4. **These** or **those** (plural, modifying **people**)

5. **These** or **those** (plural, referring to **tools**)

6. **That** or **this** (singular, modifying **road**)

7. **This, that,** or **that, this** (singular, referring to **photograph;** used in contrast to each other)

8. **That kind** (agreeing with singular **dog**)

9. **Those sorts, solve** (agreeing with plural **problems**)

10. **That kind** (agreeing with singular **hat**)

Possessive Pronouns

Possessive forms of pronouns indicate ownership.

> That guitar is **his,** although I have one that looks just like it.
>
> If you forgot your key, I can lend you **mine.**

Possessive adjectives (adjectives, p. 161) are closely related to possessive pronouns; however, possessive adjectives act as modifiers for nouns, while possessive pronouns act as nouns (possessive pronouns, p. 63).

Possessive adjective:

> **Your** coat is hanging in the closet. (**Your** modifies the noun **coat.**)

Possessive pronoun:

> The coat in the closet is **yours.** (**Yours** is a pronoun; **coat** is its antecedent.)

The following table shows the possessive adjectives and pronouns for first, second, and third person.

Possessive pronouns singular/plural	*Possessive adjectives singular/plural*
my / our	mine /ours
your / your	yours / yours
his, her, its / their	his, hers, its / theirs

Common Pitfall: Possessive Pronouns and Apostrophes

Because an **apostrophe** and **s** added to the end of a noun indicates possession, many writers try to add apostrophes to possessive pronouns (apostrophes, p. 239).

> *Incorrect:* your's, their's, it's, her's
> *Correct:* yours, theirs, its, hers
>
> *Incorrect:* That coat is her's.
> *Correct:* That coat is hers.
>
> *Incorrect*: The box was missing it's lid.
> *Correct:* The box was missing its lid.

Writers also confuse possessives with contractions, which use apostrophes to indicate omitted letters. This confusion is compounded by the fact that the adjectives and contractions are pronounced exactly alike.

> **Their** = belonging to them
> **They're** = contraction of "they are"

Your = belonging to you
You're = contraction of "you are"

Its = belonging to it
It's = contraction of "it is"

Whose = belonging to who
Who's = contraction of "who is"

If you are in doubt as to which form to use in writing, try expanding the contraction to see if it still makes sense.

That tree has lost **it's/its** leaves.
Incorrect: That tree has lost **it is** leaves.
Correct: That tree has lost **its** leaves. ("the leaves belonging to it"—**its** is the possessive form)

Example Problems

Supply the correct possessive pronoun form.

1. For a woman: This is ___ flute; it is _____.

   Answer: **her** (adjective form), **hers** (pronoun form)

2. For a group of people: This is _____ house; it is _____.

   Answer: **their** (adjective form), **theirs** (pronoun form)

3. For me: These are _____ shoes; they are _____.

   Answer: **my** (adjective form), **mine** (pronoun form)

Work Problems

Choose the correct possessive pronoun form.

1. **Her/hers** leadership style has **its/it's** advantages.

2. I prefer **my/mine** method, but **their/they're** method also works.

3. If **your/you're** going to the park, can you take **her/hers** dog for a walk?

4. **Its/it's** a long way to the museum.

5. Are these recommendations **your/yours** or **their/theirs?**

6. **Their/they're** not finished with the exercise yet.

7. **My/mine** pencil is broken. May I borrow **your/yours?**

8. I fear **our/ours** best effort is not enough, but **its/it's** all we can do.

9. I liked **your/you're** proposal, but others questioned **its/it's** feasibility.

10. Some people like **their/theirs/they're** coffee with cream and sugar, but for me, **its/it's** best black.

Worked Solutions

1. **Her, its. Her** modifies **leadership style,** and **its** modifies **advantages.** "It is advantages" would not make sense.

2. **My, their. My** and **their** are possessive adjectives modifying **method.** "They are method" would not make sense.

3. **You're, her.** "You are going" is required for the sentence to make sense. **Her** is a possessive adjective modifying **dog.**

4. **It's.** A possessive would not make sense in this context; the verb in "it is" is required.

5. **Yours, theirs.** Both are possessive pronouns referring to **recommendations.**

6. **They're.** A possessive would not make sense in this context. The verb in "they are" is required.

7. **My, yours. My** is a possessive adjective modifying **pencil; yours** is a possessive pronoun referring to **pencil.**

8. **Our; it's. Our** is a possessive adjective modifying **best effort. It's** is a contraction of **it is:** "it is all we could do." The possessive **its** would not make sense in this case.

9. **Your, its. Your** is a possessive adjective; "I liked you are proposal" would not make sense. **Its** is a possessive adjective modifying **feasibility.** "Questioned it is feasibility" would not make sense.

10. **Their, it's. Their** is a possessive adjective modifying **coffee. It's** includes the personal pronoun **it,** referring to the antecedent **coffee:** "for me, it (coffee) is best black."

Reflexive and Intensive Pronouns

Reflexive pronouns are used when the object of a verb in a sentence is the same as its subject.

> I told **myself** it would never work.
> He cut **himself** shaving.

Reflexive pronouns do not change forms for case.

The following table shows singular and plural reflexive pronouns for first, second, and third persons.

Singular	*Plural*
myself	ourselves
yourself	yourselves
himself, herself, itself	themselves

Intensive pronouns are identical in form to reflexive pronouns, but they are used for emphasis, to intensify the meaning of the sentence. In such cases, the sentence would make sense even if the intensive pronoun was omitted.

> *Correct:* No one else would clean the kitchen, so I did it **myself.**
> *Correct:* No one else would clean the kitchen, so I did it.

Informal, spoken English sometimes replaces simple personal pronouns with reflexive/intensive forms, even though the reflexive pronoun is not needed:

> *Informal:* Liu and **myself** interviewed the applicant. (Liu and **I** interviewed the applicant.)
> *Informal:* A person like **yourself** would do well in this job. (A person like **you** would do well in this job.)

In formal writing, however, reflexives should only be used where they are grammatically required, as many teachers and editors frown upon the misuse of reflexives. Reflexives should not replace personal pronouns, but supplement them.

Reciprocal Pronouns

The **reciprocal** pronouns **each other** and **one another** are used to indicate a mutual or "reciprocal" action by the subjects of the verb. The two pronouns are used interchangeably.

> My sister and I help **each other** study for our college classes.
> If the players would cooperate with **one another,** the team would win more games.

Example Problems

Supply the correct reflexive, intensive, or reciprocal pronoun.

1. After the little girl had learned to tie her shoes, she always wanted to do it _____.

    Answer: **herself** (intensive, emphasizing that the girl did not want help)

2. Watch out! You might hurt _____.

    Answer: **yourself** (reflexive, because the subject and object are the same)

3. Whenever those two start talking to _____, I cannot get a word in edgewise.

    Answers: **each other** or **one another** (reciprocal). "Talking to themselves" would mean that each person was not speaking to the other person.

Work Problems

Supply the correct reflexive, intensive, or reciprocal pronoun.

1. If you want something done right, you have to do it _____.

2. Margaret and Tim bumped into_____ in the hallway.

3. I think we should take _____ out to dinner tonight.

4. I _____ would not want to take such a risk, but you must do what you think is best.

5. He talked _____ into auditioning for the play.

6. In my family, we know we can rely on _____ for support.

7. Sarah taught _____ to play the piano.

8. Because Mike was ill, Elizabeth had to finish the gardening _____.

9. When you talk to _____, do you get an answer?

10. Aaron has turned _____ into an expert potter.

Worked Solutions

1. **Yourself** (intensive, referring to **you**)

2. **Each other** or **one another** (reciprocal, referring to **Margaret and Tim**)

3. **Ourselves** (reflexive, referring to **we**). **Each other** or **one another** would also be acceptable.

4. **Myself** (intensive, referring to **I**)

5. **Himself** (reflexive, referring to **he**)

6. **One another** or **each other** (reciprocal, referring to the members of **my family**)

7. **Herself** (reflexive, referring to **Sarah**)

8. **Herself** (intensive, referring to **Elizabeth**)

9. **Yourself** (reflexive, referring to **you**)

10. **Himself** (reflexive, referring to **Aaron**)

Indefinite Pronouns

Indefinite pronouns do not refer to a specific antecedent. Instead, they refer to people, places, things, or ideas in a general way.

> **Nobody** likes a sore loser.
>
> Do not worry about **anything.**

Common indefinite pronouns include the following:

all	either, neither	one, oneself
any, anyone, anybody, anything	few	no one, none, nobody
both	everyone, everybody, everything	other, others
each	many, most	some, someone, somebody

Most indefinite pronouns, such as **nobody, someone,** or **anything,** are treated as singular and, therefore, take singular verbs.

> **Someone** <u>is</u> playing a trick on you.
> **Anything** <u>is</u> possible.

The indefinite pronouns **everyone, everybody,** and **everything** are also considered singular. The presence of the word "every" does not make them plural.

> **Everyone** <u>is</u> going on the field trip.
> **Everything** <u>was</u> ready for the party.

Exceptions are **both, many, few, all, some,** and **others,** which are treated as plural.

> **Many** <u>are</u> called, but **few** <u>are</u> chosen.

Many indefinite pronouns can also be used as adjectives, modifying nouns (adjectives, p. 161).

> **Few** plants are tough enough to grow in an arctic environment. (**Few** modifies **plants.**)
> **Each** antique plate is now safe in the cupboard. (**Each** modifies **antique plate.**)

Like indefinite pronouns, collective nouns (p. 35) such as **group, team,** or **jury,** pose agreement problems. Collective nouns may be singular or plural, depending on the context. (See also lack of agreement, p. 214.)

Example Problems

Choose the correct verb form to agree with the indefinite pronoun.

1. Many **finish/finishes** the marathon, but some **do/does** not.

   Answer: **finish, do.** (**Many** and **some** are plural.)

2. Everyone who **want/wants** to come **is/are** welcome.

   Answer: **wants, is.** (**Everyone** is singular.)

3. Until all **agree/agrees** on a verdict, the jury will continue to deliberate.

   Answer: **agree.** (**All** is plural.)

Work Problems

Supply the correct verb form to agree with the indefinite pronoun.

1. Everybody **say/says** that new movie is great.

2. If no one **volunteer/volunteers,** then we will have to do the work.

3. **Is/Are** the others coming with you?

4. Most **is/are** coming, but not all.

5. Both **was/were** involved in the accident.

6. Everything **is/are** going to be okay.

7. **Is/Are** anyone at home?

8. Some **is/are** going to disagree, but I think the plan is good.

9. Everyone **struggle/struggles** when learning a new language.

10. If someone **ask/asks** for me, please tell me immediately.

Worked Solutions

1. **Says** (**Everybody** is singular.)

2. **Volunteers** (**No one** is singular.)

3. **Are** (**Others** is plural.)

4. **Are** (**Most** is plural, as is **all.**)

5. **Were** (**Both** is plural.)

6. **Is** (**Everything** is singular.)

7. **Is** (**Anyone** is singular.)

8. **Are** (**Some** is plural.)

9. **Struggles** (**Everyone** is singular.)

10. **Asks** (**Someone** is singular.)

Gray Area: Sexist Language and Indefinite Pronouns

Indefinite pronouns are often used to make general observations or broadly inclusive statements. As mentioned previously, most indefinite pronouns are considered singular. In the past, it was often standard practice to use a singular male pronoun to follow indefinite pronouns. This "generic **he**" was supposed to refer to males and females generally.

> Everyone wants to do **his** best.

However, concerns over sexist language have created a desire for more gender-inclusive constructions.

> Everyone wants to do **his or her** best.
> *or*
> Everyone wants to do **their** best.

Although the second sentence violates the general rule requiring agreement with antecedents, many writers and speakers prefer to use forms of **they** because these forms are not gender specific. This is a common practice, but it is still criticized by grammatical purists.

To avoid the problem, rewrite the sentence so that a "generic **he**" would not be necessary. Usually, the simplest solution is to replace the singular indefinite pronoun with a plural alternative (underlined in the following example).

> <u>All people</u> want to do **their** best.

Work Problems

Rewrite the following sentences to avoid the use of a "generic he."

1. Anyone who wants to attend must complete his registration by Friday.

2. A careful painter will make sure he cleans his brushes after each use.

3. Without good study skills, a student may find himself overwhelmed by his assignments.

Worked Solutions

Other correct answers in addition to those given below are possible.

1. **Any employees** who want to attend must complete **their** registration by Friday.

2. **Careful painters** will make sure **they** clean **their** brushes after each use.

3. Without good study skills, **students** may find **themselves** overwhelmed by **their** assignments.

Interrogative Pronouns

Interrogative pronouns introduce questions.

> **What** is the answer?
> **Which** color do you like best?

Interrogative pronouns are **who/whom/whose**, **which**, and **what**. The pronoun **who/whom** always refers to people, and **whose** indicates possession.

Remember that the same rules regarding **who** and **whom** as relative pronouns apply to them as interrogative pronouns. If the interrogative pronoun is the subject, use **who;** if it is the object, use **whom.**

> **Whom** did you see there? (you saw whom → whom is the object)
> **Who** brought the cake? (who brought it → who is the subject)
> **Whose** sweater is this?

Which refers to one item out of a group, or a specific item.

> **Which** puppy do you want to buy?
> **Which** of the players is your son?
> **Which** woman sang the solo?

What refers broadly to things, ideas, concepts, actions, or abstractions.

> **What** are you doing?
> **What** did he say?
> **What** time is it?

Other interrogative words used to introduce questions are **when, where, why,** and **how** (sentence types: declarative, imperative, and interrogative moods, p. 202). These words act as adverbs (adverbs, p. 163) rather than pronouns.

Example Problems

Supply the correct interrogative pronoun.

1.   _____ will be driving the bus?

     Answer: **who** (referring to a person)

2.   _____ can we do to help you?

     Answer: **what** (referring to a general concept)

3.   _____ woman in the photo is your mother?

     Answer: **which** (referring to one out of a group)

Work Problems

Supply the correct interrogative pronoun.

1.   _____ did Mr. Montoya hire to replace me?

2.   _____ is the solution?

3.   _____ of these chairs would look best in our living room?

4.   _____ needs a ride to the basketball game?

5. _____ student was chosen as class president?

6. _____ do you want for your birthday?

7. _____ will speak at the conference?

8. _____ happened after I left?

9. _____ can I trust with this information?

10. _____ cat is the friendliest one?

Worked Solutions

1. **Whom** (referring to a person, object of the verb **hire**)

2. **What** (referring to a general concept)

3. **Which** (referring to one out of a group of chairs)

4. **Who** (referring to a person, subject of the verb **needs**)

5. **Which** (referring to one specific student)

6. **What** (referring to a thing)

7. **Who** (referring to a person, subject of the verb **will speak**)

8. **What** (referring to an unknown occurrence)

9. **Whom** (referring to a person, object of the verb **can trust**)

10. **Which** (referring to one cat out of several)

Chapter Problems

Problems
Select the correct form of the pronoun.

1. Karla asked Steve to take out the garbage for **she/her,** but **he/him** would not do it.

2. Mr. Mendez gave Jane and **I/me/myself** the job of pruning the hedge.

3. John considered **he/him/himself** lucky when **he/him** found an affordable apartment.

4. If **they/them** keep **their/they're** goals in mind, nothing will stop **they/them.**

5. It was **I/me/myself** and **he/him/himself** who ended up as finalists in the competition.

Supply the correct relative pronoun.

6. This shipment _____ you sent to us was not complete.

7. The children _____ went to the play all got to meet the actors.

8. The statue _____ they are restoring is 3,000 years old.

9. The test consisted of questions _____ were grouped by topic.

10. The singers _____ you heard were from Russia.

Determine whether the following sentences contain errors and correct any you find.

11. Jay and myself already had dinner; you should have your's.

12. Everybody that are ready can begin now.

13. I like these chocolate candy, but them mints are better.

14. Can anyone tell me who wrote this embarrassing memo?

15. Mr. Richards met my girlfriend and I in the park.

16. That lamp has lost it's shade. If its not too much trouble, could you buy a new one?

17. Many people enjoyed the show, but some was disappointed.

18. I told him those sort of parts do not fit, but he tried to use it anyway.

19. This is the worst film that I have ever seen.

20. This is the kind of book what you want to read over and over.

21. The man who you met was not my teacher.

22. Warren Company was the firm who's bid was accepted.

23. Ryan and her went to the store.

24. The students which are working together will have a meeting this afternoon.

25. Every citizen should cherish his right to vote.

26. Caroline or Marcia will need to give their input.

27. Mrs. Lee is the woman who taught me how to cook.

28. What of the available options did you choose?

29. If their not going to help us, us boys will have to set up the tent ourselves.

30. She and I are the best of friends, but Jacques does not like either her or me.

Answers and Solutions

1. **Her, he. Her** is the object of the preposition **for; he** is the subject of the verb **would.**

2. **Me.** Both **Jane** and **me** are objects of the verb **gave. Myself** is unnecessary in this context.

3. **Himself, he. Himself** is a reflexive pronoun because **John** is both the subject and the object of the verb **considered. He** is the subject of the verb **found.**

4. **They, their, them. They** is the subject of the verb **keep. Their** is a possessive personal adjective modifying **goals.** Note that the contraction **they're** would not make sense: "if they keep they are goals in mind. . . . " **Them** is the object of the verb **stop.**

5. **I, he.** Both are predicate nominatives, following the construction **it is.**

6. **That** or **which.** Either is acceptable to refer to a thing (**this shipment**).

7. **Who** or **that. Who** is preferable because it is referring to people. **Who** is in the nominative case because it is the subject of the verb **went.** The relative pronoun **which** should not refer to people.

8. **That** or **which.** Either is acceptable to refer to a thing (**the statue**).

9. **That** or **which.** Either is acceptable to refer to things (**questions**).

10. **Whom** or **that. Whom** is preferable because it is referring to people. **Whom** is in the objective case because it is the object of the verb **heard.** The relative pronoun **which** should not refer to people.

11. Jay and **I** already had dinner; you should have **yours.** The reflexive **myself** should not be used as a subject. **Your's** attempts to add an unnecessary apostrophe to a possessive pronoun.

12. Everybody **who is** ready can begin now. **Everybody** is singular and requires a singular verb for agreement. **That** might be acceptable as a relative pronoun in this case, although **who** is be a better choice in terms of style.

13. I like **this chocolate candy** [or **these chocolate candies**], but **these** [or **those**] mints are better. **These** does not agree in number with the noun it modifies. **Them** is not used as demonstrative; either **these** or **those** agrees with **mints** in number.

14. Can anyone tell me who wrote this embarrassing memo? No errors. **Who** is the subject of the verb **wrote,** so it is correctly in the nominative case.

15. Mr. Richards met my girlfriend and **me** in the park. **Me** is the object of the verb **met.**

16. That lamp has lost **its** shade. If **it's** not too much trouble, could you buy a new one? In the first sentence, the contraction does not make sense: "The lamp has lost it is shade." In the second sentence, the contraction is required for the sentence to make sense: "If it is not too much trouble. . . ." The possessive adjective **its** does not use an apostrophe.

17. Many people enjoyed the show, but some **were** disappointed. The indefinite pronoun **some** is considered plural, so it requires a plural verb for agreement.

18. I told him **those sorts of parts do** not fit, but he tried to use **them** anyway. *or* I told him **that sort of part does** not fit, but he tried to use **it** anyway. Expressions such as **this sort of** or **those kinds of** must carry agreement throughout the sentence, either all plural or all singular.

19. This is the worst film that I have ever seen. No errors. **This** is a singular demonstrative pronoun referring to the singular noun **film,** and it is the subject of the singular verb **is.** **That** is a relative pronoun correctly referring to a thing (**film**). Notice that in this case, **that** could be omitted from the relative clause because it is not the subject of the relative clause.

20. This is the kind of book **that** [or **which**] you want to read over and over. **What** is not a relative pronoun. Relative pronouns **that** and **which** can both refer to a thing (**book**). **That/which** could be omitted because it is not the subject of the relative clause.

21. The man **whom** you met was not my teacher. **Whom** is the object of the verb **met.** (To make the relative clause clearer, try rephrasing it: You met the man; you met him.) **Whom** could be omitted because it is not the subject of the relative clause.

22. Warren Company was the firm **whose** bid was accepted. **Who's** is a contraction of **who is.** "The firm who is bid was accepted" does not make sense. **Whose** is relative pronoun indicating possession. (**Their bid** was accepted.)

23. Ryan and **she** went to the store. Both **Ryan** and **she** are subjects of the verb **went,** so the nominative case is required.

24. The students **who** are working together will have a meeting this afternoon. The relative pronoun **which** should not be used to refer to people.

25. Every citizen should cherish **his or her** right to vote. *or* **All citizens** should cherish **their** right to vote. Nothing is grammatically incorrect about the sentence, but it is an example of the use of a "generic he" after an indefinite pronoun. Such expressions should be rephrased to be nonsexist.

26. Caroline or Marcia will need to give **her** input. Compound subjects joined by **or** need a singular pronoun for agreement.

27. Mrs. Lee is the woman who taught me how to cook. No errors. **Who** is relative pronoun correctly referring to a person (**woman**). **Who** is the subject of the verb **taught.**

28. **Which** of the available options did you choose? **Which** refers to one out of a group and is required before the preposition **of** in this construction. It would also be correct to say, "What option did you choose?"

29. If **they're** not going to help us, **we** boys will have to set up the tent ourselves. **Their** is a possessive adjective and does not make sense in this construction ("if they are not going to help us"). **We** is an appositive to the subject **boys,** so it must be in the nominative case.

30. She and I are the best of friends, but Jacques does not like either her or me. No errors. **She** and **I** are subjects of the verb **are** and are, therefore, correctly in the nominative case. **Her** and **me** are objects of the verb **like** and are, therefore, correctly in the objective case.

Supplemental Chapter Problems

Problems

Supply the missing pronouns.

1. Mary and Liam are dance partners. _____ entered a dance contest, but first prize did not go to _____.

2. Mrs. Dvorak made _____ a cup of coffee.

3. I need your opinion about some birdhouses I am making. Do you think _____ birdhouses are large enough? What about _____?

4. The surprise party _____ you threw for Jennifer was a big success. _____ are you going to do for _____ this year?

5. Mr. Lopez organizes trips for students _____ want to see the United States. The students _____ you met at the train station were friends of _____.

6. _____ is my favorite television show. I enjoy shows _____ make me think.

7. _____ students are entering the speech contest? _____ will they speak about?

8. Juan and Margo are dating. _____ often go out with _____.

9. I cut _____ on some broken glass in the kitchen. Do not go in there until I clean _____ up.

10. _____ is a great opportunity. _____ will be able to turn it down.

Select the correct case for the pronoun.

11. Mr. Leon assigned the case to Irene and **I/me.**

12. It was **he/him who/whom** you met in the park.

13. Tell **they/them** to hurry up. **They/them** are about to be late.

14. The artist **who/whom** made this necklace for **I/me** is now famous.

15. The police officer **who/whom** found Mike and **I/me** in the alley thought that **we/us** were burglars.

Supply the missing relative pronouns.

16. Where is the book _____ you borrowed?

17. The salespeople _____ sell the most units will get a bonus.

18. There is the man _____ dog bit me.

19. If there is anyone _____ you want to meet, I will introduce you.

20. The tenants _____ apartments were damaged by the smoke had to stay in a hotel.

Determine whether the following sentences contain errors and correct any you find.

21. Who will benefit from the new tax laws?

22. Us fans must support our team.

23. Mark or Greg will give their support to our proposal.

24. They will give theirselves a headache listening to such loud music.

25. Anyone what says I was not at the meeting is mistaken.

26. If your going to the concert, can I go along?

27. Michaela's mother is the woman who I most admire.

28. We will meet she and Tim at the restaurant at seven o'clock.

29. People which have seen the new building are impressed.

30. I lost my notes, so I had to borrow their's.

Answers

1. **They, them** (personal pronouns, p. 51)

2. **Herself** (reflexive and intensive pronouns, p. 65)

3. **These, those** (demonstrative pronouns, p. 60)

4. **That** (relative pronouns, p. 57), **what** (interrogative pronouns, p. 70), **her** (personal pronouns, p. 51)

5. **Who, whom** (relative pronouns, p. 57), **his** (possessive pronouns, p. 63)

6. **This** or **that** (demonstrative pronouns, p. 60), **that** or **which** (relative pronouns, p. 57)

7. **Which, what** (interrogative pronouns, p. 70)

8. **They** (personal pronouns, p. 51), **each other** or **one another** (reciprocal pronouns, p. 66)

9. **Myself** (reflexive pronouns, p. 65), **it** (personal pronouns, p. 51)

10. **This** or **that** (demonstrative pronouns, p. 60), **no one** or **nobody** (indefinite pronouns, p. 67)

11. **Me** (personal pronouns, p. 51)

12. **He, whom** (personal pronouns, p. 51)

13. **Them, they** (personal pronouns, p. 51)

14. **Who, me** (personal pronouns, p. 51)

15. **Who, me, we** (personal pronouns, p. 51)

16. **That** or **which** (relative pronouns, p. 57)

17. **Who** or **that** (relative pronouns, p. 57)

18. **Whose** (relative pronouns, p. 57)

19. **Whom** or **that** (relative pronouns, p. 57)

20. **Whose** (relative pronouns, p. 57)

21. No errors.

22. **We** fans must support our team. (common pitfall: "we" and "us" as appositives, p. 52)

23. Mark or Greg will give **his** support to our proposal. (agreement of pronouns with antecedents, p. 55)

24. They will give **themselves** a headache listening to such loud music. (reflexive pronouns, p. 65)

25. Anyone **who** says I was not at the meeting is mistaken. (relative pronouns, p. 57)

26. If **you're** going to the concert, can I go along? (possessive pronouns, p. 63)

27. Michaela's mother is the woman **whom** I most admire. (relative pronouns, p. 57)

28. We will meet **her** and Tim at the restaurant at 7 o'clock. (personal pronouns, p. 51)

29. People **who** have seen the new building are impressed. (relative pronouns, p. 57)

30. I lost my notes, so I had to borrow **theirs**. (possessive pronouns, p. 63)

Chapter 3
Verbs

Verbs are words that express action. Verbs can also express states of being or conditions. In a sentence, verbs have a **subject** (the doer of the action). Verbs can also have an **object** (the receiver of the action). Verbs agree in number and person with their subjects, for example: I *am,* he *is,* they *are.*

Verbs express **tense;** that is, the time at which the action occurred. The most common verb tenses are **past, present,** and **future,** but English also has **progressive** and **perfect** forms of each of these tenses as well. Sometimes tense is expressed by a change in the form of the verb, and sometimes tense is expressed by "helping verbs" or **auxiliary verbs,** usually forms of *to be, to have,* or *to do,* which supplement the main verb.

Verbs also express **voice** and **mood.** The voice can be **active** (where the subject does the action) or **passive** (where the action is done by an unspecified or implied subject). Mood can be **indicative, imperative** (for expressing commands), or **subjunctive** (for expressing desired, hypothetical, or uncertain events). **Modal auxiliaries** (must, could, and would) express possible, conditional, or required actions, and are often followed by subjunctive verb forms.

Some verbs require more than one word to express their meaning. These are called **phrasal verbs.** Finally, some word forms derived from verbs actually have quite different grammatical functions. **Gerunds** and **infinitives** act as nouns, while **participles** act as modifiers.

Transitive and Intransitive Verbs: Direct Objects

Some verbs do not require any objects to express their meaning. The action they express is complete by itself. These are called **intransitive verbs.**

Subject | Verb
The sun | shines.
He | slept.
The dog | will bark.

However, some verbs require an object (the receiver of the action) to complete their meaning. These are called **transitive** verbs. Transitive verbs cannot make sense unless they are followed by a **direct object.** A direct object tells *who* or *what* received the action of the verb.

Subject | Verb | Direct Object
Jorge | mailed | a letter. (*What* did Jorge mail? A letter.)
Julia | bought | a bicycle. (*What* did Julia buy? A bicycle.)
We | saw | our friends. (*Whom* did we see? Our friends.)

Some verbs can be either transitive or intransitive, depending on how they are used.

Intransitive: My arm **hurts.**

Transitive: I **hurt** my arm. (*What* did I hurt? My arm.)

In this example, the verb *to hurt* has two distinct meanings. The intransitive form means "to have a sensation of pain." The transitive form means "to cause injury to."

Example Problems

Are the following verbs transitive or intransitive?

1. Talk

   Intransitive. Talk does not take an object. For example: *We talked for hours. She is talking on the phone.*

2. Run

   Either, depending on the meaning. Intransitive: *Mitch runs in marathons.* Transitive: *Mitch runs the drill press at the factory.* (*What* does he run? The drill press.)

3. Seal

   Transitive. Seal always requires an object. For example: *I sealed the envelope. They sealed the agreement.*

Work Problems

Underline any direct objects in the following sentences.

1. After the game, we ate ice cream and went to a movie.

2. I returned the DVDs to the video rental store.

3. If you like peanuts and chocolate, you should try this candy bar.

4. Arizona is hot and dry much of the year.

5. What did you buy your mom for her birthday?

Worked Solutions

1. After the game, we ate <u>ice cream</u> and went to a movie.

   Ice cream is the direct object of **ate. Went** does not take an object; it is followed here by a prepositional phrase (**to a movie**).

2. I returned the <u>DVDs</u> to the video rental store.

    DVDs is the direct object of **returned.**

3. If you like <u>peanuts</u> and <u>chocolate</u>, you should try this <u>candy bar</u>.

    Peanuts and **chocolate** are both direct objects of the verb **like; candy bar** is the direct object of the verb **try.**

4. No direct objects.

    Is, a linking verb (linking verbs, p. 83), does not take an object. **Hot** and **dry** are adjectives, not nouns, so they cannot be objects. Technically, they are predicate adjectives (predicates, p. 188) in this sentence.

5. <u>What</u> did you buy your mom for her birthday?

    What is the direct object of the verb **buy.** (**What** is also an interrogative pronoun.) This direct object is difficult to see because the sentence is a question, so normal word order is inverted. Put the sentence in normal word order and the direct object becomes clearer: *You bought your mom <u>what</u> for her birthday.* (By the way, **mom** is an indirect object. These are covered in the next section.)

Indirect Objects

If a verb has a direct object, it can also have an **indirect object.** An indirect object tells *to whom* or *for whom* the action of the verb was done.

> **Subject | Verb | Indirect Object | Direct Object**
> Jorge | mailed | Clarice | a letter. (*To whom* did he send it? To Clarice.)
> Julia | bought | her sister | a bicycle. (*For whom* did she buy it? For her sister.)

Indirect objects are usually living beings like people or animals, but direct objects can be either people or things. If a verb has only one object, it will be a direct object.

Indirect objects usually come between the verb and the direct object. It is possible to restate these sentences using the prepositions *to* and *for*. While we can still think of the word following the preposition as an indirect object, some grammarians would say that the indirect object has instead become the object of a preposition (Prepositions, p. 151).

> **Subject | Verb | Direct Object | Indirect Object**
> Jorge | mailed | a letter | to Clarice.
> Julia | bought | a bicycle | for her sister.

Look at the following sentences. Do they have indirect objects?

1. Carol called Mike a liar.

2. Carol called Mike a cab.

3. Picasso's talent made him famous.

4. Picasso's paintings give me pleasure.

In Sentence 1, **Mike** is a direct object. In Sentence 2, **Mike** is an indirect object. So, how can we tell the difference? To determine if a word is an indirect object, try placing it at the end of the sentence with the word *to* or *for*.

> Carol called a liar *for Mike*. Carol called a liar *to Mike*.
>
> (This makes no sense, unless Mike suddenly needs to find a liar; therefore, **Mike** is a direct object.)

> Carol called a cab *for Mike*.
>
> (This sentence still makes sense; therefore, **Mike** is an indirect object.)

In Sentence 1, **liar** does not function as a direct object. Instead, it is an **object complement** of the direct object **Mike.** Object complements describe, modify, or rename direct objects. (See objects, p. 190, for more about object complements.) Try the test on Sentences 3 and 4.

> Picasso's talent made famous *for him* or *to him*.
> Picasso's paintings give pleasure *to me*.

Sentence 3 does not have an indirect object; **famous** is an object complement. Sentence 4 does have a direct object (**pleasure**) and an indirect object (**me**).

Example Problems

What is the indirect object in this sentence?

1. Terri gave me a ride to school.

    Answer: **Me.** Terri gave *what?* A **ride** (direct object). To *whom?* to **me** (indirect object).

2. My father sent extra money to my sister at college.

    Answer: **My sister. My sister** is the object of a preposition, but it also answers the question, to *whom* did he send money? Therefore, it is an indirect object. (**Money** is the direct object.)

3. The suppliers sent the shipment to Minneapolis.

    Answer: **No indirect object. Shipment** is the direct object of **sent.** Even though **Minneapolis** follows the preposition *to,* **Minneapolis** cannot be an indirect object because it is not a living being. It does not answer the question, *to whom* or *for whom* was the shipment sent? Instead, it is a prepositional phrase describing *where* the shipment went.

Work Problems

Draw a single line under any direct objects. Draw a double line under any indirect objects.

1. The teacher asked Janelle a question about the assignment.

2. After the wedding, the bride threw her bouquet to her bridesmaids.

3. That horrible music is driving me crazy.

4. Newspapers provide their communities news and advertising services.

5. Marcus plays basketball well, but football gives him problems.

Worked Solutions

The bolded section stands for the double-underline mentioned in the instructions for this section.

1. The teacher asked **Janelle** a <u>question</u> about the assignment.

   This is a rare case where the *to-for* test does not work well to root out the indirect object because the preposition typically used with **ask** is *of:* "The teacher asked a question *of Janelle.*" Regardless, **Janelle** is still an indirect object.

2. After the wedding, the bride threw <u>her bouquet</u> to her **bridesmaids.**

   While **bridesmaids** is also the object of a preposition, it is still functioning as an indirect object.

3. That horrible music is driving <u>me</u> crazy.

   Crazy is an object complement, not a direct object. **Crazy** is an adjective, not a noun, so it cannot be an object itself.

4. Local newspapers provide their **communities** <u>news</u> and <u>advertising services</u>.

   The *to-for* test works well here: ". . . provide news and advertising *to their communities.*"

5. Marcus plays <u>basketball</u> well, but football gives **him** <u>problems</u>.

   Basketball is the direct object of **plays. Problems** is the direct object of **gives,** and **him** is the indirect object of **gives** ("gives problems *to him*").

Linking Verbs

A **linking verb** joins a **subject** to a **subject complement** (also called a **predicate noun** or **predicate adjective**), a word or phrase that describes or explains the subject. (See predicates, p. 188.) The most common linking verb is the verb *to be.*

> Kayaking **is** my favorite sport.
> My grandmother **was** an expert pilot.

Other common linking verbs are **seem, appear, look, feel, sound, taste,** and **smell.**

> This shirt **feels** comfortable.
> That cake **smells** delicious.

Linking verbs are always intransitive. If a verb takes a direct object, it is not a linking verb.

> The dog **smelled** the garbage. (Transitive verb with direct object **garbage**)
> The garbage **smelled** awful. (Linking verb to subject complement **awful**)

Example Problems

Identify the linking verb in each sentence.

1. Mary told me that she feels sick today.

   Answer: **Feels.** The complement is **sick,** telling how Mary feels.

2. That idea sounds crazy to me.

   Answer: **Sounds.** The complement is **crazy,** telling how the idea sounds.

Work Problems

Use linking verbs to complete the following sentences.

1. Chocolate _____ wonderful.

2. Chocolate mousse _____ my favorite dessert.

3. From below, clouds _____ fluffy and light.

4. Simone _____ beautiful in her new dress.

5. Their idea _____ good at the time.

Worked Solutions

1. Tastes

2. Is

3. Seem or appear

4. Looks

5. Sounded or seemed

(For Questions 1 and 3–5, a form of the verb *to be* would also be an appropriate answer.)

Verb Tenses

Tense indicates the time at which an action takes place. We usually speak of tense as representing **past, present,** or **future,** but in English each of these tenses also has **perfect** and **progressive** forms.

> *Present:* I **eat** an apple every day.
> *Present Progressive:* She **is eating** her lunch right now.
> *Past:* He **ate** dinner already.
> *Past Perfect:* They **had eaten** something that made them sick.

Most English tenses are formed using helping verbs or auxiliary verbs, usually forms of the verbs **be, do,** or **have.** Changes in tense can also involve changes to the base form of the verb. With the exception of the verb **be,** the base form of all English verbs is the same as the first person singular present tense form.

Simple Present Tense

As its name implies, simple present tense indicates actions occurring in the present.

> The cat **sees** the bird.
> She **knows** the answer.

Simple present tense also indicates habitual, customary, repeated, or permanent actions or conditions.

> My karate class **meets** on Thursdays.
> Dave **smokes** too many cigarettes.
> I **drink** a cup of coffee before I **go** to work.
> Horned toads **live** in the desert.

English simple present verbs change forms to agree in **number** and **person** with the subject of the verb. For most verbs, simply add an **–s** to the end of the verb for third person singular, as shown in the table that follows.

	Singular	*Plural*
First person	I eat	We eat
Second person	You eat	You eat
Third person	He/She/It eats	They eat

However, if the base form of the verb ends in **–s, –sh, –ch, –x, –z,** or **–o,** add **–es.** If the base form ends in **consonant + y,** change the **y** to **i** before adding **–es.**

	Singular	*Plural*
First person	I catch	We catch
Second person	You catch	You catch
Third person	He/She/It catches	They catch

	Singular	*Plural*
First person	I hurry	We hurry
Second person	You hurry	You hurry
Third person	He/She/It hurries	They hurry

The most common English verb, *to be*, is **irregular,** meaning that it does not follow this pattern.

I **am**	We **are**
You **are**	You **are**
He/She/It **is**	They **are**

Another common verb, *to have*, is irregular only for third person singular: He/She/It **has.**

To form the negative of a simple present tense verb, use the auxiliary verb **do.**

> **Present tense form of do + not + base form of another verb**

The verb **do** becomes the one that agrees with the subject. The auxiliary **do** is also required to make a simple present tense sentence into a question, in which case **do** comes at the beginning of the sentence, in front of the subject. (See sentence types: declarative, imperative, and interrogative moods, p. 202, for more about questions.)

> The cat **sees** the bird.
> *Question:* **Does** the cat **see** the bird?
> *Negative:* The cat **does not see** the bird.

> My karate class **meets** on Thursdays.
> *Question:* **Does** my karate class **meet** on Thursdays?
> *Negative:* My karate class **does not meet** on Thursdays.

Only the simple present tense verb *to be* does not use the **do** auxiliary.

> The sky **is** blue.
> **Is** the sky blue?
> The sky **is not** blue.

Example Problems

Change the verb in the first sentence to fit in the second sentence.

1. We enjoy running. Marcus also _____ running.

   Answer: **Enjoys.** (third person singular, add **–s** to the base form)

2. They go to the beach. Kate also _____ to the beach.

   Answer: **Goes.** (third person singular, ends in **–o,** so add **–es**)

3. I carry a backpack. Carmen also _____ a backpack.

   Answer: **Carries.** (third person singular, ends in **consonant + y,** change **y** to **i,** and then add **–es**)

Work Problems

Supply the simple present tense form of the verb indicated.

1. (Teach) Mr. Lee _____ tae kwan do at the community center.

2. (Invite) The seniors _____ everyone to the spring dance.

3. (Guarantee) The manufacturer _____ this product for one year.

4. (Testify) Dr. Juarez often _____ in court as an expert witness.

5. (Eat) We usually _____ lunch at the corner café.

Worked Solutions

1. **Teaches** (third person singular, ends in **–ch,** add **–es**)

2. **Invite** (third person plural, no change needed)

3. **Guarantees** (third person singular, add **–s**)

4. **Testifies** (third person singular, ends in **consonant + y,** change **y** to **i,** and then add **–es**)

5. **Eat** (first person plural, no change needed)

Simple Past Tense

Simple past tense indicates an action that took place in the past.

> Alfred Hitchcock **directed** many great films.
> The cat **chased** the bird.
> I **ate** breakfast this morning.
> We **saw** a Broadway play when we **visited** New York.

To form the simple past of most English verbs, simply add **–ed** to the base form. If the base form ends in **consonant + y,** change the **y** to **i** before adding **–ed.**

> talk → talk**ed**
> need → need**ed**
> carry → carr**ied**

If the base form ends in **consonant + e,** add **–d.**

> bake → bake**d**
> arrive → arrive**d**

If the base form ends in **vowel + consonant,** double the consonant if the last syllable is stressed or the word has only one syllable.

> permit → permitted
> transmit → transmitted
> step → stepped
> plan → planned

However, many common English verbs are irregular in past tense. These verbs change forms completely in simple past. For example:

> see → **saw**
> eat → **ate**
> take → **took**
> do → **did**

For a table of irregular past tense verb forms, see p. 98 following the section on past perfect tense.

To form the negative of a simple past tense verb, use:

> **Did (the simple past tense form of do) + not + base form of another verb**

To form a question in simple past tense, move the auxiliary **did** to the beginning of the sentence, in front of the subject.

> The cat **chased** the bird.
> **Did** the cat **chase** the bird?
> The cat **did not chase** the bird.

Only the irregular verb *to be* does not use the **did** auxiliary.

> They **were** tired of waiting.
> **Were** they tired of waiting?
> They **were not** tired of waiting.

Example Problems

Following the examples above, change the simple past tense sentences to questions, and then give a negative answer.

1. Farah **asked** me to meet her at the mall.

   Answer: **Did** Farah **ask** me to meet her at the mall?

   Answer: Farah **did not ask** me to meet her at the mall.

   For questions using simple past tense, the auxiliary verb **do** becomes the verb in past tense, while the original verb changes to its base form. For negatives, **not** goes between **did** and the base form of the verb.

2. My boss **told** me to go home early.

    Answer: **Did** my boss **tell** me to go home early?

    Answer: My boss **did not tell** me to go home early.

    Told is an irregular simple past tense form; the base form is **tell.** Otherwise, the rules are the same as for Sentence 1.

Work Problems

Change the verb in each sentence from simple present to simple past tense.

1. Helen eats her lunch at noon.

2. Her friends wait for her in the park.

3. They go to a restaurant.

4. She stops to feed the birds by the fountain.

5. She seldom varies this routine.

Worked Solutions

1. Helen **ate** her lunch at noon. (irregular past tense form)

2. Her friends **waited** for her in the park. (regular form, add **–ed** to base form)

3. They **went** to a restaurant. (irregular past tense form)

4. She **stopped** to feed the birds by the fountain. (regular form, base form is a single syllable ending in **vowel + consonant,** so double the final letter before adding **–ed)**

5. She seldom **varied** this routine. (regular form, base form **vary** ends in **consonant + y,** so change **y** to **i,** and then add **–ed)**

Simple Future Tense

Simple future tense indicates an action that has not yet taken place.

> We **will go** to Germany next summer.
> They **will meet** you at the coffee shop at seven o'clock.
> The contractor **will finish** the project by Friday.

The pattern for forming simple future tense is as follows:

> **Will + base form of verb**

Will is one of a small group of verbs called **modal auxiliaries** that do not vary in form (modal auxiliaries, p. 116).

To form the negative of a simple future verb, place **not** between the auxiliary **will** and the base verb. To form a question, move **will** to the beginning of the sentence, in front of the subject.

They **will meet** you at the coffee shop.

Will they **meet** you at the coffee shop?

They **will not meet** you at the coffee shop.

Example Problems

Change each simple past tense sentence to a simple future tense sentence, and then turn the future tense sentence into a question.

1. The bookstore **sent** you the package.

    Answer: The bookstore **will send** you the package.

    Answer: **Will** the bookstore **send** you the package?

    Sent is an irregular past tense verb; the base form, required for future tense, is **send.** For questions, the auxiliary verb moves to the beginning of the sentence.

2. Dave **talked** to the central office.

    Answer: Dave **will talk** to the central office.

    Answer: **Will** Dave **talk** to the central office?

    Talked is a regular past tense form; just remove the **–ed** to find the base form.

Work Problems

Change the verbs in these sentences from simple past to simple future tense.

1. The children saw a puppet show.

2. He became a famous artist.

3. Brian decided to paint his house green.

4. The judge rendered her verdict on the case.

5. Her decision was unpopular.

Worked Solutions

1. The children **will see** a puppet show. (**Saw** is an irregular simple past tense form; the base form is **see.**)

2. He **will become** a famous artist. (**Became** is an irregular simple past tense form; the base form is **become.**)

3. Brian **will decide** to paint his house green. (**Decided** is a regular form; simply remove the **–d** to find the base form.)

4. The judge **will render** her verdict on the case. (**Render** is a regular form; simply remove the **–ed** to find the base form.)

5. Her decision **will be** unpopular. (Nearly all forms of the verb *to be* are irregular, but the base form is simply **be.**)

Present Progressive Tense

Present progressive tense indicates an action currently in progress or actively taking place.

> She **is talking** to her friends right now.
> We **are negotiating** with a new supplier.
> The cookies **are baking,** and they will be ready soon.

The pattern for forming present progressive tense is as follows:

> **Present tense form of be + present participle**

The present participle is the base form of the verb with **–ing** added to the end. If the base form of the verb ends in **consonant + e**, drop the **e** before adding **–ing**. If the base form of the verb ends in **vowel + consonant,** double the consonant if the word has only one syllable. (An exception to this pattern is **oo + consonant,** as in *look* or *cook*.)

> march → **marching**
> ache → **aching**
> hit → **hitting**
> **But:** snoop → **snooping**

To form the negative, place **not** between the auxiliary **be** and the present participle. To form a question, move the auxiliary to the beginning of the sentence, before the subject.

> She **is talking** to her friends.
> She **is not talking** to her friends.
> **Is** she **talking** to her friends?

The verb **go** is a special case among present progressive tense verbs. **Go** is often used in a specific construction:

> **Present tense form of be + going + to + *base form of another verb***

This construction always expresses actions that are going to happen in the future, and it is often used interchangeably with simple future tense.

> We **are going to** *have* a barbecue on Saturday.
> I **am going to** *tell* him what I really think.
> The Cubs **are going to** *win* the World Series this year.

Of course, it is also possible to use **go** as an ordinary present progressive tense verb.

> I **am going** to the movies with Lisa.

Example Problems

Should the verbs in the following sentences be in simple present or present progressive tense?

1.　I (take) judo lessons.

　　Answer: Either tense could be appropriate, depending on the context.

　　"I **take** judo lessons. My class meets three times a week." (Present tense is appropriate because this is a habitual or repeated event.)

　　"I **am taking** judo lessons. I am learning a lot." (Present progressive tense is appropriate because the speaker is emphasizing the ongoing process of learning judo.)

2.　My neighbors (restore) their Victorian house.

　　Answer: Present progressive tense is more appropriate because restoring the house is an ongoing process: "My neighbors **are restoring** their Victorian house." Compare this usage of present perfect progressive tense: "My neighbors **are restoring** their Victorian house. They **have been restoring** it for more than two years." (present perfect progressive tense, p. 104)

Work Problems

Change the verb in each sentence from simple present to present progressive tense.

1.　Carrie walks her dog.

2.　The workers repair the damaged building.

3.　The client considers the proposal.

4.　We save money to buy a new car.

5.　I drive to work.

Worked Solutions

1.　Carrie **is walking** her dog. **Is** (third person singular) agrees with **Carrie;** to form the present participle, simply add **–ing** to the base form of the verb.

2.　The workers **are repairing** the damaged building. **Are** (third person plural) agrees with **workers;** to form the present participle, simply add **–ing** to the base form of the verb.

3.　The client **is considering** the proposal. **Is** (third person singular) agrees with **client;** to form the present participle, simply add **–ing** to the base form of the verb.

4.　We **are saving** money to buy a new car. **Are** (first person plural) agrees with **we;** to form the present participle, drop the final **e** and add **–ing** to the base form of the verb.

5.　I **am driving** to work. **Am** (first person singular) agrees with **I;** to form the present participle, drop the final **e** and add **–ing** to the base form of the verb.

Past Progressive Tense

Past progressive tense indicates an event that was in progress at a particular point in the past.

She **was cooking** dinner when I called.

While you **were wasting** time, I **was doing** all the work.

We **were watching** television at eight o'clock.

The pattern for forming past progressive is as follows:

Simple past tense form of *to be* + present participle

To be is irregular in simple past tense and also agrees with the subject in number and person.

I was	We were
You were	You were
He/She/It **was**	They **were**

Example Problems

Change the simple past tense verb to past progressive.

1. We looked for you last night.

    Answer: We **were looking** for you last night.

    Were (first person plural) agrees with the subject **we.** To form the present participle of **look,** simply add **–ing.**

2. The party went well.

    Answer: The party **was going** well.

    Was (third person singular) agrees with the subject **party. Went** is the irregular past tense form of the verb **go.** To form the present participle, add **–ing** to the base form. (By itself, this sentence does not make much sense in past progressive tense. It would be more helpful to put a specific, single event in the sentence to contrast with the progressive action, such as: The party was going well *until the couch caught on fire.*)

Work Problems

Supply the past progressive form of the verb indicated.

1. (Take) My sister _____ out the garbage when she saw a stray cat.

2. (Scrounge) The cat _____ for food in the garbage cans.

3. (Look) The cat's owners _____ for it.

4. (Drive) They _____ down our street.

5. (Carry) My sister _____ the cat home when they saw her.

Worked Solutions

1. My sister **was taking** out the garbage when she saw a stray cat. **Was** (third person singular) agrees with **my sister;** remove the **e** from the base form **take** before adding **–ing** to form the present participle.

2. The cat **was scrounging** for food in the garbage cans. **Was** (third person singular) agrees with **cat;** remove the **e** from the base form **scrounge** before adding **–ing.**

3. The cat's owners **were looking** for it. **Were** (third person plural) agrees with **the cat's owners;** simply add **–ing** to the base form **look.**

4. They **were driving** down our street. **Were** (third person plural) agrees with **they;** remove the **e** from the base form **drive** before adding **–ing.**

5. My sister **was carrying** the cat home when they saw her. **Was** (third person singular) agrees with **my sister;** add **–ing** to the base form **carry.**

Future Progressive Tense

Future progressive tense indicates an event that will be in progress at a specific point in the future.

My family **will be taking** a vacation the first week in June.
We **will be staying** at a resort in Florida.
My uncle **will be running** the family business while we are gone.

The pattern for forming future progressive tense is as follows:

Will be + present participle

To form the negative, place **not** between **will** and **be.** To form a question, move **will** to the beginning of the sentence, before the subject.

Juan **will be directing** work on the project.
Will Juan **be directing** work on the project?
Juan **will not be directing** work on the project.

Example Problems

Change each simple past tense sentence to a future progressive tense sentence, and then turn the sentence into a question.

1. Students designed the costumes for the play.

   Answer: Students **will be designing** the costumes for the play.

   Answer: **Will** students **be designing** the costumes for the play?

   Design is a regular verb form; simply add **–ing** to make the present participle. **Will be** is an invariable form; it does not change to show agreement with number or person.

2. The factory upgraded its computers.

    Answer: The factory **will be upgrading** its computers.

    Answer: **Will** the factory **be upgrading** its computers?

    Upgrade is a regular verb form, but you must remove the final **e** before adding **–ing.**

Both of the preceding sentences would make just as much sense in simple future tense as in future progressive tense.

    Students **will design** the costumes for the play.
    The factory **will upgrade** its computers.

Using future progressive tense simply places somewhat more emphasis on the idea of a process taking place.

Work Problems
Supply the future progressive form of the verb indicated.

1. (Seek) The company _____ a replacement for the CEO.

2. (Clean) I _____ my basement on Saturday.

3. (Host) The club _____ a dinner for new members.

4. (Fly) Mariah and Ben _____ to Jamaica tomorrow.

5. (Prepare) The caterers _____ the food for the wedding.

Worked Solutions

1. **Will be seeking** (Add **–ing** to the base form to make the present participle; the auxiliary **will be** does not change forms for number or person.)

2. **Will be cleaning** (Add **–ing** to the base form to make the present participle.)

3. **Will be hosting** (Add **–ing** to the base form to make the present participle.)

4. **Will be flying** (Add **–ing** to the base form to make the present participle.)

5. **Will be preparing** (Remove the final **e,** and then add **–ing** to the base form to make the present participle.)

Present Perfect Tense

Despite its name, present perfect tense normally does not refer to actions occurring in the present. Instead, it most often refers to actions completed in the past that have some consequence or effect on the present situation.

> I **have tried** to tell him to slow down, but he will not listen.
>
> Mr. Jones **has ordered** a new couch for his house, but it has not arrived yet.
>
> Stan **has broken** his leg, so he cannot go on the ski trip with us.

Present perfect tense also refers to continuous actions begun in the past and extending into the present.

> I **have lived** in California for three years.
>
> My mother **has wanted** to visit India since she was a little girl.

The pattern for forming present perfect tense is as follows:

> **Simple present tense form of have + past participle of the verb**

For most verbs, the past participle is the same as the **simple past** form.

> try → **tried**
>
> look → **looked**

However, many common English verbs have irregular past and past participle forms. For a table of irregular past tense verb forms, see p. 98 following the section on past perfect tense.

To form the negative of present perfect tense, insert **not** between the auxiliary and the past participle. To form a question, move the auxiliary to the beginning of the sentence.

> Stan **has broken** his leg.
>
> **Has** Stan **broken** his leg?
>
> Stan **has not broken** his leg.

Example Problems

Should the verbs in the following sentences be in simple past or present perfect tense?

1. I (be) in college for five years. This year, I will finally graduate.

   Answer: Present perfect is more appropriate than simple past tense for this sentence: "I **have been** in college for five years." The second sentence indicates that this is an action begun in the past and continuing in the present.

2. My perceptions of Japan (change) a lot during my stay in Tokyo.

   Answer: Either present perfect or simple past tense could be appropriate, depending on the context. If the speaker is still living in Tokyo, it would be more appropriate to say "my perceptions **have changed**" because this implies a situation begun in the past and continuing in the present. If the speaker lived in Tokyo for a brief period last year, it would be more appropriate to say "my perceptions **changed**" because the action was completed in the past.

3. We (visit) many museums since we arrived in New York.

> *Answer:* Present perfect tense is more appropriate: "We **have visited** many museums since we arrived in New York." The time marker **since we arrived** is a good hint that this situation is continuing in the present.

Work Problems

Change the simple past tense verbs to present perfect.

1. The rose bush grew rapidly.

2. They broke their promises too many times.

3. The mayor failed to understand the voters' wishes.

4. The accountants mismanaged the company's finances.

5. This cruise ship was in service for more than 10 years.

Worked Solutions

1. **Has grown. Has** (third person singular) agrees with **rose bush; grown** is the irregular past participle of the verb **grow.**

2. **Have broken. Have** (third person plural) agrees with **they; broken** is the irregular past participle of the verb **break.**

3. **Has failed. Has** (third person singular) agrees with **mayor; failed** is the regular past participle of the verb **fail.**

4. **Have mismanaged. Have** (third person plural) agrees with **accountants; mismanaged** is the regular past participle of the verb **mismanage.**

5. **Has been. Has** (third person singular) agrees with **cruise ship; been** is the regular past participle of the verb **be,** seen here in its simple past form **was.**

In changing the verbs to present perfect tense, it is implied that a past action has some effect on the present situation, which might only be apparent from the context.

> The rose bush has grown rapidly; *now it produces beautiful flowers.*
>
> The mayor has failed to understand the voters' wishes, *so he will lose this election.*

Past Perfect Tense

Past perfect tense indicates an action that preceded another action in the past.

> The building **had burned** completely by the time the fire department arrived.
>
> I **had visited** London several times before I decided to move there.

Past perfect tense is often used in narratives, with **said.**

> She **said** that she **had talked** to you last night.
> We **told** Mr. James that you **had washed** his car.

The pattern for forming past perfect tense is as follows:

Had + past participle

For regular English verbs, the past participle is the same as the simple past tense form (ending in –**ed**). However, many irregular past tense verbs exist in English. Some have identical forms for simple past tense and past participle, but others do not. If in doubt as to the past tense forms of a particular verb, consult a dictionary. A table of some common irregular past tense verbs follows.

Common irregular past tense verbs		
Base Form	*Simple Past*	*Past Participle*
be (irregular present: I am, he/she/it **is,** you/we/they **are**)	I /he/she/it **was,** you/we/they **were**	been
beat	beat	beaten
become	became	become
begin	began	begun
bend	bent	bent
bite	bit	bitten
bleed	bled	bled
blow	blew	blown
break	broke	broken
bring	brought	brought
build	built	built
buy	bought	bought
come	came	come
catch	caught	caught
choose	chose	chosen
dig	dug	dug
dive	dove or dived	dived
do	did	done
draw	drew	drawn
drink	drank	drunk

Base Form	Simple Past	Past Participle
drive	drove	driven
eat	ate	eaten
fall	fell	fallen
feed	fed	fed
feel	felt	felt
find	found	found
fly	flew	flown
forbid	forbade	forbidden
freeze	froze	frozen
get	got	gotten
give	gave	given
go	went	gone
grow	grew	grown
hang	hung	hung
have	had	had
keep	kept	kept
know	knew	known
lay	laid	laid
lead	led	led
lie	lay	lain
leave	left	left
lose	lost	lost
make	made	made
mean	meant	meant
meet	met	met
pay	paid	paid
prove	proved	proven or proved
read (pronounced "reed")	read (pronounced "red")	read (pronounced "red")
ride	rode	ridden
rise	rose	risen
run	ran	run

(continued)

Common irregular past tense verbs *(continued)*		
Base Form	*Simple Past*	*Past Participle*
say	said	said
see	saw	seen
sell	sold	sold
send	sent	sent
shake	shook	shaken
shoot	shot	shot
show	showed	shown or showed
shrink	shrank	shrunk
sing	sang	sung
sit	sat	sat
sleep	slept	slept
speak	spoke	spoken
spend	spent	spent
spring	sprang	sprung
stand	stood	stood
steal	stole	stolen
stink	stank	stunk
strike	struck	struck
swear	swore	sworn
sweep	swept	swept
swim	swam	swum
swing	swung	swung
teach	taught	taught
take	took	taken
tear	tore	torn
tell	told	told
think	thought	thought
throw	threw	thrown
wear	wore	worn
win	won	won
write	wrote	written

A few verbs do not change form or pronunciation for simple past or past participle. Common examples are:

bet	put
cost	quit
cut	set
hit	shut
hurt	spread
let	

To form the negative, place **not** between **had** and the past participle. To form a question, move **had** to the beginning of sentence, before the subject.

> She **had taken** a wrong turn.
> **Had** she **taken** a wrong turn?
> She **had not taken** a wrong turn.

Past perfect tense is often accompanied by **yet, never,** and **already.** These words go between **had** and the past participle:

> She knew that she **had** *already* **taken** a wrong turn.

Example Problems

Put the indicated verbs into simple past or past perfect tense.

1. My father (ask) me to mow the lawn, but I (do) it already.

    Answer: **Asked, had done.** The action of mowing the lawn was completed before the father asked about it.

2. Everyone else (go) home by the time we (finish) cleaning up.

    Answer: **Had gone, finished.** The action of leaving was completed before the task of cleaning was finished.

Work Problems

Put the indicated verbs in simple past or past perfect tense. Place the adverb in its correct location in the sentence.

1. Katrina wore the same wedding dress her mother (wear).

2. The leaves (fall, [already]) even though it was only October.

3. They told the police they (see, not) the accident happen.

4. I (skate, [never]) until this winter.

5. He had a bump on his head where the ball (hit) him.

Worked Solutions

1. **Had worn** (**Worn** is an irregular past participle.)

2. **Had already fallen** (**Fallen** is an irregular past participle; **already** goes between **had** and the participle.)

3. **Had not seen** (**Seen** is an irregular past participle; **not** goes between **had** and the participle.)

4. **Had never skated** (**Skated** is a regular past participle; **never** goes between **had** and the participle.)

5. **Had hit** (**Hit** is an irregular past participle that does not change forms.)

Common Pitfall: "Lie" versus "Lay"

Two commonly confused verbs are **lie** and **lay.** The confusion becomes more understandable when we look at the past tense forms, which resemble each other.

Present	*Past*	*Past Participle*
lay	laid	laid
lie	lay	lain

Lie is an intransitive verb meaning *to recline.*

(Present) I often **lie** in bed and read a book.
(Past) The cat **lay** on top of the television.
(Past perfect) His coat **had lain** on the floor for days before he hung it up.

Lay is a transitive verb meaning *to put or place (something).*

(Present) Please **lay** that package on my desk.
(Past) I **laid** my book down when I answered the phone.
(Past perfect) I forgot where I **had laid** my glasses.

Future Perfect Tense

Future perfect tense indicates an event that will be completed by a specific point in the future.

We **will have finished** the project by the end of the week.
The movie **will have ended** before we can get there.
She **will have left** her house by now.

The pattern for forming future perfect tense is as follows:

Will have + past participle

To form the negative, place **not** between **will** and **have.** To form a question, move **will** to the beginning of the sentence, in front of the subject.

> They **will have gone** by now.
> **Will** they **have gone** by now?
> They **will not have gone** by now.

Example Problems

Change the verbs from simple past to future perfect tense.

1. The author gave his speech.

   Answer: The author **will have given** his speech. The verb **give** changes from simple past to the past participle form.

2. The chef cooked the meal.

   Answer: The chef **will have cooked** the meal. The verb **cook** is regular; simply add **–ed** to the base form for both simple past and past participle forms.

Work Problems

Supply the future perfect tense of the verb indicated.

1. By this time tomorrow, we (take) the test.

2. The surgeon (complete) the operation soon.

3. He (ask) her to marry him.

4. The birds (fly) south for the winter.

5. The tide (go) out already.

Worked Solutions

1. **Will have taken** (**Taken** is an irregular past participle.)

2. **Will have completed** (**Completed** is a regular past participle; the base form ends in **e,** so add **–d.**)

3. **Will have asked** (**Asked** is a regular past participle; simply add **–ed** to the base form.)

4. **Will have flown** (**Flown** is an irregular past participle.)

5. **Will have gone** (**Gone** is an irregular past participle.)

Present Perfect Progressive Tense

Present perfect progressive tense indicates an ongoing event begun in the past and continuing into the present.

> She **has been looking** tired lately.
> We **have been taking** dance lessons for three weeks now.

The pattern for forming present perfect progressive tense is as follows:

> **Present tense form of have + been + present participle**

To form the negative, place **not** between the **have** auxiliary and **been.** To form a question, move the **have** auxiliary to the beginning of the sentence, in front of the subject.

> She **has been looking** tired.
> **Has** she **been looking** tired?
> She **has not been looking** tired.

Example Problems

Should the verbs in the following sentences be in present perfect progressive or simple past tense?

1. Everyone in the choir (ask) about you.

    Answer: Either is correct, depending on the context. "Everyone in the choir **asked** about you" would imply that the asking occurred at a single gathering. "Everyone in the choir **has been asking** about you" would imply that the asking has been repeated, and has gone on recently.

2. Marianne (go) to an acupuncturist for treatment.

    Answer: Either is correct, depending on the context. "Marianne **went** to an acupuncturist for treatment" would imply that she went once, and then stopped. "Marianne **has been going** to an acupuncturist for treatment" would imply that she went several times, and continues to go back.

Work Problems

Supply the present perfect progressive tense form of the verb indicated.

1. Vlad (act) strangely since he got back from Transylvania.

2. My neighbors (talk) about moving, but they have not done it yet.

3. Our basketball team (practice) handoffs and passing.

4. It feels like we (walk) forever.

5. John (write) poetry for as long as I have known him.

Worked Solutions

1. **Has been acting. Has** (third person singular) agrees with **Vlad;** to form the present participle of **act** simply add **–ing.**

2. **Have been talking. Have** (third person plural) agrees with **neighbors;** to form the present participle of **talk** simply add **–ing.**

3. **Has been practicing. Has** (third person singular) agrees with **team;** to form the present participle of **practice,** remove the final **e** and add **–ing.**

4. **Have been walking. Have** (first person plural) agrees with **we;** to form the present participle of **walk,** simply add **–ing.**

5. **Has been writing. Has** (third person singular) agrees with **John;** to form the present participle of **write,** remove the final **e** and add **–ing.**

Past Perfect Progressive Tense

Past perfect progressive tense indicates an ongoing event that was completed in the past, prior to some other past event.

> We **had been looking** for a house for six months when we found this one.
> Mark **had been applying** for other jobs before he was laid off.

The pattern for forming past perfect progressive tense is as follows:

> **Had + been + present participle**

To form the negative, place **not** between **had** and **been.** To form a question, move **had** to the beginning of the sentence, in front of the subject.

> We **had been looking** for a house.
> **Had** we **been looking** for a house?
> We **had not been looking** for a house.

Example Problems

Change the present progressive verb to past perfect progressive.

1. She is running to answer the phone.

    Answer: She **had been running** to answer the phone.

2. We are learning a new dance routine.

    Answer: We **had been learning** a new dance routine.

    The past tense form **had** does not change forms for number or person. **Been,** the past participle of the verb **be,** also does not change.

Neither of these sentences makes much sense without a context for the event: She had been running to answer the phone *when she tripped over the cat.*

We had been learning a new dance routine *when the choreographer suddenly changed it.*

Work Problems
Supply the past perfect progressive form of the verb indicated.

1. (Anticipate) I _____ a new challenge when this job offer came along.

2. (Wait) He _____ for the right time to announce his candidacy.

3. (Howl) The dog _____ for days before his owners came home.

4. (Wish) The little boy _____ for a new bicycle for his birthday.

5. (Burn) The fire _____ for nearly an hour before anyone saw the smoke.

Worked Solutions

1. **Had been anticipating** (Remove the final **e** before adding **–ing** to the base form of the verb; **had been** does not change forms for number or person.)

2. **Had been waiting** (Add **–ing** to the base form of the verb to form the present participle.)

3. **Had been howling** (Add **–ing** to the base form of the verb to form the present participle.)

4. **Had been wishing** (Add **–ing** to the base form of the verb to form the present participle.)

5. **Had been burning** (Add **–ing** to the base form of the verb to form the present participle.)

Future Perfect Progressive Tense
Future perfect progressive tense indicates an ongoing event that will be completed by a certain point in the future.

The party **will have been going** for ages by the time we arrive.

In just half an hour from now, we **will have been working** for 14 hours straight.

The pattern for forming future perfect progressive tense is as follows:

Will have been + present participle

To form the negative, place **not** between the auxiliaries **will** and **have.** To form a question, move **will** to the beginning of the sentence, in front of the subject.

They **will have been preparing** the food.

Will they **have been preparing** the food?

They **will not have been preparing** the food.

Example Problems

Change the verbs from present perfect to future perfect progressive tense.

1. The stage crew has painted the set.

    Answer: The stage crew **will have been painting** the set. **Paint** is a regular verb; simply add **–ing** to the base form to form the present participle.

2. The baseball team has taken batting practice.

    Answer: The baseball team **will have been taking** batting practice. The verb **take** has an irregular past participle, but drop the final **e** from the base form before adding **–ing** to form the present participle. The auxiliaries **will** and **have** never change forms as part of a future perfect progressive verb.

Work Problems

Supply the future perfect progressive form of the verb indicated.

1. The stew (cook) for at least three hours.

2. I am sure they will be tired; they (work) all day.

3. By the time we finish, we (restore) this house for years.

4. As of July 24, I (live) in the United States for a decade.

5. By tomorrow, Jeremy and Lita (date) for an entire week.

Worked Solutions

1. **Will have been cooking** (Add **–ing** to the base form **cook** to make the present participle.)

2. **Will have been working** (Add **–ing** to the base form **work** to make the present participle.)

3. **Will have been restoring** (Remove the final **e** from the base form **restore,** and then add **–ing** to make the present participle.)

4. **Will have been living** (Remove the final **e** from the base form **live,** and then add **–ing** to make the present participle.)

5. **Will have been dating** (Remove the final **e** from the base form **date,** and then add **–ing** to make the present participle.)

Voice

Voice is the form of a verb that indicates whether the subject is doing the action of the verb or receiving the action of the verb. In **active** voice, the subject does the action of the verb.

Subject + verb + object. = Doer of action + **verb** + *receiver of action.*

Yun **caught** *the ball.*

Karen **fixed** *the problem.*

In **passive** voice, the active subject and the direct object change places, and the subject receives the action of the verb.

> Subject + verb by object. = *Receiver of action* + **verb** <u>by</u> doer of action.
>
> *The ball* **was caught** <u>by</u> Yun.
> *The problem* **was fixed** <u>by</u> Karen.

Changing a verb from active to passive voice requires adding a form of the verb *to be* as an auxiliary and changing the main verb to its past participle form, as follows.

	Active	*Passive*
Simple Present	I **advise** her.	She **is advised** by me.
Simple Past	I **advised** her	She **was advised** by me.
Simple Future	I **will advise** her.	She **will be advised** by me.
Present Progressive	I **am advising** her.	She **is being advised** by me.
Past Progressive	I **was advising** her.	She **was being advised** by me.
Future Progressive	I **will be advising** her.	She **will be being advised** by me.
Present Perfect	I **have** advised her	She **has been advised** by me.
Past Perfect	I **had** advised her.	She **had been advised** by me.
Future Perfect	I **will have advised** her.	She **will have been advised** by me.
Modal	I **must advise** her.	She **must be** advised by me.

If the doer of the action is stated in a passive sentence, the word **by** introduces the doer.

> Lionel *was kicked* **by** a mule.

However, the doer of the action can be omitted, especially if the doer is unknown or impersonal.

> Colin's car **was stolen.** (We do not know who the thief was.)
> The policy **was revised** in 1998. (Anyone working then might have revised it.)

Only transitive verbs can become passive (transitive and intransitive verbs: direct objects, p. 79). In fact, a simple test for determining if a verb is transitive is to try to make it passive.

Common Pitfall: Passive Voice

Novice writers tend to overuse passive voice. To combat this, many writing teachers advise students never to use passive voice.

Passive voice places the emphasis on the result of the action or the receiver of the action, rather than the actor or the action itself. This is appropriate in cases where the actor is unknown, unimportant, impersonal, or anonymous. Passive voice often expresses policies or rules.

> Smoking **is prohibited** in all areas of the building.

Scientific writing often uses passive voice to describe procedures or experiments.

> A solution of one part sodium chloride and three parts water **was prepared.**

Passive voice can also be a kind of scapegoat, to avoid saying who did what.

> The new regulation **was approved** without debate or public comment.

Who approved it, and *why* did they do so in secret? This passive sentence does not tell us.

Too many sentences in passive voice make a written passage wordy, sluggish, and dull. Use passive voice only where it is absolutely needed so that it will not lose its effect.

Example Problems

Are these sentences active or passive?

1. The committee was told that no more funds were available.

   Answer: Passive. The main verb of this sentence, **was told,** is in passive voice. **Committee** is receiving the action of the verb, but we do not know who told the committee this news because the doer of the action is not specified.

2. The horse was eating oats when we found him.

   Answer: Active. The main verb of this sentence, **was eating,** might look like a passive verb because it uses **was.** However, it is actually in past progressive tense; one good clue is the fact that **eating** is a present participle, while passive voice uses a past participle. The subject of the sentence, the horse, is doing the eating. If this sentence were passive, it would say, "The oats **were being eaten by** the horse."

Work Problems

Change each sentence from passive to active or from active to passive.

1. This house is being built by my community service group.

2. Brian loaded the instruments into the van.

3. The club is recruiting new members.

4. Access to this area is restricted to authorized personnel only.

5. The mad scientist created a horrible monster.

6. A great time was had by everyone at the picnic.

7. This castle was built by King Ludwig in 1869.

8. The board was asked by the investors to provide details about the merger.

9. This soup tastes awful.

10. The telephone was invented by Alexander Graham Bell.

Worked Solutions

1. My community service group is building this house.

    This sentence was passive. To make it active, move the doer of the action, **community service group,** to the beginning of the sentence and change the passive verb, **is being built (by),** to present progressive tense.

2. The instruments were loaded into the van by Brian.

    This sentence was active. To make it passive, move the doer of the action, **Brian,** to the end of the sentence and change the simple past tense verb, **loaded,** to the passive form, **were loaded (by).**

3. New members are being recruited by the club.

    This sentence was active. To make it passive, move the doer of the action, **club,** to the end of the sentence and change the present progressive verb, **is recruiting,** to the passive form, **are being recruited (by).**

4. This passive sentence is extremely difficult to make active because the actor (the one doing the restricting) is not specified. The only way to do it is to completely rewrite the sentence and supply an actor. One possibility is: "The owners restrict access to this area to authorized personnel only."

5. A horrible monster was created by the mad scientist.

    This sentence was active. To make it passive, move the doer of the action, **mad scientist,** to the end of the sentence and change the simple past tense verb, **created,** to the passive form, **was created (by).**

6. Everyone at the picnic had a great time.

    This sentence was passive. To make it active, move the doer of the action, **everyone,** to the beginning of the sentence and change the passive verb, **was had (by),** to the active simple past form, **had.**

7. King Ludwig built this castle in 1869.

    This sentence was passive. To make it active, move the doer of the action, **King Ludwig,** to the beginning of the sentence and change the passive verb, **was built (by),** to the active simple past form, **built.**

8. The investors asked the board to provide details about the merger.

    This sentence was passive. To make it active, move the doers of the action, **investors,** to the beginning of the sentence and change the passive verb, **was asked (by),** to the active simple past form, **asked.**

9. Trick question! It is impossible to make this verb passive because it is intransitive. In fact, **taste** is a linking verb, and linking verbs are intransitive by definition (linking verbs, p. 83).

10. Alexander Graham Bell invented the telephone.

    This sentence was passive. To make it active, move the doer of the action, **Alexander Graham Bell,** to the beginning of the sentence and change the passive verb, **was invented (by),** to the active simple past form, **invented.**

Mood

We usually speak of English verbs as having three main **moods: indicative** mood, **imperative** mood, and **subjunctive** mood.

Indicative is the usual mood of most verbs. It simply declares that an action is so. An indicative verb can be in any person, number, or tense.

> I **will be building** the new cabinets. *(future progressive)*
> Keiko **enjoys** hiking and rockclimbing. *(simple present)*
> The city council **had considered** the same proposal before. *(past perfect)*

Verbs in **imperative** mood give orders, instructions, or commands. Imperative verbs usually come at the beginning of a sentence. The implied subject of a verb in imperative mood is always **you** (either singular or plural).

> **Deliver** this letter to Ms. Zhang.
> **Meet** me at the ice skating rink.
> **Take** this medicine with milk or food.

Verbs in **subjunctive** mood indicate desired, demanded, or hypothetical situations—or situations that are contrary to fact. The subjunctive form is the same as the base form of the verb, so it usually looks identical to simple present, except in third person singular.

> The doctor recommends that my father **get** a knee replacement.
> They asked that Maria **go** with them.
> I suggest that you **be** silent during the testimony.

The only **past** subjunctive verb is **were.**

> If I **were** you, I would reconsider that job offer.
> She acted as if she **were** my mother.
> If that **were** to happen, it would be a disaster.

Subjunctive mood usually follows expressions such as **ask that, demand that, wish that, suggest that, recommend that, insist that,** and so on. Subjunctives also follow expressions such as **it is important that, it is desirable that, it is necessary that,** and so on. The subjunctive verb **were** most commonly appears with "if" clauses (special types of clauses: "if" clauses, p. 198).

Subjunctive mood is rare in contemporary English, though it used to be more common. One of the best known (and most misinterpreted) instances of subjunctive mood occurs in the song "America the Beautiful," written around the year 1900.

> America, America!
> God **shed** his grace on thee,
> And **crown** thy good with brotherhood. . . .

The verb **shed** is not in simple past tense. Like **crown,** it is subjunctive, expressing a wished-for situation: "(May) God shed his grace on thee. . . ."

Example Problems

Identify the mood of the verb in each sentence.

1. **Do not take** his criticism personally.

   Answer: **Imperative. Do not take** is an order or command: (**You**) do not take his criticism personally. Commands can be negative as well as positive: **Take** his criticism personally.

2. I **was** happy to see some sunny weather.

   Answer: **Indicative.** The verb simply states a fact.

3. She wished that she **were** lying on the beach in Hawaii.

   Answer: **Subjunctive.** The verb expresses a wished-for situation, one that is currently contrary to fact.

Work Problems

Identify the indicative, imperative, or subjunctive verbs in each sentence.

1. The circumstances require that I handle the problem personally.

2. Find your sister and tell her that I want to see her.

3. No one told me you were coming.

4. Stop worrying; everything will be fine.

5. The owners asked that we not use their facilities.

6. Anyone can see this will end in disaster.

7. Think carefully and remain calm when you take the test.

8. I wish you were here because I miss you.

9. They insisted that Mr. Dourif unlock the doors.

10. Suppose it were true.

Worked Solutions

1. **Require** = indicative; **handle** = subjunctive.

   Require states a fact; **handle** indicates a demanded situation.

2. **Find** = imperative; **tell** = imperative; **want** = indicative.

    Find and **tell** give an order; **want** simply states a fact. By the way, **to see** is an infinitive.

3. **Told** = indicative; **were coming** = indicative.

    Both verbs simply state the facts. **Told** is simple past; **were coming** is past progressive.

4. **Stop** = imperative; **will be** = indicative.

    Stop gives an order; **will be** (simple future tense) states a fact.

5. **Asked** = indicative; **(not) use** = subjunctive.

    Asked states a fact; **(not) use** indicates a demanded situation.

6. **(Can) see** = indicative; **will end** = indicative.

    Both verbs simply state facts. **See** uses the modal auxiliary **can; will end** is simple future tense.

7. **Think** = imperative; **remain** = imperative; **take** = indicative.

    Think and **remain** give orders; **take** simply states a fact.

8. **Wish** = indicative; **were** = subjunctive; **miss** = indicative.

    Wish states a fact; **were** indicates a situation contrary to fact; **miss** states a fact.

9. **Insisted** = indicative; **unlock** = subjunctive.

    Insisted (simple past tense) states a fact; **unlock** indicates a demanded situation.

10. **Suppose** = imperative; **were** = subjunctive.

    Suppose gives an order; **were** indicates a situation contrary to fact.

Phrasal Verbs

Many English verbs require more than one word to express their meanings. These are called **phrasal verbs.** Compare the single-word verbs with the phrasal verbs in these sentences.

> She **put** her hat on the table.
> She **put on** her hat and her coat.

> The sunflower **turned** toward the light.
> I **turned off** the light when I left the room.

Usually the word attached to a phrasal verb looks like a **preposition,** such as *out, in, off, up,* or *on* (prepositions and compound prepositions, p. 151). However, when these words are essential parts of a phrasal verb, they no longer function as prepositions and are instead called **particles.**

Phrasal verbs are extremely common in English. The following are a few familiar examples:

break down	hand out	take off
carry on	pass out	take on
figure out	put off	touch down
get up	put up with	turn on
give in	send off	turn up
hand in	stand by	use up

Like single-word verbs, phrasal verbs can be transitive or intransitive, depending on their meaning. For example:

Transitive: **Take off** those wet clothes before you catch cold. *(remove)*
Intransitive: I am going to **take off** after the meeting is over. *(leave)*
Intransitive: The plane finally **took off** after the wings were de-iced. *(took flight)*

Phrasal verbs are either **separable** or **inseparable.** If a phrasal verb is separable, its direct object can come between the verb and the particle.

Correct: She **put on** *her coat.*
Correct: She **put** *her coat* **on.**
Correct: I cannot **figure out** *this problem.*
Correct: I cannot **figure** *this problem* **out.**

Inseparable phrasal verbs must stay together.

Correct: She could not **deal with** *the situation.*
Incorrect: She could not **deal** *the situation* **with.**
Correct: I need to **read up on** *modern philosophy.*
Incorrect: I need to **read up** *modern philosophy* **on.**

Some grammarians would say that only separable verbs are true phrasal verbs. They would call inseparable phrasal verbs **prepositional verbs.**

Gray Area: The Particle at the End of the Sentence

A common English grammar rule says that sentences cannot end with a preposition. This rule was derived from languages like Latin and French, in which it is grammatically impossible to put a preposition at the end of a sentence. Unfortunately, the rule is nonsensical when applied to English, and nowhere is this more evident than with phrasal verbs. As Winston Churchill supposedly said:

"This is the sort of English up with which I will not put."

Churchill's sarcastic statement uses a phrasal verb, **put up with,** to make its point. The innocent phrasal verb appears to use prepositions, so purists insist that it must be split if it appears at the end of a sentence. As this quotation shows, splitting up the verb and its particles makes the sentence ridiculous.

Example Problems

Is this phrasal verb separable or inseparable?

1. Take back

   Answer: **Separable.** Try putting the verb into a sentence: I will **take back** my book. I will **take** my book **back.**

2. Look up

   Answer: **Separable. Look up** the definition. **Look** the definition **up.**

3. Come across

   Answer: **Inseparable.** I **came across** the answer. *But not:* I **came** the answer **across.**

Work Problems

Underline the phrasal verb(s) in each sentence. Correct any that are wrongly separated.

1. We will take up the project again after the holiday break.

2. You cannot carry this way on and expect to hand your paper in on time.

3. Remember to turn off the lights when you leave the room.

4. He threw up his hands in disgust.

5. What has become my glasses of? I cannot do them without.

6. We need to talk over this new proposal.

7. Given time, we can work out a solution.

8. Ali asked if we could come over to his office and look over his accounts.

9. Turn the volume up. I cannot hear what that guy is going on about.

10. Put down that bag. Pick this box up.

Worked Solutions

1. We will <u>take up</u> the project again after the holiday break. (The phrasal verb **take up** means *resume* in this context, and it is separable: **Take** it **up.**)

2. You cannot **carry on** this way and expect to <u>hand</u> your paper <u>in</u> on time. (**Carry on** is not separable; **hand in** is separable.

3. Remember to <u>turn off</u> the lights when you leave the room. (**Turn off** is separable: **Turn** them **off.**)

4. He <u>threw up</u> his hands in disgust. (**Threw up** in this context is separable: **Threw** them **up.**)

5. What has **become of** my glasses? I cannot **do without** them. (Both **become of** and **do without** are inseparable.)

6. We need to <u>talk over</u> this new proposal. (**Talk over** is separable: **Talk** it **over.**)

7. Given time, we can <u>work out</u> a solution. (**Work out** is separable: **Work** it **out.**)

8. Ali asked if we could <u>come over</u> to his office and <u>look over</u> his accounts. (**Come over** is inseparable, but **look over** is separable.)

9. <u>Turn</u> the volume <u>up</u>. I cannot hear what that guy is <u>going on about</u>. (**Turn up** is separable; **going on about** is inseparable.)

10. <u>Put down</u> that bag. <u>Pick</u> this box <u>up</u>. (Both **put down** and **pick up** are separable.)

Modal Auxiliaries

Modal auxiliaries are a small group of auxiliary verbs that indicate ability, possibility, permission, or obligation.

>   We **might** be able to fix the engine ourselves.
>   You **should** talk to a dentist about your sore tooth.
>   **Can** I park my car here?
>   If I had enough money, I **would** travel around the world.
>   He **could** easily afford his own apartment, but he prefers to live with his parents.

The following list contains some modal auxiliaries.

can	could
may	might
shall	should
will	would
must	

Modal auxiliaries do not change forms for number, person, or tense. They always precede any other verb forms in the sentence, including other auxiliaries like *be, have,* or *do.* When used in present tense, modals are followed by the base form of the verb.

>   Maybe they **should** *have asked* Yoko what she thinks.
>   We **might** *order* a pizza after practice.
>   You **must** *consider* every alternative.

To form the negative with a modal, place **not** immediately after the modal and before any other auxiliary verbs. To form a question, move the modal to the beginning of the sentence, before the subject.

>   **Should** they *have asked* Yoko what she thinks?
>   Maybe they **should not** *have asked* Yoko what she thinks.

The negative of **can** is one word, **cannot.**

> I **cannot** run as fast as Kendra.

In this chapter, we have already seen the modal auxiliary **will,** which is used to create future tense verb forms. It can also express a definite intent or decision on the speaker's part.

> Tomorrow, the president **will** deliver the State of the Union address.
> I **will** finish this project even if it kills me.

Can indicates an ability to do something. The past tense is **could.**

> A penguin **can** survive freezing water because it is well insulated.
> Navigating the rapids **can** be dangerous.
> I **could** not see the fireworks from where I stood.

May and **might,** often used interchangeably, indicate possibilities or uncertain events. **May** can also indicate permission to do something.

> It **may** rain tomorrow.
> We **might** have to reschedule our game.
> You **may** keep that umbrella, if you want it.

Must indicates a necessity or obligation, or expresses certainty about an assumption.

> You **must** get a license before you become a truck driver.
> If she stayed home, she **must** be sick.

Should indicates something that is appropriate or advisable.

> You **should** try to study more.
> Americans **should** eat more fruits and vegetables.

Could and **would** sometimes function as the past tense forms of **can** and **will.** More often, they indicate hypothetical or wished-for situations. They are often used with **if** clauses (special types of clauses: "if" clauses, p. 198) or in combination with subjunctive verbs.

> I wish I **could** afford a motorcycle.
> I **would** love to have one.
> If I were rich, I **would** buy a dozen.0

Some grammarians include **ought to, need, dare,** and **used to** as modals or semimodals. **Used to** expresses a habitual action in the past, one that is no longer being repeated. **Used to** can be used interchangeably with **would** in this sense, but because **would** also has other meanings, it requires an indication of past time to make sense.

> We **used to** *go* to the beach every summer.
> *Or:* When I was a child, we **would** *go* to the beach every summer.
> He **used to** *smoke* three packs of cigarettes each day.
> *Or:* Before he got sick, he **would** *smoke* three packs of cigarettes each day.

Have to, meaning *to be required or forced to do something,* can be used interchangeably with **must,** but **have to** is not considered a modal because it varies for tense and person.

> She **has to** *turn in* the assignment by noon or she will fail the class.
> *Or:* She **must** *turn in* the assignment by noon or she will fail the class.
> They **will have to** *demolish* the old building before they start new construction.
> *Or:* They **must** *demolish* the old building before they start new construction.

Must cannot indicate past tense. Use **had to** instead.

> I locked myself out of my apartment, so I **had to** *call* the manager.
> *Not:* I locked myself out of my apartment, so I **must** *call* the manager.

Gray Area: "Can" versus "May"

An often-repeated grammar rule says that **can** indicates an ability to do something, while **may** indicates what is allowed or permitted.

> **Can** she run a mile in less than six minutes?
> **May** I have another piece of cake?

In reality, this distinction in meaning is often difficult to make, so **can** and **may** are sometimes used interchangeably.

> You **may** keep that umbrella, if you want it.
> You **can** keep that umbrella, if you want it.
> (Is the speaker granting you permission to keep the umbrella, or informing you that you have the ability to keep it?)

In general, **may** is preferable for polite requests or suggestions. **Would, could,** and **might** can also introduce polite requests: *Could* you carry this for me? *Would* you like another cup of coffee?

Gray Area: "Will" versus "Shall"

Formerly, **shall** was used as the first person form of **will** to express future tense. Using **will** in first person implied intent or definite decision. When **shall** was used in second or third person, it expressed obligation.

In modern American English, **shall** has generally been replaced by **will. Shall** is reserved mainly for contexts in which the speaker wants to sound formal or extremely polite.

However, when **shall** and **will** introduce questions, they have an important distinction in meaning. **Shall** asks for a preference or offers a polite suggestion, while **will** indicates future tense.

> **"Shall** we get a cup of coffee?" means "Do you want to get a cup of coffee?"
> **"Will** we get a cup of coffee?" involves speculation about future events, such as: "Do they serve coffee at this restaurant?" or "Is coffee included in the price of the meal?"

Example Problems

Choose the appropriate modal auxiliary to introduce the question.

1. **Shall/Will** we take my car?

    Answer: **Either, depending on context.** Use **shall** if the speaker is making a polite offer. Use **will** if the speaker is asking about future events. For example: "Will we have to take my car, or will we be able to ride with someone else?"

2. **Shall/Will** we have to pay to park in this lot?

    Answer: **Will.** The speaker is asking about events that will occur in the future.

3. **Can/May** I offer you something to eat?

    Answer: **May.** The speaker is making a polite offer.

4. **Can/May** you explain this problem for me?

    Answer: **Can.** The speaker is asking whether you are able to explain the problem.

Work Problems

Select the appropriate modal auxiliary for each sentence.

1. You could/should not drink and drive.

2. I must/may go surfing tomorrow if the waves are not too high.

3. The flood could/should cause widespread damage.

4. The result can/will be the same no matter what you do.

5. She can/may play the violin, and she sings beautifully as well.

6. If he were taller, he may/would make a good basketball player.

7. Should/would we put the eggs in the refrigerator?

8. Do not send invitations yet because we could/might have to change the date.

9. The jury may/should not believe his testimony.

10. The manufacturer guarantees that it may/will replace defective parts.

Worked Solutions

1. **Should.** (**Should** is appropriate because the speaker is giving advice; using **could not** indicates that you are not capable of drinking and driving.)

2. **May.** (**May** states a possibility; **must** indicates that the speaker is obliged to go surfing.)

3. **Could.** (**Could** states what the flood is capable of doing; **should** indicates that the flood needs to cause damage.)

4. **Will.** (**Will** states an event with absolute certainty; **can** indicates that something is capable of happening.)

5. **Can.** (**Can** states that she is capable of playing the violin; **may** indicates only a possibility.)

6. **Would.** (**Would,** often paired with **if** clauses, states something that will likely happen if a particular condition is met; **may** indicates only a possibility.)

7. **Should.** (**Should** asks for advice or opinion; **would** speculates about future events.)

8. **Might.** (**Might** indicates a possibility that may or may not happen; **could** implies that we are capable of changing the date.)

9. Either, depending on the context. (**Should not believe** says that he is untrustworthy; **may not believe** simply states that is it possible the jury will not believe him.)

10. **Will.** (**Will** indicates certainty about future events; a guarantee that only **may** replace parts is not much good.)

Gerunds

A gerund is a **verbal;** that is, a word form derived from a verb. Even though they are derived from verbs, verbals perform grammatical functions that real verbs cannot. Gerunds are verbals that act as **nouns** (Nouns and Articles, p. 33).

> **Moving** to a new city is always stressful.
> I enjoy **listening** to music and **reading** books.
> **Mentioning** this to Barbara would be a big mistake.

Gerunds look identical to present participles (**base form of verb + –ing**), but they do not act like present participles. In the first sentence, the gerund **moving** is acting as the noun subject of the sentence.

> Moving is stressful.
> **subject** *(noun)* **linking verb complement** *(adjective)*

In the second sentence, the gerunds **listening** and **reading** are direct objects of the verb **enjoy.**

Gerunds are often part of phrases. **Moving to a new city** includes the gerund and a prepositional phrase modifying it, but grammatically, it is one unit in the sentence, acting as a subject.

Gray Area: Possessives with Gerunds

English speakers and writers sometimes puzzle over what to do with nouns or pronouns that come before gerunds.

> *Informal:* I appreciated **Jane** helping us clean up the mess. *(noun)*
> *More acceptable:* I appreciated **Jane's** helping us clean up the mess. *(possessive noun)*

Informal: Ron's parents did not approve of **him** getting married. *(personal pronoun)*

More acceptable: Ron's parents did not approve of **his** getting married. *(possessive adjective)*

Although the **noun/pronoun + gerund** combination is not uncommon and would make sense to most English speakers, editors and writing teachers generally recommend using a possessive before a gerund.

Example Problems

Identify the gerunds in these sentences.

1. Managing the store is becoming a burden for Stella.

    Answer: **Managing. Becoming** is not a gerund; it is part of the present progressive tense verb **is becoming.**

2. I am looking forward to meeting you in person.

    Answer: **Meeting. Looking** is part of the present progressive verb **am looking.**

Work Problems

Supply the gerund form of the verb indicated.

1. (Read) and (write) are vital skills.

2. (Jog) has never been my favorite form of exercise.

3. (Hear) Maya Angelou speak was inspiring.

4. We cannot ask him to help without (alert) him to our plans.

5. Practice (swing) the bat with a fluid motion.

6. He made a living by (repair) antique cars.

7. They do not seem to have time for anything but (drink) and (stay) out late.

8. The manager's responsibilities are (supervise) employees and (schedule) work shifts.

9. (Decide) what to do with our profits was not difficult.

10. I warned him that (program) the new server would take several days.

Worked Solutions

1. **Reading, writing.** (For **read,** add **–ing;** for **write,** remove the final **e** before adding **–ing.**)

2. **Jogging.** (Double the consonant because the word has only one syllable.)

3. **Hearing.** (Add **–ing** to the base form.)

4. **Alerting.** (Add **–ing** to the base form.)

5. **Swinging.** (Add **–ing** to the base form.)

6. **Repairing.** (Add **–ing** to the base form.)

7. **Drinking, staying.** (Add **–ing** to the base form.)

8. **Supervising, scheduling.** (Remove the final **e** before adding **–ing** to the base form.)

9. **Deciding.** (Remove the final **e** before adding **–ing** to the base form.)

10. **Programming.** (The consonant must be doubled at the end of the base form, **program,** when adding **–ing** or **–ed;** not all two-syllable words require this, for example: profiting, debiting.)

Infinitives

Like gerunds, **infinitives** are verbals that act as **nouns.**

> I wanted **to go** with you. (**To go** is the direct object of the verb **want.**)
>
> **To become** a ballerina is her greatest ambition. (**To become** is the subject of the verb **is.**)
>
> We hope **to open** our new store soon. (**To open** is the direct object of the verb **hope.**)

The pattern for forming infinitives is as follows:

To + base form of the verb

Like gerunds, infinitives are often part of phrases: **To become a ballerina** is the entire subject of the second sentence.

Some verbs that take verbal complements must be followed by infinitives.

> The doctor *advised* her **to get** treatment quickly.
>
> We *expect* **to sign** the agreement soon.
>
> Unfortunately, Mike *forgot* **to give** me his phone number.

Typically these are words expressing preference or intent, or giving orders or permission. Some common examples are as follows:

agree	decide	permit
allow	encourage	plan
ask	expect	prefer
choose	forget	require
command	hope	want
	intend	

However, some verbs take gerund complements, and others can take either a gerund or an infinitive depending on the context. Unfortunately, no reliable rules exist for determining what kind of verb complement is required.

To form the negative of an infinitive, place **not** in front of the infinitive.

> She asked me **not to tell** you.
>
> Because I was not feeling well, I decided **not to go** swimming.

Gray Area: Split Infinitives

An often-repeated grammar rule says that infinitives should never be "split," meaning that no words should come between **to** and the base form of the verb:

> *Split:* We need **to** *completely* **revise** our strategic plan.
>
> *Not split:* We need **to revise** our strategic plan *completely.*

This rule was derived from Latin and Greek, where the infinitive is one word, so it is grammatically impossible to split it. However, nothing is grammatically incorrect about splitting an English infinitive, so the decision to split or not to split is a matter of style, not grammar. Gene Roddenberry thought a split infinitive was good enough for the introduction to his *Star Trek* TV series: "**To** *boldly* **go** where no man has gone before." And not splitting an infinitive sometimes makes the meaning unclear or the sentence awkward, as seen in the following example:

> The company plans **to** *more than* **triple** its production in the coming year.

It is impossible to avoid splitting this infinitive without rewriting the sentence. Do whatever makes the meaning clear and the writing easy to read.

Example Problems

Identify the infinitives in these sentences.

1. I plan to fly to New York next week.

   Answer: **To fly. To New York** is a prepositional phrase, not an infinitive. It tells where I plan to fly.

2. My teacher advised me to take the test so that I can go to college.

   Answer: **To take. To college** is another prepositional phrase.

3. We needed to break the window to get into the house.

   Answer: **To break, to get.** In this sentence, the expression **in order** could be inserted to clarify the meaning of the second infinitive: "We needed to break the window *in order* to get into the house."

Work Problems

Supply a gerund or an infinitive for the verb indicated.

1. Jiang Li enjoys (read) mystery stories.

2. Someday I want (visit) Moscow.

3.   My saxophone teacher asked me (come) to his performance.

4.   Do you like (live) in Seattle?

5.   They expect (arrive) on time.

6.   The coach advised the team (practice) more often.

7.   Remind me (buy) a carton of milk.

8.   Giorgio hopes (attend) college in the United States.

9.   I remember (hear) him say that he loves coconut cream pie.

10. Remember (lock) the door when you leave.

Worked Solutions

1.   Gerund: **Reading.**

2.   Infinitive: **To visit.**

3.   Infinitive: **To come.**

4.   Gerund: **Living.**

5.   Infinitive: **To arrive.**

6.   Infinitive: **To practice.**

7.   Infinitive: **To buy.**

8.   Infinitive: **To attend.**

9.   Gerund: **Hearing.**

10. Infinitive: **To lock.** (**Remember** is an example of a verb that can take either a gerund or an infinitive complement, depending on the context. In this sentence, where **remember** is in imperative mood, an infinitive is required. In Sentence 9, a gerund is required.)

Participles

A **participle** is yet another verbal, a word derived from a verb. Participles are verbals that act as **adjectives** (adjectives, p. 161).

That **dripping** faucet kept me awake all night.
Dried meat and **preserved** fruit were staples for our ancestors.
This movie is **boring.**
A **broken** clock stood on the mantelpiece.

Participles can look like present participles (**base form of verb + –ing**) or like past participles (**base form + –ed** for regular verbs, or the various irregular past participles). Participles in present form usually describe what a thing *does*. Participles in past form usually describe what *was done to* a thing.

Do not confuse adjective participles with participles that are part of verbs.

>   She **is buying** a **talking** bird for her daughter.

Is buying is the verb **buy** in present progressive tense. **Talking** is a participle modifying the noun **bird.**

Participles frequently occur in participial phrases.

>   The woman **sitting in front of me** was so tall I could not see the stage.
>   **Knowing you would disapprove,** I could not lie to him.
>   **Calling the horse's name,** she ran through the snowstorm.

When a participial phrase comes at the beginning of the sentence, it should modify the subject of the sentence. If it does not, it is called a **dangling participle** (misplaced or "dangling" modifiers, p. 209).

>   *Dangling participle, incorrect:* Walking through the forest, **the trees** were beautiful.
>   It sounds like the beautiful trees were walking!
>   *Correct:* Walking through the forest, **we** saw many beautiful trees.
>   We saw the trees while we were walking.

Example Problems

Identify the function of each **–ing** verb form in these sentences.

1.   I was thinking of taking some time off. I need a relaxing vacation.

>   *Answer:* **Thinking** is part of the past progressive verb **was thinking. Taking** is a gerund, part of the gerund phrase **taking some time off** (and also a direct object—it tells what I was thinking of). **Relaxing** is a participle, an adjective modifying the noun **vacation.**

2.   Asking for a raise would be a bad idea in this time of shrinking revenues.

>   *Answer:* **Asking** is a gerund; the entire gerund phrase **asking for a raise** is the subject of the sentence. **Shrinking** is a participle, an adjective modifying the noun **revenues.**

Work Problems

Supply the correct participial form of the verb indicated.

1.   Mario cannot go on our (hike) trip because he has a (break) ankle.

2.   The museum has a (sign) copy of a work (paint) by Rembrandt.

3.   That (chime) clock is (annoy).

4. My neighbor's (squawk) parrot is keeping me awake at night.

5. Ming Yue gave me an (engrave) bracelet for my birthday.

6. My little sister has a (talk) doll.

7. The (stain) glass windows spread (color) light across the room.

8. The (injure) man could see the (flash) red lights of the ambulance.

9. A beautifully (wrap) gift lay on the (polish) table.

10. The earliest (write) language is Sumerian.

Worked Solutions

1. **Hiking, broken.** (Remove the final **e** of **hike** before adding **–ing;** the past participle form of **break** is irregular. **Hiking** describes what we do on the trip: We **hike. Broken** describes what happened to the ankle: Mario **broke** it.)

2. **Signed, painted.** (Add **–ed** to the base forms **sign** and **paint.** Both participles describe what Rembrandt did to the artwork: He **painted** it and **signed** it.)

3. **Chiming, annoying.** (Add **–ing** to the base form **annoy;** drop the final **e** on **chime** before adding **–ing.** Both participles describe what the clock does: It **chimes,** and it **annoys.**)

4. **Squawking.** (Add **–ing** to the base form **squawk. Squawking** describes what the parrot does: It **squawks.**)

5. **Engraved.** (Add **–d** to the base form **engrave** because it already ends in **e. Engraved** describes what was done to the bracelet: The jeweler **engraved** it.)

6. **Talking.** (Add **–ing** to the base form **talk. Talking** describes what the doll does: It **talks.**)

7. **Stained, colored.** (Add **–ed** to the base forms **stain** and **color. Stained** describes what was done to the glass: Someone **stained** it, and **colored** describes what the glass does to the light: The glass **colors** it.)

8. **Injured, flashing.** (Add **–d** to the base form **injure** because it already ends in **e;** add **–ing** to the base form **flash. Injured** describes what happened to the man: Something **injured** him; **flashing** describes what the lights are doing: They **are flashing.**)

9. **Wrapped, polished.** (Add **–ed** to the base forms **wrap** and **polish;** double the **p** on **wrap** because the word has only one syllable. Both participles describe what was done to the objects: Someone **wrapped** the gift and **polished** the table.)

10. **Written.** (**Write** has an irregular past participle form. **Written** describes what was done to the language: The Sumerians **wrote** it.)

Chapter Problems

Problems

Draw one line under any direct objects. Draw two lines under any indirect objects.

1. His announcement caused everyone a terrible shock.

2. I deliver pizza on weekends. I always appreciate the customers who give me tips.

3. The earthquake severely damaged the frescoes in the old church, but conservators have repaired the worst damage.

4. Mick played his newest recording for me, but I did not like it.

5. We took down the curtains and washed all the windows.

Are the boldface verbs transitive or intransitive?

6. The flowers **smelled** heavenly. They **filled** the room with sweet perfume.

7. She **placed** the vase on the table. The sun **shone** through the cut glass vase.

8. The birds **were singing** outside the window. I **heard** their happy music.

Supply the correct form of the verb indicated.

9. Last year, I (go) to Disneyland. I (see) theme parks before, but none like this.

10. My sister always (want) (ride) the roller coaster. Personally, I (like, not) them.

11. I am happy (watch) instead of (ride). The (spin) teacups are all I (stand, can).

12. While we (be) there, I (hear) my parents (talk).

13. They (discuss) what they (want) (do) next.

14. My mother (tell) my father that she (love, would) (see) (Sleep) Beauty's castle.

15. She (say) that she (wish) she (be) a princess so that she (live, can) in a castle.

16. (Imagine) my surprise when I (learn) my mother (want) (be) a fairy-tale princess.

17. I (can, believe, not) it. She (seem, always) so practical.

18. Since then, I (think) of my mother differently. Maybe someday I (buy) her a crown.

Identify the underlined verbs or verbals. (Indicate tense, voice, mood, gerund, participle, and so on.)

19. Kelly and Tasha <u>are riding</u> their bikes out to the park. The park <u>has</u> a beautiful lake.

20. <u>Fishing</u>, <u>swimming</u>, and <u>boating</u> <u>are enjoyed</u> by adults and children alike.

21. <u>To fish</u>, you <u>must get</u> a <u>fishing</u> license first. State laws <u>require</u> that everyone <u>do</u> this.

22. Kelly and Tasha <u>have been looking forward to</u> a swim.

23. Tasha <u>would swim</u> every day if she <u>could get away from</u> school.

24. Kelly <u>prefers</u> to <u>lie</u> in the sun and <u>read</u> a book <u>borrowed</u> from the library.

25. Tasha <u>is taking off</u> her shoes as she <u>runs</u> toward the shore.

26. Kelly <u>shouts</u>, "<u>Put</u> your shoes <u>on!</u>"

27. Kelly <u>is</u> concerned because she once <u>cut</u> her foot on a piece of glass <u>hidden</u> in the sand.

28. But Tasha, <u>splashing</u> in the water, <u>is having</u> too much fun <u>to worry</u> about <u>broken</u> glass.

Answers and Solutions

The bolded section of Questions 1-5 stands for the double-underline mentioned in the instructions for this section.

1. His announcement caused **everyone** <u>a terrible shock</u>.

2. I deliver <u>pizza</u> on weekends. I always appreciate <u>the customers</u> who give **me** <u>tips</u>.

3. The earthquake severely damaged <u>the frescoes</u> in the old church, but conservators have repaired <u>the worst damage</u>.

4. Mick played <u>his newest recording</u> for **me,** but I did not like <u>it</u>.

5. We took down <u>the curtains</u> and washed all <u>the windows</u>.

6. The flowers **smelled** heavenly: *intransitive.* **Smell** is a linking verb, which by definitive is intransitive. **Heavenly** is a predicate adjective describing how the flowers smelled.

   They **filled** the room with sweet perfume: *transitive.* The direct object is **room.** (*What* did they fill? The room.)

7. She **placed** the vase on the table: *transitive.* The direct object is **vase.** (*What* did she place? The vase.)

   The sun **shone** through the cut glass vase: *intransitive.* Nothing receives the action of the verb **shine. Through the cut glass vase** is a prepositional phrase describing where the sun was shining.

8. The birds **were singing** outside the window: *intransitive.* In this case, nothing receives the action of the verb **sing.** However, **sing** can also be transitive: The birds sang *songs.* (**Songs** is the direct object of **sing;** *what* did they sing? Songs.)

   I **heard** their happy music: *transitive.* **Their happy music** is the direct object of the verb hear. (*What* did I hear? Music.)

9. **Went:** simple past tense, for an action completed in the past.

   Had seen: past perfect, describing an action completed prior to another action in the past.

10. **Wants:** simple present tense, for a habitual or permanent condition.

    To ride: infinitive, acting as a complement to the verb **want.**

    Do not like: simple present tense, describing a habitual or permanent condition. The negative requires the auxiliary verb **do** followed by **not.**

11. **To watch:** infinitive, acting as a complement to the verb phrase **am happy.**

    Ride (or **riding**): Because two infinitives are acting as complements to the same verb, the **to** of the second infinitive can be omitted. The gerund **riding** would also be acceptable, but as a matter of style it is preferable to have two verbs of the same type.

    Spinning: present participle modifying **teacups;** tells what the teacups do.

    Can stand: modal auxiliary + base form of the verb, indicating an ability to do something.

12. **Were:** simple past tense, for an action completed in the past.

    Heard: simple past tense (an irregular form).

    Talking: gerund, acting as a direct object of the verb **heard.**

13. **Were discussing:** past progressive tense, for a continuing action in the past. (It is appropriate in this case because **heard** describes a single action that occurred during the process of another action, the conversation.)

    Wanted: simple past tense, for an action completed in the past. (Simple past tense is often used in narratives to describe states of mind.)

    To do: infinitive, acting as the complement of the verb **want.**

14. **Told:** simple past tense (an irregular form), for an action completed in the past.

    Would love: modal auxiliary + base form of the verb, indicating a hypothetical situation.

    To see: infinitive, acting as the complement of the verb **love.**

    Sleeping: participle, modifying the noun **Beauty,** telling what the fairy-tale princess did.

15. **Said:** simple past tense (an irregular form), for an action completed in the past.

    Wished: simple past tense, for an action completed in the past.

    Were: simple past tense, for an action completed in the past.

    Could live: modal auxiliary + base form of the verb, expressing a hypothetical or wished-for situation.

16. **Imagine:** imperative, expressing an order or command.

    Learned: simple past tense, for an action completed in the past.

    Wanted: simple past tense, for an action completed in the past.

    To be: infinitive, complement of the verb **want.**

17. **Could not believe:** modal auxiliary + base form of the verb; for the negative, **not** follows the auxiliary. **Could** is acting as the past tense form of **can,** indicating an ability to do something.

    Had always seemed (or **always seemed**): past perfect, describing an action completed prior to another action in the past. The modifier **always** goes between the auxiliary **had** and the main verb. It would also be acceptable to use the simple past, **always seemed,** but past perfect is more appropriate in this case because the speaker's past perceptions have now changed.

18. **Think:** simple present tense, for a habitual or permanent condition.

    Will buy: simple future tense.

19. <u>Are riding</u> = present progressive tense; <u>has</u> = simple present. (All verbs are in indicative mood and active voice unless stated otherwise.)

20. <u>Fishing</u>, <u>swimming</u>, <u>boating</u> = gerunds; <u>are enjoyed</u> = passive voice, simple past tense.

21. <u>To fish</u> = infinitive; <u>must get</u> = modal auxiliary + base form of the verb; <u>fishing</u> = participle; <u>require</u> = simple present tense; <u>do</u> = subjunctive.

22. <u>Have been looking forward to</u> = phrasal verb, present perfect progressive tense.

23. <u>Would swim</u> = modal auxiliary + base form of the verb; <u>could get away from</u> = modal auxiliary + a phrasal verb.

24. <u>Prefers</u> = simple present; <u>to lie</u> = infinitive; <u>read</u> = infinitive. (It shares its **to** particle with the previous infinitive.) <u>Borrowed</u> = participle, part of a participial phrase.

25. <u>Is taking off</u> = present progressive tense, phrasal verb; <u>runs</u> = simple present.

26. <u>Shouts</u> = simple present tense; <u>put on</u> = imperative mood, phrasal verb (separable).

27. <u>Is</u> = linking verb; <u>cut</u> = simple past tense (an irregular verb that does not change); <u>hidden</u> = participle.

28. <u>Splashing</u> = participle, part of a participial phrase; <u>is having</u> = present progressive tense; <u>to worry</u> = infinitive; <u>broken</u> = participle.

Supplemental Chapter Problems

Problems

Draw one line under any direct objects. Draw two lines under any indirect objects.

1. Show Mr. Montoya the blueprints for the new building.

2. The manager assigned Reiko to supervise the project.

3. That dealer sold me a defective car.

Change these sentences from active to passive or passive to active.

4. The singers will perform a Renaissance motet.

5. The old statue had been damaged by vandalism and pollution.

6. The rights to the movie were bought by a Hollywood studio.

Correct any errors of verb usage in this paragraph.

7. My neighbor, Mr. Boudreaux, enjoy to garden. He can making anything grow.

8. In fact, he are a master gardener. He taked classes to get his certification.

9. Last summer, my mother's rose bushes turn brown.

10. All the blossoms dried up and falls off.

11. No one can figuring out what happens to them.

12. Mom have asked Mr. Boudreaux helping her.

13. He is knowing right away what the problem is being.

14. The roses had been infect by a fungus.

15. Mr. Boudreaux put fungicide on them and will have been keeping the leaves dry.

16. Soon the roses had become healthy again.

17. I told you, Mr. Boudreaux may grow anything.

18. No one would growing flowers like he might.

Underline all the verbs or verbals and indicate tense, voice, mood, gerund, participle, and so on.

19. Mr. Thomas asked that you wait here until he arrives.

20. An alien spacecraft shooting laser beams hovered over the city.

21. My grandfather has promised to give me his enameled watch when I graduate from high school.

22. If you had mentioned the meeting, I could have told you it was canceled.

23. The acting club will be staging a production of *Hamlet* in the spring.

24. I was looking forward to visiting my aunt, but we may not have time to go to her house.

25. Smoking has been shown to cause cancer.

26. By the time I finish work, the movie will have been playing for half an hour.

27. Do not drive on Orange Street. Take Main Street instead.

28. I was hoping to meet a recording star when I visited Nashville.

29. The waxed floor was slippery and dangerous.

30. Mara would love to win the lottery.

Answers

The bolded section of Questions 1–3 stands for the double-underline mentioned in the instructions for this section.

1. Show **Mr. Montoya** <u>the blueprints</u> for the new building. (transitive and intransitive verbs: direct objects, p. 79; indirect objects, p. 81)

2. The manager assigned <u>Reiko</u> to supervise the project.

3. That dealer sold **me** <u>a defective car</u>. (direct and indirect objects, pp. 79–83)

4. A Renaissance motet will be performed by the singers.

5. Vandalism and pollution had damaged the old statue.

6. A Hollywood studio bought the rights to the movie. (voice, p. 107)

7. My neighbor, Mr. Boudreaux, **enjoys gardening**. He can **make** anything grow. (simple present tense, p. 85; gerunds, p. 120; infinitives, p. 122; modal auxiliaries, p. 116)

8. In fact, he **is** a master gardener. He **took** classes to get his certification. (simple present tense, p. 85; simple past tense, p. 87)

9. Last summer, my mother's rose bushes **turned** brown. (simple past tense, p. 87)

10. All the blossoms dried up and **fell** off. (simple past tense, p. 87; irregular past tense verb forms, p. 98)

11. No one **could figure out** what **was happening** to them. (modal auxiliaries, p. 116; past progressive tense, p. 93)

12. Mom **asked** Mr. Boudreaux **to help** her. (simple past tense, p. 87; infinitives, p. 122)

13. He **knew** right away what the problem **was.** (simple past tense, p. 87; irregular past tense verb forms, p. 98)

14. The roses had been **infected** by a fungus. (voice, p. 107; past perfect tense, p. 97)

15. Mr. Boudreaux put fungicide on them and **kept** the leaves dry. (simple past tense, p. 87; irregular past tense verb forms, p. 98)

16. Soon the roses **became** healthy again. (simple past tense, p. 87; irregular past tense verb forms, p. 98; past perfect tense, p. 97)

17. I told you, Mr. Boudreaux **can** grow anything. (modal auxiliaries, p. 116)

18. No one **can grow** flowers like he **can.** (modal auxiliaries, p. 116)

19. Mr. Thomas <u>asked</u> (simple past tense, p. 87) that you <u>wait</u> (mood [subjunctive], p. 111) here until he <u>arrives</u> (simple present tense, p. 85).

20. An alien spacecraft <u>shooting</u> (participles, p. 124) laser beams <u>hovered</u> (simple past tense, p. 87) over the city.

21. My grandfather <u>has promised</u> (present perfect tense, p. 96) <u>to give</u> (infinitives, p. 122) me his enameled watch when I <u>graduate</u> (simple present tense, p. 85) from high school.

22. If you <u>had mentioned</u> (past perfect tense, p. 97) the <u>meeting</u> (gerunds, p. 120), I <u>could have told</u> (modal auxiliaries, p. 116; present perfect tense, p. 96) you it <u>was canceled</u> (passive voice, p. 108; simple past tense, p. 87).

23. The <u>acting</u> (participles, p. 124) club <u>will be staging</u> (future progressive tense, p. 94) a production of *Hamlet* in the spring.

24. I <u>was looking forward to</u> (phrasal verbs, p. 113; past progressive tense, p. 93) <u>visiting</u> (gerunds, p. 120) my aunt, but we <u>may not have</u> (modal auxiliaries, p. 116) time <u>to go</u> (infinitives, p. 122) to her house.

25. <u>Smoking</u> (gerunds, p. 120) <u>has been shown</u> (passive voice, p. 108; present perfect tense, p. 96) <u>to cause</u> (infinitives, p. 122) cancer.

26. By the time I <u>finish</u> (simple present tense, p. 85) work, the movie <u>will have been playing</u> (future perfect progressive tense, p. 106) for half an hour.

27. <u>Do not drive</u> (mood [imperative], p. 111) on Orange Street. <u>Take</u> (mood [imperative], p. 111) Main Street instead.

28. I <u>was hoping</u> (past progressive tense, p. 93) <u>to meet</u> (infinitives, p. 122) a <u>recording</u> (participles, p. 124) star when I <u>visited</u> (simple past tense, p. 87) Nashville.

29. The <u>waxed</u> (participles, p. 124) floor <u>was</u> (linking verbs, p. 83) slippery and dangerous.

30. Mara <u>would love</u> (modal auxiliaries, p. 116) <u>to win</u> (infinitives, p. 122) the lottery.

Chapter 4
Conjunctions

Conjunctions are words that connect (or "conjoin") other words, phrases, or clauses. This chapter will cover the four main types of conjunctions.

- ❑ **Coordinating conjunctions** (and, but, or)
- ❑ **Correlative conjunctions** (either . . . or, not only . . . but also)
- ❑ **Subordinating conjunctions** (because, although, while)
- ❑ **Conjunctive adverbs** (for example, nevertheless)

Coordinating Conjunctions

Coordinating conjunctions connect words or groups of words of the same grammatical type, such as nouns, verbs, or adjectives, or of the same grammatical structure, such as phrases or clauses.

Common coordinating conjunctions include the following:

- ❑ **and**
- ❑ **but**
- ❑ **or**
- ❑ **nor**
- ❑ **for**
- ❑ **so**
- ❑ **yet**

Notice that the word **for,** here listed as a conjunction, can also be used as a preposition (prepositions and compound prepositions, p. 151). The word's function within the sentence, not the word itself, determines whether it is a preposition or a conjunction.

The following sentences give two examples of the use of coordinating conjunctions. The first sentence connects nouns, and the second connects verb phrases.

> The chef prepared chicken **and** pasta for dinner.
> You can go with us **or** stay home.

But and **yet** show a contrast between the items they connect. **But** can also mean "except" or "notwithstanding."

> The project was challenging, **but** we finished it on time.
> The orange juice was tart **yet** refreshing.

Or shows a choice or offers alternatives between the items it connects.

> He wants a tennis racket **or** a video game for his birthday.
> On my day off, I will go to the beach **or** the mountains.

When a coordinating conjunction connects more than two items, the conjunction usually appears between the last two items in the series. Commas separate the items in the series (gray area: the serial comma, p. 231).

> *Correct:* For this craft project, you will need scissors, glue, green felt, **and** silk flowers.
> *Incorrect:* You will need scissors **and** glue **and** green felt **and** silk flowers.

However, conjunctions may be included for emphasis.

> I cannot believe you ate a whole steak **and** an enormous potato **and** a chicken leg **and** a salad **and** a big slice of cheesecake!

For, so, and **nor** usually connect independent clauses (clauses, p. 195). **For** and **so** show a cause/effect relationship or explain why something is so.

> I could not find your house, **so** I called to ask for directions.
> She could not speak, **for** her heart was filled with grief.

Nor usually connects negative statements. An independent clause following **nor** always has its subject and verb inverted, as if it were a question (clauses, p. 195).

> He would not say why he was leaving, **nor** would he say where he was going.
> They did not repair my car, **nor** did they give me a refund.

Nor can also appear as part of the correlative conjunction (correlative conjunctions, p. 137) **neither . . . nor,** in which it can connect nouns, verbs, or other grammatical units.

When a coordinating conjunction connects independent clauses, the conjunction is usually preceded by a comma, unless both clauses are very short (commas, p. 229).

Independent clauses joined by coordinating conjunctions create **compound sentences** (sentence types: compound and complex, p. 200).

Gray Area: Beginning a Sentence with "And"

Nothing is grammatically wrong with placing **and** or other coordinating conjunctions at the beginning of a complete sentence, although this practice should be used sparingly. Novice writers should be especially careful not to begin **sentence fragments** (sentence fragments, p. 208) with conjunctions.

> *Incorrect:* We hung the wallpaper and painted the walls. And laid new tile.
> *Correct:* We hung the wallpaper and painted the walls. And we laid new tile.
> *Correct:* We hung the wallpaper, painted the walls, and laid new tile.

Although the second sentence is technically correct, the third sentence is preferable, because it is less wordy and flows more smoothly.

Correlative Conjunctions

Correlative conjunctions function like coordinating conjunctions, but they have two parts.

- ❑ **Either . . . or**
- ❑ **Not only . . . but (or "but also")**
- ❑ **Neither . . . nor**
- ❑ **Both . . . and**
- ❑ **Whether . . . or**
- ❑ **As . . . as**

Here are some examples of sentences that have correlative conjunctions.

> **Both** the police **and** the FBI were investigating the crime.
> **Either** he goes, **or** I do.
> **Neither** Miriam **nor** Josh will agree to write the script.
> The rescue workers brought **not only** food **but** blankets.

Example Problems

What grammatical elements are connected by the coordinating conjunction, and what is the relationship between those elements?

1. T.S. Eliot wrote poems and plays.

   Answer: Two nouns, objects of the verb *wrote*. **And** shows that Eliot wrote both kinds of things.

2. The waves were high, so we had to go back to shore.

   Answer: Two independent clauses. **So** indicates that the first clause explains the result in the second clause.

3. The stars are beautiful but cold.

   Answer: Two adjectives, both subject complements. **But** shows a contrast between the two qualities described.

Work Problems

Supply the missing coordinating conjunction.

1. I went downstairs ____ opened the door.

2. Mickey _____ Angela were standing outside.

3. Mickey did not have a coat, _____ did Angela.

4. I asked them to come in, _____ they would not.

5. You must wear a coat in the winter _____ you will freeze.

Underline the conjunction(s) in each sentence.

6. If you will move the furniture, then I will rent a shampooing machine and clean the carpet.

7. Neither pleading nor argument would change the judge's verdict, but the defendant vowed to appeal.

8. The movie was not only long but also dull, and it put me to sleep.

9. I was hungry and wanted either a cheeseburger or a hamburger.

10. She did not know whether she was on the right path or hopelessly lost, for night was coming and the forest was dark.

Worked Solutions

1. **and** (The speaker did two things, which were in sequence.)

2. **and** (Both people were there.)

3. **nor** (Two negative statements are linked.)

4. **but** (The second clause contrasts with the first.)

5. **or** (Two alternative actions are presented.)

6. If you will move the furniture, <u>then</u> I will rent a shampooing machine <u>and</u> clean the carpet. (correlative conjunction **if . . . then** and coordinating conjunction **and**)

7. <u>Neither</u> pleading <u>nor</u> argument would change the judge's verdict, <u>but</u> the defendant vowed to appeal. (correlative conjunction **neither . . . nor** and coordinating conjunction **but**)

8. The movie was <u>not only</u> long <u>but also</u> dull, <u>and</u> it put me to sleep. (correlative conjunction **not only . . . but also** and coordinating conjunction **and**)

9. I was hungry for <u>either</u> a cheeseburger <u>or</u> a hamburger. (correlative conjunction **either . . . or**)

10. She did not know <u>whether</u> she was on the right path <u>or</u> hopelessly lost, <u>for</u> night was falling <u>and</u> the forest was dark. (correlative conjunction **whether . . . or** and coordinating conjunctions **for** and **and**)

Subordinating Conjunctions

Subordinating conjunctions connect **subordinate clauses** to **independent clauses** (clauses, p. 195). An independent clause has both a subject and a verb, and it can stand alone as a complete thought. A subordinate clause has a subject and a verb, but it depends on the independent clause for its meaning. Note that the subordinate clause always includes the subordinating conjunction.

[I went to the gym] [**even though** I was already tired.]

[independent clause] [**subordinating conjunction** + subordinate clause]

Some common subordinating conjunctions include:

after	since
although	than
as, as if, as though	though
because	unless
before	until
even, even if, even though	when
except	where
if	while

Some examples of sentences using subordinating conjunctions are:

We will go to Ethan's house **after** we finish practice.

I enjoyed talking to him **because** he has such a good sense of humor.

Deanna will not join the band **unless** she can be the lead singer.

Many subordinating conjunctions express relationships having to do with time (such as **before, after, while, when,** and **until**). These words also function as adverbs (adverbs, p. 163), but when they link independent and subordinate clauses, they become subordinating conjunctions. They tell *when* the action in the independent clause occurred in relation to the action in the subordinate clause.

He used to be a mechanic **before** he became a teacher.

(*When* was he a mechanic? **Before** he became a teacher)

Marcia waited in the lobby **while** Evan talked to the desk clerk.

(*When* did Marcia wait in the lobby? **While** Even talked to the desk clerk.)

The subordinating conjunction **because** explains *why* something happens.

I love this club **because** they play the newest music.

(*Why* do I love this club? **Because** they play the newest music.)

Since can express either an explanation (synonymous with **because**) or a time relationship (sometimes used with **ever**).

We cannot buy lunch **since** we do not have any money.

(This is an explanation; it tells why we cannot buy lunch.)

He has been afraid to go diving **ever since** he was bitten by a shark.

(This is a time relationship; it tells when his fear began.)

Subordinating conjunctions such as **although, except, even though,** and **though** express exceptions (cases where some usual rule does not apply) or indicate a condition that exists despite some other condition.

She was an excellent basketball player **even though** she was not very tall.

(This expresses an exception: Most basketball players are tall.)

I loved my apartment **although** it was small and cramped.

(Despite its smallness, I still loved my apartment.)

A subordinate clause introduced by **if** (special types of clauses: "if" clauses, p. 198) expresses a condition that must be met, and the independent clause describes what will happen when that condition is met. **Unless** can also express conditions or requirements.

You can play on the team **if** you come to practice regularly.

You cannot play on the team **unless** you come to practice regularly.

No punctuation is needed before a subordinating conjunction. Notice, however, that if the order of the clauses is reversed, a comma is always required after the subordinate clause.

[**Subordinating conjunction** + subordinate clause], [independent clause]

Before he became a teacher, he used to be a mechanic.

While Evan talked to the desk clerk, Marcia waited in the lobby.

The relative pronouns **that, which, who, whom,** and **whose** also function much like subordinating conjunctions because they introduce subordinate clauses (relative pronouns, p. 57).

Gray Area: Using "Than" with Personal Pronouns

Some grammarians insist that the word **than** can only be used as a subordinating conjunction. Therefore, they argue, when **than** is followed by a personal pronoun, the pronoun must be in the nominative case because it is the subject of the subordinate clause (personal pronouns, p. 51). For example:

Tom is much taller than **I.**

(It is assumed that the rest of the subordinate clause has been omitted: "Tom is much taller than I am tall.")

Others insist that in this situation, **than** is being used as a preposition (prepositions and compound prepositions, p. 151). Therefore, pronouns following it should be in the objective case.

Tom is much taller than **me.**

One way to avoid the problem in your writing is to always include the "assumed" verb in the subordinate clause:

Preferable: She is more qualified for the position **than he is.**

Not: She is more qualified for the position **than him.**

Not: She is more qualified for the position **than he.**

Gray Area: "As" versus "Like"

Some grammarians insist that **like** can only be used as a preposition (prepositions and compound prepositions, p. 151), not a conjunction, so it should only introduce nouns or pronouns. These grammarians recommend the use of the conjunctions **as, as if,** or **as though** to introduce clauses.

preposition [noun]

She sings **like** [a bird].
Her perfume smelled **like** [roses].

subordinating conjunction [subordinate clause]

I felt **as if** [I would die of happiness].
The sky looked **as if** [it would soon rain].

However, just as with **than,** there are many examples of **like** being used both as a preposition and as a conjunction. Many writers and speakers would see no difference between "I felt like I wanted to cry" and "I felt as if I wanted to cry," except that the second example is more formal sounding.

Common Pitfall: "Than" versus "Then"

Writers often confuse the words **than** and **then** because they sound alike when spoken. Remember that **than** is used to make comparisons and **then** is used to indicate a point in time.

Incorrect: You reacted more calmly **then** I would have.
Correct: You reacted more calmly **than** I would have.

Incorrect: They changed clothes and **than** they went swimming.
Correct: They changed clothes and **then** they went swimming.

Example Problems

Supply the missing subordinating conjunction.

1. I enjoy Mr. Allen's classes _____ he respects all his students.

    Answer: **because** (The second clause explains why the speaker enjoys this teacher's classes.)

2. We will have to wait _____ the bus arrives.

    Answer: **until** (The bus will arrive at an unspecified point in the future; the speakers must wait up to that point.)

3. You must buy a ticket _____ you can ride the roller coaster.

    Answer: **before** (The action in the first clause must take place prior to the action in the second clause. It would also be acceptable to use **so** or **so that,** although this would change the meaning of the sentence slightly.)

Work Problems

Supply the missing subordinating conjunction.

1. The governor will raise taxes _____ budget cuts can save enough money.

2. The mayor supported the plan _____ he had serious reservations about it.

3. I will do my homework _____ my favorite TV show is over.

4. Miguel is younger _____ I am by three days.

5. You can have a pet _____ you promise to take care of it.

6. Fortunately, the soccer game was over _____ the rain began.

7. My best friend is never home _____ I try to call him.

8. Everyone likes Julia _____ she is friendly and easygoing.

9. He must be rich _____ he drives such an expensive car.

10. The actor kept auditioning _____ he finally got a role.

Worked Solutions

1. **Unless** (Saving enough money would prevent the need to raise taxes.)

2. **Even though** or **although** (The mayor supported the plan despite his reservations about it.)

3. **After** (The two actions will take place in sequence. **When** or **as soon as** would also be acceptable answers.)

4. **Than** (Two things are being compared.)

5. **If** (Having a pet is conditional on your agreeing to take care of it.)

6. **Before** or **when** (The two actions took place in sequence.)

7. **When** or **whenever** (Every time I call, he is not there.)

8. **Because** (The conditions in the second clause caused the conditions in the first clause.)

9. **Since** (The conditions in the second clause are giving evidence of the condition in the first clause. **Because** would also be correct.)

10. **Until** (The action in the first clause took place up to the point specified in the second clause.)

Conjunctive Adverbs

Conjunctive adverbs act as conjunctions because they connect independent clauses. They act as adverbs because they also modify one of the independent clauses (adverbs, p. 163).

> We spent the afternoon in the park; **later,** we went for a bicycle ride by the lake.
>
> The kiln was broken; **consequently,** we could not finish our ceramics project.

Some common conjunctive adverbs include the following:

- ❑ afterwards
- ❑ anyway
- ❑ besides
- ❑ consequently
- ❑ eventually
- ❑ finally
- ❑ for example, for instance
- ❑ however
- ❑ instead
- ❑ later
- ❑ likewise
- ❑ nevertheless
- ❑ next
- ❑ now
- ❑ otherwise
- ❑ still
- ❑ then
- ❑ therefore
- ❑ thus
- ❑ unfortunately

Conjunctive adverbs only connect independent clauses; that is, clauses that can stand on their own as complete thoughts. Conjunctive adverbs are usually preceded by a semicolon and followed by a comma (semicolons, p. 233; commas, p. 229).

> I would like to buy a new car; **however,** I will settle for a used one.
>
> You need to study more; **otherwise,** you will flunk calculus.

If the two independent clauses are very short and closely related, it is also acceptable to use a comma rather than a semicolon before the conjunctive adverb, and no comma after it.

The same idea expressed by a conjunctive adverb can often be expressed by a coordinating conjunction (coordinating conjunctions, p. 135).

> I would like to buy a new car, **but** I will settle for a used one.

The choice between conjunctive adverbs and coordinating conjunctions is purely a matter of style and personal preference. Conjunctive adverbs tend to sound more formal than coordinating conjunctions.

> I could not find your house; **therefore,** I called to ask for directions.
>
> I could not find your house, **so** I called to ask for directions.

Independent clauses joined by conjunctive adverbs can also be separated into complete sentences by placing a period after the first independent clause.

> I could not find your house. Therefore, I called to ask for directions.

Example Problems

Combine the two sentences into one sentence using a conjunctive adverb.

1. I like seafood. I am allergic to shellfish.

   Answer: I like seafood; **however,** I am allergic to shellfish.

   (The second sentence is showing a contrast or exception to the first. Notice that a semicolon comes before the conjunctive adverb and a comma comes after it.)

2. They spent the entire day fishing. They fried their catch for dinner.

   Answer: They spent the entire day fishing; **afterwards,** they fried their catch for dinner.

   (**Later** would also be an acceptable answer. The action in the second sentence follows the action in the first sentence.)

Work Problems

Combine the two sentences into one sentence using a conjunctive adverb. Remember to use correct punctuation.

1. Howard Hughes was incredibly rich. He did not have a happy life.

2. The work must be done by Tuesday. We will fall behind schedule.

3. The store is already closed. You do not have any money.

4. She enjoys all kinds of sports. She loves to play basketball.

5. Mr. Truong cannot attend the meeting. Ms. Madsen will go in his place.

6. We had a romantic dinner at a French restaurant. We went for a walk on the beach.

7. The old building stayed vacant for many years. The city tore it down.

8. It was a difficult time for me. I learned many valuable lessons from my experience.

9. We had planned to go to the zoo today. The rain canceled our plans.

10. I stopped to visit my mother on my way to California. I stayed with friends in Los Angeles.

Worked Solutions

1. Howard Hughes was incredibly rich; **however,** he did not have a happy life.

2. The work must be done by Tuesday; **otherwise,** we will fall behind schedule.

3. The store is already closed; **besides,** you do not have any money. (or **anyway**)

4. She enjoys all kinds of sports; **for example,** she loves to play basketball. (or **for instance**)

5. Mr. Truong cannot attend the meeting; **instead,** Ms. Madsen will go in his place. (or **therefore**)

6. We had a romantic dinner at a French restaurant; **afterwards,** we went for a walk on the beach. (or **later,** or **next**)

7. The old building stayed vacant for many years; **finally,** the city tore it down. (or **eventually**)

8. It was a difficult time for me; **still,** I learned many valuable lessons from my experience. (or **nonetheless,** or **however**)

9. We had planned to go to the zoo today; **however,** the rain canceled our plans. (or **unfortunately**)

10. I stopped to visit my mother on my way to California; **afterwards,** I stayed with friends in Los Angeles. (or **later,** or **then**)

Chapter Problems

Problems

For each sentence, underline the conjunction(s) and name the type of conjunction.

1. I must either walk or take the bus while my car is being repaired.

2. I enjoy both rap music and classical music; however, I do not like country or reggae.

3. If you want to quit smoking, then you should develop a plan.

4. The union wanted either higher wages or more vacation, but the company would not compromise.

5. The game was postponed because the field was muddy and slippery.

Supply the missing conjunction.

6. Employees can wear jeans, slacks, _____ skirts in the office, _____ not shorts.

7. Dave held the ladder _____ Don climbed up to the roof.

8. French fries are delicious; _____, they are also high in fat.

9. The police did not catch the thieves, _____ did they have any suspects.

10. The concert went on ____ the lead singer was sick.

11. I have not played baseball ____ I broke my arm.

12. My new cell phone is small ____ lightweight.

13. I dropped my camera ____ I leaned out the window to take a picture.

14, Writing the paper was harder ____ she had expected.

15. _____ you tell me which shirt you want, _____ I will buy it for you.

Determine whether the following sentences contain errors and correct any you find. Pay close attention to punctuation.

16. She did not know how to play the piano but she was eager to learn.

17. Bring a salad either a casserole to the potluck dinner.

18. I went to the restaurant at seven o'clock my friends were not there.

19. He did chores, while the other children went outside to play.

20. Cinderella's stepsisters were cruel but selfish.

21. I like you better than him.

22. If we finish early, than we can go home.

23. The work was both exhausting and rewarding.

24. I liked the job and it did not pay well.

25. We will make either chicken nor spaghetti for dinner.

Answers and Solutions

1. I must <u>either</u> walk <u>or</u> take the bus <u>while</u> my car is being repaired. (correlative conjunction **either . . . or** and subordinating conjunction **while**)

2. I enjoy <u>both</u> rap music <u>and</u> classical music; <u>however</u>, I do not like country <u>or</u> reggae. (correlative conjunction **both . . . and,** conjunctive adverb **however,** and coordinating conjunction **or**)

3. If you want to quit smoking, <u>then</u> you should develop a plan. (subordinating conjunction **then**)

4. The union wanted <u>either</u> higher wages <u>or</u> more vacation, <u>but</u> the company would not compromise. (correlative conjunction **either . . . or** and coordinating conjunction **but**)

5. The game was postponed <u>because</u> the field was muddy <u>and</u> slippery. (subordinating conjunction **because** and coordinating conjunction **and**)

6. **Or, but** (The first three options are choices, while the final option is a contrast.)

7. **While** (Two actions are going on at the same time.)

8. **Unfortunately** or **however** (The second clause contrasts unfavorably with the first one.)

9. **Nor** (Two negative statements are linked.)

10. **Even though** or **although** (The action in the first clause happened despite the circumstances in the second clause.)

11. **Since** (The condition in the first clause began with the condition in the second clause and has continued forward in time.)

12. **And** (Both adjectives describe the cell phone.)

13. **When** or **as** (The action in the first clause happened at the same point that the action in the second clause happened.)

14. **Than** (The conjunction indicates a comparison.)

15. **If . . . then** (A conditional relationship exists between the two actions.)

16. She did not know how to play the piano, but she was eager to learn. (Because **but** is linking two independent clauses, a comma must precede it.)

17. Bring **either** a salad **or** a casserole to the potluck dinner. (**Either** cannot be used alone as a conjunction. It would also be correct to omit **either** and use only **or.**)

18. I went to the restaurant at seven o'clock; **however,** my friends were not there. OR I went to the restaurant at seven o'clock, **but** my friends were not there. (Without some kind of conjunction, the two clauses become a run-on sentence.)

19. He did chores while the other children went outside to play. (A comma is not needed before a subordinating conjunction.)

20. Cinderella's stepsisters were cruel **and** selfish. (**Cruel** and **selfish** are similarly bad qualities, so **but,** which shows a contrast, is not appropriate.)

21. I like you better than **I like** him. OR I like you better than **he likes you**. (While it is not necessarily incorrect to use an objective pronoun after **than,** in this case the sentence is unclear as originally written.)

22. If we finish early, **then** we can go home. (**Then,** not **than,** is used to indicate a sequence in time.)

23. No errors.

24. I liked the job, **but** it did not pay well. OR I liked the job; **however,** it did not pay well. OR I liked the job **even though** it did not pay well. (**And** is incorrect because the two clauses are contrasting. Notice that punctuation is required to separate the independent clauses.)

25. We will make either chicken **or** spaghetti for dinner. (**Either . . . nor** is not a correlative conjunction. No punctuation is needed after the **or;** only two items are listed, and no independent clauses are involved.)

Supplemental Chapter Problems

Problems

Supply the missing conjunction.

1. I listen to the radio _____ I am driving.

2. Sensible eating _____ moderate exercise will help you lose weight.

3. _____ pleading _____ threatening made any difference.

4. The chair is broken, _____ I cannot offer you a seat.

5. The toy store sells dolls, board games, _____ model airplanes.

6. Everyone told him he would never succeed; _____, he never gave up hope.

7. When she was young, my mother wanted to be a pilot _____ an archaeologist.

8. The legislature repealed the law _____ it was too restrictive.

9. The governor signed the bill _____ it was approved by the legislature.

10. I could not decide _____ to say what I really thought _____ tell a polite lie.

11. The company must _____ lay off workers _____ go bankrupt.

12. Can you return my book to the library _____ it closes?

13. Being a fashion model and a teacher, my aunt is _____ beautiful _____ intelligent.

14. I am tired of that song _____ I hear it all the time.

15. He is not a good cook, _____ he tries hard.

Determine whether the following sentences contain errors and correct any you find. Pay close attention to punctuation.

16. If I promise to keep it a secret, than will you tell what is going on?

17. Mr. Ramon is a good administrator, but, not a good teacher.

18. Sleet is neither snow neither rain.

19. The ingredients for the stew are beef and noodles and carrots and broth and potatoes.

20. She is my grandfather's age although, she looks much younger.

21. He has been successful in business because he is so well organized.

22. Both my sister or my brother play saxophone.

23. No one asked the tenants what they wanted consequently the remodeling project was a failure.

24. When they went scuba diving they saw colorful fish.

25. This computer game is exciting yet action packed.

Answers

1. **When** or **while** (subordinating conjunctions, p. 138)

2. **And** (coordinating conjunctions, p. 135)

3. **Neither, nor** (correlative conjunctions, p. 137)

4. **So** (subordinating conjunctions, p. 138) (Notice that using **therefore** in this instance would have required a semicolon after the first independent clause.)

5. **And** (coordinating conjunctions, p. 135)

6. **Nonetheless** or **nevertheless** (conjunctive adverbs, p. 143)

7. **Or** (coordinating conjunctions, p. 135)

8. **Because** (subordinating conjunctions, p. 138)

9. **After** (subordinating conjunctions, p. 138)

10. **Whether . . . or** (correlative conjunctions, p. 137)

11. **Either . . . or** (correlative conjunctions, p. 137)

12. **Before** (subordinating conjunctions, p. 138)

13. **Both . . . and** or **not only . . . but also** (correlative conjunctions, p. 137)

14. **Because** (subordinating conjunctions, p. 138)

15. **But** (coordinating conjunctions, p. 138)

16. If I promise to keep it a secret, **then** will you tell what is going on? (correlative conjunctions, p. 137)

17. Mr. Ramon is a good administrator but not a good teacher. (coordinating conjunctions, p. 135)

18. Sleet is neither snow **nor** rain. (correlative conjunctions, p. 137)

19. The ingredients for the stew are beef, noodles, carrots, broth, and potatoes. (coordinating conjunctions, p. 135)

20. She is my grandfather's age although she looks much younger. (subordinating conjunctions, p. 138)

21. No errors.

22. Both my sister **and** my brother play saxophone. (correlative conjunctions, p. 137)

23. No one asked the tenants what they wanted; consequently, the remodeling project was a failure. (conjunctive adverbs, p. 143)

24. When they went scuba diving, they saw colorful fish. (subordinating conjunctions, p. 138)

25. This computer game is exciting **and** action packed. (coordinating conjunctions, p. 135)

Chapter 5
Prepositions

Prepositions are words that modify a noun or pronoun by describing a relationship between it and the remainder of the sentence. Prepositions describe two primary types of relationships: place and time. The noun or pronoun that the preposition points to is called the **object** of the preposition. In the sentences below, the preposition is in bold, and the object of the preposition is underlined.

The cat was hiding **under** the <u>chair</u>. (describes a place: **under** the chair)

Please place the vase **on** the <u>table</u>. (describes a place: **on** the table)

We only owned that car **for** a <u>month</u>. (describes a length of time: **for** a month)

Prepositions and Compound Prepositions

The following list shows the most common prepositions. Note that some of these words can be other parts of speech, depending on their use. The word *up*, for instance, can be a noun, verb, adverb, adjective, or preposition.

Common Prepositions			
aboard	about	above	across
after	against	along	alongside
amid	amidst	among	around
as to	at	before	behind
below	beneath	beside	besides
between	beyond	but	by
concerning	despite	down	due to
during	except	for	from
in	inside	into	like
near	of	off	on
onto	out	over	past
per	round	since	through
throughout	till	to	toward
towards	under	until	unto
up	upon	up to	via
with	within	without	

Compound prepositions are several words that together function as a single preposition. Compound prepositions combine at least one preposition with a noun or adjective. The English language contains many compound prepositions; the following table lists some of the more common ones.

Compound Prepositions			
ahead of	as far as	because of	by means of
contrary to	in addition to	in back of	in case of
in lieu of	in light of	in regard to	in spite of
instead of	next to	out of	

Prepositions that form in this manner with verbs are not called compound prepositions; they are **phrasal verbs** (phrasal verbs, p. 113). Examples of phrasal verbs include *put on*, *stand by*, and *use up*.

Common Pitfall: Misused Prepositions

Some prepositions are commonly misused because the writer mistakes one meaning for another. The word **except** means without, minus an object, or excluding a certain event. **Besides** means with, plus an object, or including a certain event.

> *Incorrect:* Maria asked for all the books by Fitzgerald besides *The Great Gatsby*. (Incorrect if the intent of the sentence is that Maria did not want *The Great Gatsby*.)
> *Correct:* Maria asked for all the books by Fitzgerald except *The Great Gatsby*.

> *Incorrect:* Except volleyball, Maria plays basketball and soccer. (Incorrect if the intent of the sentence is that Maria plays all three sports.)
> *Correct:* Besides volleyball, Maria plays basketball and soccer.

The word **between** refers to a choice involving exactly two things. **Among** refers to a choice involving more than two things. The most common mistake is to use between in cases where **among** should be used.

> *Incorrect:* I had to choose between going to the movie, ice skating, and having dinner with my parents.
> *Correct:* I had to choose among going to the movie, ice skating, and having dinner with my parents.

> *Incorrect:* I had to choose among blue and red paint.
> *Correct:* I had to choose between blue and red paint.

Common Pitfall: The Double Preposition

It is not necessary to use two prepositions together. In most cases, one preposition is sufficient.

> *Incorrect:* Do not go **beyond toward** the water.
> *Correct:* Do not go **toward** the water.

Incorrect: He walked **around by** the fence.

Correct: He came **by** the fence.

Correct: He walked **around** the fence.

Gray Area: Prepositions at the End of a Sentence

A hard-and-fast rule of grammar used to be "never end a sentence with a preposition." This rule was created by grammarians who had studied Latin and were carrying over rules from that language into the English language. Modern usage does not adhere to this rule as strictly. If a writer feels it is necessary to capture dialog or simplify the structure of a sentence by putting a preposition at the end, it is permissible to do so. However, sentences can sometimes be recast so that a preposition at the end is not necessary.

Acceptable: What kind of trouble is she <u>in</u>?

Acceptable: He had no idea what he was there <u>for</u>.

Better: He had no idea why he was there.

Example Problems

For each sentence, identify the preposition or compound preposition and its object.

1. Tell me about the movie you saw.

    Answer: **about** and **movie. About** is the preposition, and **movie** is its object.

2. The geese soared high above the clouds.

    Answer: **above** and **clouds.** Above is the preposition, and clouds is its object.

3. If she is still shopping at the mall, then she will be late for the play.

    Answer: **at, mall, for,** and **play. At** is a preposition, and **mall** is its object; **for** is also a preposition, and **play** is its object.

4. I would like a hamburger instead of this bratwurst.

    Answer: **instead of** and **bratwurst. Instead of** is a compound preposition, and **bratwurst** is its object.

Work Problems

In the following sentences, find the preposition or compound preposition and its object. Also, correct any misused prepositions.

1. Is that dog barking at me?

2. Do you know the way to San Jose?

3. I cannot leave until 5:00, but I can get there in time.

4. I must choose between the black boots, the brown mules, and the navy blue pumps.

5. I saw these shoes in a catalog I received from my friend.

6. You should put on a jacket.

Worked Solutions

1. **At, me. At** is a preposition, and **me** is its object. (prepositions and compound prepositions, p. 151.)

2. **To, San Jose. To** is a preposition, and its object is the compound, proper noun **San Jose.** (prepositions and compound prepositions, p. 151.)

3. **Until, 5:00, in, time. Until** is a preposition, and its object is **5:00; in** is also a preposition, and its object is **time.** (prepositions and compound prepositions, p. 151.)

4. **Between** is the preposition, and its objects are **boots, mules,** and **pumps. Between** is the incorrect preposition because it describes a choice among more than two things. The correct preposition is **among.** (misused prepositions, p. 152.)

5. **In, catalog, from, friend. In** is a preposition, and its object is **catalog. From** is also a preposition, and its object is **friend.** (prepositions and compound prepositions, p. 151.)

6. Trick question! **On** looks like a preposition, but it is not; it is part of the phrasal verb **put on.** (phrasal verbs, p. 113.)

Prepositional Phrases

A **prepositional phrase** consists of the preposition or compound preposition, its object (a noun or pronoun), and a set of determiners (articles, adjectives, or pronouns) which modify the object. The most common construction of a prepositional phrase is as follows:

> Preposition + determiner + object
> *Example:* into the seats

In this sentence, **into** is the preposition, **the** is an article that acts as a determiner because it modifies the object, and **seats** is a noun which is the object of the phrase.

A sentence can be formulated as follows:

> She hit the ball into the cheap seats.

A breakdown of the sentence is as follows:

She	hit	the ball	into the cheap seats.
Noun	Verb	Object complement	Prepositional phrase

The English language contains only about 150 prepositions and compound prepositions, but it contains tens of thousands of adjectives. You can create an almost endless number of prepositional phrases. Following are a few examples.

aboard the ship	at the ballpark
concerning the subscription	during the game
from the boy	in lieu of a test
like a bird	off the ground
since the flood	until the work ends
via the expressway	with respect to the library

All the above phrases, whether simple or complex, adhere to the preposition + determiner + object, or compound preposition + determiner + object construction.

A **predicate preposition** is a prepositional phrase following a form of the verb *to be* and telling where the subject of the sentence is. (predicates, p. 188.) In the sentences below, the form of the verb *to be* is underlined and the predicate preposition is in bold.

> The dog <u>is</u> **in the neighbor's backyard.**
> My keys <u>were</u> **on the kitchen counter.**

Example Problems

Find the prepositional phrases in the following sentences.

1. Aside from the weather, we had a good time.

   Answer: In this sentence, **aside from the weather** is the prepositional phrase; **aside from** is the compound preposition, **the** is the determiner, and **weather** is the object of the preposition.

2. We drove toward Miami.

   Answer: In this sentence, the phrase **toward Miami** is the prepositional phrase; **toward** is the preposition, and **Miami** is the object of the preposition.

3. The towels are in the hallway closet.

   Answer: In this sentence, **in the hallway closet** is the prepositional phrase; it is also a predicate preposition because it follows **are,** which is a form of the verb *to be*, and it modifies **towels,** which is the subject of the sentence.

Work Problems:

Find the prepositional phrases in the following sentences.

1. Contrary to what she was told, Caroline went toward the river for a swim.

2. The ship sank anyway, despite all our efforts.

3. Up to that point, things had gone well.

4.   We never went through the house.

5.   Within a few hours of learning the news, Jeff called his parents.

Worked Solutions

In the following answers, the prepositional phrases are underlined.

1.   <u>Contrary to what she was told</u>, Caroline went <u>toward the river</u> <u>for a swim</u>. (prepositional phrases, p. 154.)

2.   The ship sank anyway, <u>despite all our efforts</u>. (prepositional phrases, p. 154.)

3.   <u>Up to that point</u>, things had gone well. (prepositional phrases, p. 154.)

4.   We never went <u>through the house</u>. (prepositional phrases, p. 154.)

5.   <u>Within a few hours</u> <u>of learning the news</u>, Jeff called his parents. (prepositional phrases, p. 154.)

Chapter Problems

Problems

Underline the prepositional phrases in the following sentences.

1.   Sue was beside herself with laughter.

2.   He went in through the out door.

3.   During the night, the dog slept and seldom moved.

4.   Between you and me, we ought to have a good time.

5.   In place of screws, I used nails.

6.   Becky got into the boat for the short trip.

7.   Jessica was ahead of Jackie in her assigned housework.

8.   The lawyer accepted my research in lieu of payment.

9.   Throughout the living room there was a scent of popcorn and candy.

10. We found him at the ballgame.

11. He got here by way of the subway.

12. The prisoner made his way past the sleeping guards.

13. Next to the house was a brand new car.

14. Until we hear otherwise, the cat is presumed lost.

15. They searched everywhere despite the bad weather.

16. Inside the carport, our bikes were safe and dry.

Answers and Solutions

1. Sue was <u>beside herself</u> <u>with laughter.</u>

2. He went <u>in through the out door.</u>

3. <u>During the night,</u> the dog slept and seldom moved.

4. <u>Between you and me,</u> we ought to have a good time.

5. <u>In place of screws,</u> I used nails.

6. Becky got <u>into the boat</u> <u>for the short trip.</u>

7. Jessica was ahead <u>of Jackie</u> <u>in her assigned housework.</u>

8. The lawyer accepted my research <u>in lieu of payment.</u>

9. <u>Throughout the living room</u> there was a scent <u>of popcorn and candy.</u>

10. We found him <u>at the ballgame.</u>

11. He got here <u>by way of the subway.</u>

12. The prisoner made his way <u>past the sleeping guards.</u>

13. <u>Next to the house</u> was a brand new car.

14. <u>Until we hear otherwise,</u> the cat is presumed lost.

15. They searched everywhere <u>despite the bad weather.</u>

16. <u>Inside the carport,</u> our bikes were safe and dry.

Supplemental Chapter Problems

Problems

Underline the prepositional phrases in the following sentences.

1. Since moving east, he has lost touch with his old friends.

2. Under the boardwalk, there were rocks and sand.

3. In spite of what we were told, the area was secure.

4. The effort was fruitless without help.

5. Until we get some new tires, our car will limp on slowly.

6. In front of an audience, I am a showman.

7. Before we go any further, Sue said she would need more water.

8. The group headed toward the mountain.

9. A sign read, "In case of rain, the event will be cancelled."

10. Throughout the ceremony, the sun danced in and out of the clouds.

11. The students were behind in the math class.

12. The fireman told us not to go near the building.

13. Before we begin, are there any questions?

14. The third baseman flung the ball across the diamond.

15. With respect to the elders, we took a vote on whether to proceed.

16. Class was cancelled in view of the impending storm.

17. Owing to his eagerness, we jumped into the river ahead of our guide.

18. Alongside the building, there were rows and rows of rose bushes.

19. Ethel set the books outside on the shelf.

Answers

1. <u>Since moving east</u>, he has lost touch <u>with his old friends</u>. (prepositions and compound prepositions, p. 151; prepositional phrases, p. 154.)

2. <u>Under the boardwalk</u>, there were rocks and sand. (prepositions and compound prepositions, p. 151.)

3. <u>In spite</u> <u>of what we were told</u>, the area was secure. (prepositional phrases, p. 154.)

4. The effort was fruitless <u>without help</u>. (prepositions and compound prepositions, p. 151.)

5. <u>Until we get some new tires</u>, our car will limp on slowly. (prepositions and compound prepositions, p. 151; prepositional phrases, p. 154.)

6. <u>In front</u> <u>of an audience</u>, I am a showman. (prepositional phrases, p. 154.)

7. <u>Before we go any further</u>, Sue said she would need more water. (prepositional phrases, p. 154.)

8. The group headed <u>toward the mountain</u>. (prepositions and compound prepositions, p. 151.)

9. A sign read, "<u>In case</u> <u>of rain</u>, the event will be cancelled." (prepositional phrases, p. 154.)

10. <u>Throughout the ceremony</u>, the sun danced in and out <u>of the clouds</u>. (prepositions and compound prepositions, p. 151; prepositional phrases, p. 154.)

11. The students were behind <u>in the math class</u>. (prepositions and compound prepositions, p. 151.)

12. The fireman told us not <u>to go</u> <u>near the building</u>. (prepositional phrases, p. 154.)

13. <u>Before we begin</u>, are there any questions? (prepositional phrases, p. 154.)

14. The third baseman flung the ball <u>across the diamond</u>. (prepositions and compound prepositions, p. 151.)

15. <u>With respect</u> <u>to the elders</u>, we took a vote <u>on whether</u> to proceed. (prepositions and compound prepositions, p. 151; prepositional phrases, p. 154.)

16. Class was cancelled <u>in view</u> <u>of the impending storm</u>. (prepositional phrases, p. 154.)

17. <u>Owing to his eagerness</u>, we jumped <u>into the river</u> <u>ahead of our guide</u>. (prepositions and compound prepositions, p. 151; prepositional phrases, p. 154.)

18. <u>Alongside the building</u>, there were rows and rows <u>of rose bushes</u>. (prepositions and compound prepositions, p. 151; prepositional phrases, p. 154.)

19. Ethel set the books outside <u>on the shelf</u>. (prepositions and compound prepositions, p. 151.)

Chapter 6
Modifiers

Modifiers are words or groups of words that tell something about other words. Commonly, modifiers give more details about the words they modify or amplify, and can add interest or detail to sentences. Modifiers can describe, limit, or qualify other words in sentences. In this chapter, the following types of modifiers will be discussed: adjectives, adverbs (and their phrases), comparatives, superlatives, and emphasis words. This chapter also covers misplaced modifiers and dangling participles.

Adjectives and Adverbs

Usually, modifiers are found near the words they modify. These modifying words are called adjectives or adverbs, depending on how they are used. Adjectives modify nouns and pronouns. Adverbs modify adjectives, verbs, and other adverbs.

Adjectives

An **adjective** modifies a noun or pronoun in a sentence. Adjectives are sometimes characterized as describing words.

> The **first** car in line was stalled.

In this sentence, the adjective **first** modifies the noun **car.**

> A **purple** car whizzed through the intersection.

In this sentence, the adjective **purple** modifies and tells more about the noun, **car.**

> The **new** snowboard was waxed and ready to go.

In this sentence, the word **new** modifies or tell us more about the snowboard. We find out the snowboard is not used or damaged, but brand new.

Consider some constructions that make use of adjectives. All the words that precede the nouns modify, in some way, those nouns.

> **big** house, **large** horse, **beautiful** shoes, **nice** pants

Adjectives often answer the question **which.** *Which house?* The **big** house.

Example Problems

Find the adjectives in the following sentences.

1. The blue and yellow truck lumbered down the street.

    Answer: The words **blue** and **yellow** describe the *truck* in this sentence.

2. For years, we loved the small dog who gave us much happiness.

    Answer: In this sentence, the word **small** modifies and describes *the dog*.

3. The warm breezes drifted across the beach.

    Answer: In this sentence, **warm** modifies the noun *breezes*.

Work Problems

Find the adjectives in the following sentences.

1. There were several large, billowy clouds in the area.

2. If we are fast, there will be good seats.

3. The poem was short and beautiful.

4. She was radiant and beaming at her wedding.

5. This is the best novel I have read.

6. The novel is hard to read.

Worked Solutions

1. There were **several large, billowy** clouds in the area. (The **clouds** are described in number, size and shape—all descriptive words.)

2. If we are **fast,** there will be **good** seats. (In this sentence, the word **fast** modifies **we** and **good** modifies **seats.**)

3. The poem was **short** and **beautiful.** (The words **short** and **beautiful** modify the **poem.**)

4. She was **radiant** and **beaming** at her wedding. (The words **radiant** and **beaming** modify how she looked at her wedding.)

5. This is the **best** novel I have read. (In this sentence, **best** describes the type of **novel** that was read.)

6. The novel is **hard** to read. (In this sentence, the word **hard** describes the difficulty in reading the novel.)

Adverbs

Adverbs answer the questions **who, what, where, when, why, how,** and **how many** in a sentence. They modify adjectives, verbs, and other adverbs.

Adjectives	Adverbs
He is kind.	He acted **kindly** towards me.
She plays a beautiful tune.	She plays tunes **beautifully.**
They were a quick team.	The team played **quickly.**

Chad answered the door **sadly,** knowing the mailman brought bad news.

In this sentence, **sadly** modifies how Chad answered the door. More details are revealed about Chad's demeanor as he went to the door. **Who** answered the door, and **where** he was when he answered the door are known. A good deal of information is provided about this one incident in a sentence.

Adverbs modify verbs, adjectives, and other adverbs; they rarely modify nouns. They tell **how** something happens or **how** somebody does something.

Adverbs are often formed from adjectives or nouns by adding the suffix **–ly. Quick** becomes **quickly, sudden** becomes **suddenly, intelligent** becomes **intelligently, anger** becomes **angrily.**

Note: Be careful because many adverbs do not end in **–ly** (for example, **fast**). Moreover, some adjectives end in **–ly** (for example, **heavenly**).

Adjective	Example	Adverb	Example
Pretty	She was a pretty girl.	Prettily	The bird sang prettily.
Serious	He was a serious boy.	Seriously	The policeman spoke seriously.
Fast	It was a fast car.	Fast	Schumaker drives fast.
Quiet	They were quiet children.	Quietly	The woman spoke quietly.

Whole-Sentence Modifiers

Some adverbs modify a whole sentence, not just a part of one.

Luckily the car stopped in time.

In this sentence, **luckily** modifies the whole sentence; it shows that it was good luck that the car stopped in time.

Adverbs at Work

Adverbs are words that indicate:

❑ the frequency when something happens

❑ the manner in which it happens

❑ the place where it happens

❑ the time when something happens

❑ the level of intensity that something happens

Adverbs used in conjunction with articles, nouns, verbs, and adjectives add to the color of the English language. It is sometimes difficult to spot the differences between adjectives and adverbs, but with practice, you will be able to do it quickly.

Frequency

Some adverbs tell how often something is done. For example:

I always do my homework on time.

In this sentence, **always** describes the **frequency** with which the homework is done on time.

Other adverbs of frequency include those in the following list, describing high frequency (top) to low frequency (bottom).

always
constantly
nearly always
almost always
usually
generally
normally
regularly
often
frequently
sometimes
periodically
occasionally
now and then
once in a while
rarely
seldom
infrequently
hardly ever
scarcely ever
almost never
never

When something happens regularly at a fixed time, the following adverbs can be used:

Fixed time	Adverbs
Every day	Daily
Every week	Weekly
Every month	Monthly
Every year	Yearly/annually

For example:

> I get a newspaper every day. **I get the newspaper daily.**
> I pay my rent every month. **I pay my rent monthly.**

Manner

Some adverbs tell how, or the manner in which, an action is or should be performed.

> The little girl ran quickly.

In this sentence, **quickly** modifies the **manner** in which she ran.

> We hurried quietly.

In this sentence, **quietly** modifies the **manner** in which we hurried.

Place

Some adverbs indicate where something happens. For example:

> My passport is here in my bag.

In this sentence, **here** describes **where** the passport is.

Time

Some adverbs tell the time that something is done. For example:

> Yesterday, all my troubles seemed so far away.

In this sentence, **yesterday** describes **when** the troubles seemed far away.

The following adverbs refer to definite time. In other words, they indicate more precisely when something is going to or did take place.

Time	Example
A recurring specific day of the week	I go to the shops on Mondays.
Today	I have been to the shops today.
Yesterday	I went to the shops yesterday.
Next week/month/year	I am going to the shops next week.
Last week/month/year	I went to the shops last year.

The following words are adverbs of indefinite time—a good sense of when they happened or will happen is not provided.

Time	Example
Finally	I finally went to the shops.
Eventually	I eventually went to the shops.
Already	I have already been to the shops.
Soon	I am going to the shops soon.
Just	I am just going to the shops. (Just going **now** as opposed to the other interpretation, "I am just going to the **shops,** not to the museum or the train station.")
Still	I am still at the shops.

Intensifying Adverbs

Many adverbs are gradable; that is, they can be intensified. To do this, use intensifying adverbs such as **very, extremely,** or **highly.** For example:

The man drove **very** badly.

These intensifiers are not gradable however. As a rule, more than one intensifier should not be used. Do not say, "The man drove **extremely very** badly." In this case, say, "The man drove very badly," or "The man drove extremely badly."

Common Pitfall: Unnecessary Adverbs

Avoid using two or more adverbs at once to show a greater degree of an idea or concept.

Incorrect: The young lady walked down the runway **extremely very** poorly.
Correct: The young lady walked down the runway **very** poorly.
Correct: The young lady walked down the runway **extremely** poorly.

Also, redundant words or phrases, such as **repeat again** or **return back,** are poor examples of the proper use of grammar.

Example Problems

Find the adverbs in the following sentences.

1. Quietly, the children moved through the hall.

    Answer: In this sentence, the word **quietly** is the adverb. Even though the word appears at the beginning of the sentence, it is, nonetheless, an adverb.

2. We rarely take breaks during the workday.

    Answer: The adverb here is **rarely,** which tells how often the group takes a break.

3. She hurriedly exited the building.

    Answer: In this sentence, the word **hurriedly** is the adverb, modifying the word **exited,** telling in what manner the girl exited the building.

Work Problems

Find the adverbs in the following sentences.

1. I get a copy of the journal semimonthly.

2. He often reads the newspaper in the afternoon.

3. We finally went to the store after running out of coffee.

4. Dave regularly brings doughnuts to the office.

5. The group ended up playing outside.

6. Our teacher spoke to us seriously about planning for next year.

7. We are still stuck in traffic.

8. Perhaps we will go to St. Augustine next year.

9. We allowed the children to play upstairs.

10. Occasionally, there are bagels in the office.

Worked Solutions

1. I get a copy of the journal <u>semimonthly</u>.

2. He <u>often</u> reads the newspaper in the afternoon.

3. We <u>finally</u> went to the store after running out of coffee.

4. Dave <u>regularly</u> brings doughnuts to the office.

5. The group ended up playing <u>outside</u>.

6. Our teacher spoke to us <u>seriously</u> about planning for next year.

7. We are <u>still</u> stuck in traffic.

8. <u>Perhaps</u> we will go to St. Augustine next year.

9. We allowed the children to play <u>upstairs</u>.

10. <u>Occasionally</u>, there are bagels in the office.

Adjective and Adverbial Phrases

An adjective phrase is simply an entire phrase used as an adjective to modify a noun (phrases, p. 192) These modifiers usually appear beside the noun they modify, as in the following sentences:

The chair in the living room is my favorite place to watch TV.

The phrase **in the living room** modifies **chair.**

He was as cool as a cucumber.

The phrase **as cool as a cucumber** modifies **he.**

An example of how adjective modifiers work is given in the following sentence:

The red wagon is in the metal shed.

The word **red** modifies **wagon** because it describes the color of the wagon. The word **metal** modifies **shed** because it gives a detail about the type of shed where the wagon is stored. No adverbial or adjectival phrase is used here, just one modifier.

The red wagon, which is in the metal shed, is now no longer used.

In this example, the phrase **which is in the metal shed** follows **the red wagon.** The phrase modifies or tells more about the wagon and where it is located. Also, a modifier usually precedes the word or words that it modifies. Words that signal an adjective phrase include: **at, between, by for, from, in, of, on, to,** and **with.**

She was **completely** and **utterly** exhausted from her shopping.

In this example, a shopper was tired from her shopping spree. The pronoun in this sentence is **she.** The verb is a compound verb (more than one verb), **was exhausted.** The adverb modifiers are **completely** and **utterly,** which describe how the shopper felt. These two words modify the verbs in the sentence. The adverbial phrase **from her shopping** tell us more about the shopping trip.

The following words signal adverbial phrases:

although	since
as	so after
as if	than
as though	that
become	though
before	unless
even if	until
even though	when
if on the condition that	where
in order that	wherever
provided that	while

Note: If in doubt about the use of a word, consult a dictionary.

Example Problems

In the following sentences, find the adverbs or adverbial phrases.

1. The car that I drive between home and work is broken.

    Answer: In this sentence, the phrase **between home and work** is the adverbial phrase modifying **drive.**

2. At the concert, the guitarist appeared suddenly and stealthily.

    Answer: In this sentence **suddenly** and **stealthily** are the adverbs that make up an adverbial phrase.

Work Problems

In the following sentences, find the adjective and adverbial phrases. Also, determine the type of phrase used.

1. As the time came for us to leave, we began packing our bags.

2. Even though we had made preparations to leave, we did not want to go.

3. We finished dinner with few problems.

4. Patty went with us to the meeting.

5. From where we sat, the lecture was hard to see.

6. Until there were more seats, some attendees had to stand during the lecture.

7. Gary was allowed to come with us provided that we took good care of him.

8. Chris quietly made his way into the lecture, while we paid attention.

Worked Solutions

1. <u>As the time came for us to leave</u>, we began packing our bags. **Adverbial phrase**

2. <u>Even though we had made preparations to leave</u>, we did not want to go. **Adverbial phrase**

3. We finished dinner <u>with few problems</u>. **Adverbial phrase**

4. Patty went <u>with us</u> <u>to the meeting</u>. **Adverbial phrases**

5. <u>From where we sat</u>, the lecture was <u>hard to see</u>. **Adjective phrases**

6. <u>Until there were more seats</u>, some attendees had to stand <u>during the lecture</u>. **Adverbial phrase, Adjective phrase**

7. Gary was allowed to come with us <u>provided that we took good care of him</u>. **Adverbial phrase**

8. Chris quietly made his way <u>into the lecture</u>, <u>while we paid attention</u>. **Adjective phrase, Adverbial phrase**

Comparatives and Superlatives

Comparatives simply compare two people, places, or things, and can be either adjectives or adverbs. They are often created by adding **–er** to an adjective or adverb. Superlatives compare more than two persons, places, or things, and are usually created by adding the ending **–est** to either adjectives or a few adverbs.

Positives are the root forms of words found in the dictionary. To compare two or more objects, you modify the positive form of a word with either a comparative or a superlative. The positive *old* can show comparison by adding **–er,** thus creating the word *older*. Likewise, the superlative of *old* becomes *oldest*, by adding the **–est** ending to the root word.

> The **old** ship is the *USS Constitution*.
> The **older** ship of the two is the *USS Constitution*.
> The **oldest** ship in the Navy is the *USS Constitution*.

By adding the ending **–est,** more than two things can be compared. In this case, the **oldest** ship qualifies or implies that the ship is older than any other ship in the Navy. It is understood by naming this ship, and not every ship in the Navy, that enough information exists for you to know that the *USS Constitution* is older than any ship in the Navy. **Oldest** modifies **ship** in this sentence. *Note:* The name of a ship, in this case the *USS Constitution,* is italicized (italics, p. 262).

> The **old** ship is the *USS Constitution*.
> That ship is not **older than** the *USS Constitution*. (Here, two ships are being compared, one named and the other unnamed.)
> That ship is not the **oldest** in the Navy. (Here, the statement is that the oldest ship in the navy is the *USS Constitution,* and not the assumed second ship.)

Note: The word **than** is often added in the comparative form.

When comparing what two things or people do, look at what makes one different from the other. Adverbs of comparison are used to show what one thing does better or worse than the other.

The rule for forming the comparative of an adverb is: If it has the same form as an adjective, add the suffix **–er** to the end. When an adverb ends in **–ly,** however, the word **more** (or **less**) is put in front of the adverb. For example:

> Jill runs **faster** than Jack. **Fast** is the same whether adverb or adjective (without **–ly** on the end).

> Jill did her homework **more frequently than** Jack. **Frequently** is an adverb with **–ly** on the end, so add **more** before it. (When comparing two things like Jill and Jack's homework output, put **than** between the adverb and what is being compared.)

The superlative of an adverb is used when a thing or person does something to the greatest degree in a group.

The rule for forming the superlative is: If it has the same form as an adjective, add the suffix **–est** to the end of the word. When an adverb ends in **–ly, most** (or **least**) is put in front of the adverb. Superlatives can be preceded by **the,** but this is not usual. For example:

> Jill won the race because she ran the **fastest. Fast** is the same whether adverb or adjective (without **–ly** on the end).

> Professor Jones ran the **most regularly** attended lectures. **Regularly** ends in **–ly,** so add **most** before it.

Common Pitfall: Irregular Endings of Comparison Words

As just stated, most comparisons simply add **–er** and most superlatives add **–est.** However, if the word ends in **–y,** make the comparative or superlative by changing the **y** to **i** before adding **–er** or **–est,** respectively. The first three comparison words in the following list are regular; the last three end in **–y** and show the change to **i.**

Word	*Comparative*	*Superlative*
large	larger	largest
hard	harder	hardest
quick	quicker	quickest
angry	angrier	angriest
funky	funkier	funkiest
lucky	luckier	luckiest

Also, some other adjectives and adverbs are irregular in their comparative or superlative form. The following irregular **adverbs** are exceptions to the rule:

Word	*Comparative*	*Superlative*
well	better	the best
badly	worse	the worst

The following irregular **adjectives** are exceptions to the rule:

Word	Comparative	Superlative
kindly	kindlier	the kindliest
bad/badly	worse	the worst
far (geographic distance)	farther	the farthest
far (additional)	further	the furthest
good/well	better	the best
little	less	the least
more	more	the most
old (position in family)	elder	the eldest
old (age)	older	the oldest
beautiful	more beautiful	the most beautiful
intelligent	more intelligent	the most intelligent

The following are sentences where the irregular adjectives and adverbs are used in their proper context:

> **Bad** (adjective):
> He felt *bad*.
> He later felt *worse*.
> Even later, he felt the *worst* he had felt all day.

> **Badly** (adverb):
> He felt *badly* that the presentation went poorly.
> He felt *worse* that the presentation did not appeal to the board.
> He felt the *worst* that he had ever felt about a presentation.

> **Well** (adverb):
> She is *well*.
> She is doing *better*.
> She is feeling the *best* she has felt in weeks.

Common Pitfall: Double Comparisons and Superlatives

To avoid an improper use of grammar, do not add or double comparisons.

funny	funnier (not *more funnier*)	funniest (not *most funniest*)
silly	sillier (not *more sillier*)	silliest (not *most silliest*)

Common Pitfall: Adjectives and Adverbs That Should Not Be Compared

The following list contains adjectives and adverbs that are noncomparable because of their respective meanings:

Unique (adjective) Either something is unique or it is not unique. The meaning implies that something is one of a kind. Something cannot be more unique or most unique.

Absolute (adjective) An absolute adjective. Degrees of absolute do not exist. Something cannot be more absolute or most absolute.

Essential (adjective) Something is either essential or not essential. It is not possible for something to be more essential or most essential.

Immortal (adjective) Meaning *to live forever*. Something either lives forever or it does not.

Universal (adjective) Meaning *present everywhere*. Something is either universal, or it is not. Things cannot be more universal or most universal.

Example Problems

In the following sentences, find the proper use of comparatives and superlatives.

1. John is funny.

    Answer: In this sentence, there is no comparison to any other person, so the present tense and the positive form of the adjective (funny) is used.

2. The funnier of the two men was John.

    Answer: In this sentence, two men are being compared, John and an unnamed man. Because only two people are being compared, attach the **–er** ending to create the comparative form of funny (funnier).

3. Of the three men, John, Thurston, and Jeff, John is the funniest character we know.

    Answer: In this sentence, more than two people being compared, so use the root word funny and the **–est** ending for the proper superlative comparison.

Work Problems

In the following sentences, find the proper use of comparatives and superlatives.

1. The comedian was funny/funnier/funniest than the clown.

2. However, the clown was funny/funnier/funniest when he worked with the dog.

3. Bjorn was the good/better/best in the world.

4. Tom was good/better/best than Sam.

5. I am a good/better/best tennis player myself.

6. Sal is the smart/smarter/smartest student in the class, based on his high grades.

7. Susan is smart/smarter/smartest.

8. Sue does good/better/best in math classes than Sal and Susan.

9. Sam had traveled the far/farther/farthest of all the meeting attendees.

10. The jury decided that they needed far/further/furthest proof that the defendant was guilty.

Worked Solutions

1. The comedian was **funnier** than the clown. (Two people are being compared.)

2. However, the clown was **funniest** when he worked with the dog. (More than two clowns are being compared. Use the superlative. We are comparing many instances of a single clown's performance and the performances with the dog were funniest.)

3. Bjorn was the **best** in the world. (Use the superlative because Bjorn was better than any other person in the world.)

4. Tom was **better** than Sam. (Two people are being compared.)

5. I am a **good** tennis player myself. (No comparison is being made, so you only need the adjective.)

6. Sal is the **smartest** student in the class, based on his high grades. (Use the superlative to compare Sal and all the students in the class.)

7. Susan is **smart**. (No comparison or superlative degree adjective is needed. Only Susan is being described, and no other person.)

8. Sue does **better** in math classes than Sal and Susan. (Sue does better in class than the other two students, so only the comparison degree is needed. Sue is one person being compared to two people, who represent one entity. Thus, it is one person versus one entity. Use the comparative in this instance.)

9. Sam had traveled the **farthest** of all the meeting attendees. (Use the word relating to distance, not addition, in this sentence.)

10. The jury decided that they needed **further** proof that the defendant was guilty. (The jury in this case needs more proof, not distance, so the word further is used.)

Emphasis Words

Emphasis words are used to emphasize an adjective or adverb. These words compare adjectives or adverbs without necessarily referring to comparison or the superlative degree. Often, people will confuse the adjective with the adverb use of some comparison words. The result is an improper use of grammar. Some of these emphasis words are (but are not limited to):

certainly	really
extremely	somewhat
highly	such
least	sure
much	too
quite	tremendously
real	very

Real is an adjective; **really** is an adverb.

Correct: She is a *real* person.
Incorrect: She is a *really* person.

Correct: She is *really* nice.
Incorrect: She is *real* nice.

Good is an adjective; **well** is an adverb.

Correct: She did a *good* job.
Incorrect: She did a *well* job.

Correct: She did the job *well*.
Incorrect: She did the job *good*.

Sure is an adjective; **surely** is an adverb.

Correct: He is *sure* of himself.
Incorrect: He is *surely* of himself.

Correct: He is *surely* confident of his abilities.
Incorrect: He is *sure* confident of his abilities.

Misplaced Modifiers and Dangling Participles

Misplaced modifiers are words or phrases that when read in the context of a sentence lend confusion, not clarity, to the meaning. (This topic will be discussed further in Chapter 7, Sentences; see misplaced or "dangling modifiers," p. 209.) As a general rule, the closer a modifier is to the word it modifies, the clearer a sentence will be.

Incorrect: The chicken fryer seen on television **only** costs $19.95.

In this case, the word **only** modifies the wrong word, **costs.** Instead, the writer meant to modify the actual price:

Correct: The chicken fryer seen on television costs **only** $19.95.

The following modifiers (**almost, even, hardly, merely, nearly,** and **only**) should appear just before the words meant for modification.

> The red, affordable car is **merely** two thousand dollars. (The phrase **two thousand dollars** is being modified, and not any other words in the sentence.)
>
> He **almost** never goes out at night. (The word **goes** is being modified, and the adverb **never** is the complement.)

Participial phrases can also confuse the reader. Sometimes, the result is humorous. Participial phrases end in **–ing** and can be used as adjectives, modifying nouns or pronouns (participles, p. 124; phrases, p. 192).

> *Incorrect:* The evening passed by, eating popcorn and other snacks. (The evening ate popcorn?)
>
> *Correct:* We passed the evening eating popcorn and other snacks.

> *Incorrect:* After working on the assignment for hours, the rains came down in torrents. (The rains worked on the assignment?)
>
> *Correct:* After we worked outside on the assignment for hours, the rains finally came down in torrents.

Example Problems

Correct the misplaced or dangling modifiers.

1. He came in even first though he was behind at first.

   Answer: In this sentence, change the dangling modifier **even first** to **first even,** and the sentence will be correct.

2. Having a headache, the test was frustrating for Sam.

   Answer: In this sentence, the test had a headache? Corrected version: Sam had a headache while taking the test. Or, Sam had a headache while taking the frustrating test.

3. Around the age of six, my father took me to a baseball game.

   Answer: Your father was six years old when he took you to a game? Correct version: I was six years old when my father took me to a baseball game.

Work Problems

Correct the dangling and misplaced modifiers in the following sentences (your answers may vary).

1. Chris left the watch at the mall that he had bought last week.

2. Walking three days a week, the heart increases its muscle mass.

3. Having entered the theatre, the smell of popcorn overwhelmed us.

4. Because he tested well, the teacher had the student run an errand for him.

5. Being a travelling salesman, my mom seldom saw my dad.

6. To avoid flying, the airplane was not a preferred transportation for me.

7. Passing by the school building, the vandalism became clear.

8. A number of animals are killed by motor vehicles unleashed.

9. Even though the jambalaya was spicy, Joe finished the entire plate.

10. Being young, my parents did not understand me.

Worked Solutions

Note: Answers may vary; the following are a few of the possibilities.

1. At the mall, Chris left the watch that he had bought last week.

2. By walking three days a week, you can increase heart muscle mass.

3. As we entered the theatre, the smell of popcorn overwhelmed us.

4. Because the student did well on the test, the teacher had the student run an errand for him.

5. Because my dad was a travelling salesman, my mom seldom saw him.

6. Because I avoid flying, traveling by airplane was not for me.

7. As we passed by the school building, we could clearly see the vandalism.

8. A number of unleashed animals are killed by motor vehicles.

9. Even though he thought the jambalaya spicy, Joe finished the entire plate.

10. Because I was young, my parents did not understand me.

Chapter Problems

Problems

Find the adjectives in the following sentences.

1. Caroline wore an elegant gown to the ball.

2. For years, I had a silver and blue bicycle.

3. The restaurant has a first-class menu.

4. We met for a long time yesterday.

5. Sam's disposition is chipper and bright.

6. The breeze is a gentle and warm one.

7. The group was pleased to have the option of generic drugs.

8. The drama group's performance was masterful and daring.

9. The store had a small microwave oven for sale.

10. That author is both prolific and popular.

Find the adverbs in the following sentences.

11. On the driving test, she performed badly.

12. We constantly have to battle the elements while skiing.

13. Every year we take a trip across the state.

14. They finished the test slowly, behind the others.

15. The dog was carried away.

Find the adjective or adverbial phrases in the following sentences and indicate each.

16. Between you and me, I think Sam is going to win.

17. She had to go with me to the store.

18. Because I am so short, buy me a medium-sized shirt.

19. He came in from the cold.

20. We acted as if we owned the airplane.

In the following sentences, choose the correct comparatives and superlatives:

21. He is the lucky/luckier/luckiest card player I know.

22. The play went well/better/best.

23. The class was large/larger/largest than my previous class.

24. She was the angry/angrier/angriest I had ever seen her.

25. Vanilla cones are good/better/the best than strawberry, but chocolate cones are good/better/the best.

Correct the dangling and misplaced modifiers in the following sentences (your answers may vary).

26. While driving down the street, the bicycle had a flat tire.

27. Hidden in the alley, the pedestrians could not see the policeman.

28. Topped with whipped cream, most people like pumpkin pie.

29. For treatment after surgery, exercise is recommended.

30. While fixing the car, the wrench fell into the engine block.

Answers and Solutions

1. Caroline wore an **elegant** gown to the ball. (adjectives, p. 161)

2. For years, I had a **silver** and **blue** bicycle. (adjectives, p. 161)

3. The restaurant has a **first-class** menu. (adjectives, p. 161)

4. We met for a **long** time yesterday. (adjectives, p. 161)

5. Sam's disposition is **chipper** and **bright**. (adjectives, p. 161)

6. The breeze is a **gentle** and **warm** one. (adjectives, p. 161)

7. The group was **pleased** to have the option of **generic** drugs. (adjectives, p. 161)

8. The **drama** group's performance was **masterful** and **daring.** (adjectives, p. 161)

9. The store had a **small microwave** oven for sale. (adjectives, p. 161)

10. That author is both **prolific** and **popular.**

11. On the driving test, she performed **badly.** (adverbs, p. 163)

12. We **constantly** have to battle the elements while skiing. (adverbs, p. 163)

13. **Every year** we take a trip across the state. (adverbs, p. 163)

14. They finished the test **slowly,** behind the others. (adverbs, p. 163)

15. The dog was carried **away.** (adverbs, p. 163)

16. **Between you and me,** I think Sam is going to win. (Adjective phrase) (adjective and adverbial phrases, p. 168)

17. She had to go **with me to the store.** (Adjective phrase, adjective phrase, adjective phrase) (adjective and adverbial phrases, p. 168)

18. **Because I am so short**, buy me a medium-sized shirt. (Adverbial phrase) (adjective and adverbial phrases, p. 168)

19. He came **in from the cold**. (Adverbial phrase) (adjective and adverbial phrases, p. 168)

20. We acted **as if we owned the airplane.** (Adverbial phrase) (adjective and adverbial phrases, p. 168)

21. He is the **luckiest** card player I know. (comparatives and superlatives, p. 170)

22. The play went **well.** (comparatives and superlatives, p. 170)

23. The class was **larger** than my previous class. (comparatives and superlatives, p. 170)

24. She was the **angriest** I had ever seen her. (comparatives and superlatives, p. 170)

25. Vanilla cones are **better** than strawberry, but chocolate cones are **the best.** (comparatives and superlatives, p. 170)

26. While I was driving down the street, my bicycle had a flat tire. (misplaced modifiers and dangling participles, p. 175)

27. The policeman was hidden in the alley, and the pedestrians could not see him. (misplaced modifiers and dangling participles, p. 175)

28. Most people like pumpkin pie topped with whipped cream. (misplaced modifiers and dangling participles, p. 175)

29. Exercise is recommended as a treatment after surgery. (misplaced modifiers and dangling participles, p. 175)

30. While I was fixing the car, I dropped the wrench into the engine block. (misplaced modifiers and dangling participles, p. 175)

Supplemental Chapter Problems

Problems

Find the adjectives in the following sentences.

1. The Internet is ubiquitous and is easily accessed everywhere.

2. She was a tenderhearted, good soul.

3. Our horse was feisty and cantankerous.

4. The attorney considered the evidence admissible in court.

5. We were asked for collateral to buy the new house.

Find the adverbs in the following sentences.

6. We went to the class yesterday.

7. I sometimes take a different route to class.

8. The children played outside.

9. She has already been to the house.

10. They ran the course quickly and efficiently.

Find the adjective or adverbial phrases in the following sentences and indicate each.

11. We found the remote control in the living room.

12. I found the magazine while you were out.

13. They were supposed to go to the grocery store.

14. Sue left before I got there.

15. Even though she enjoyed her trip, Elaine was totally exhausted.

In the following sentences, choose the correct comparatives and superlatives.

16. He is the kind/kindlier/kindliest man I know.

17. She felt bad/worse/worst after taking the medicine.

18. The float was the large/larger/largest I had ever seen.

19. Ethel was pretty/prettier/prettiest than anyone had ever seen her.

20. Stacy was the old/older/oldest sibling in her family.

Correct the dangling and misplaced modifiers in the following sentences

21. Getting out of the car, the mall was just up ahead.

22. Running back to the house, the car sped by.

23. He served hot dogs to the men on paper plates.

24. Having read the original work, the article was fascinating.

25. To change the paper's focus, it had to be rewritten.

Answers

1. The Internet is **ubiquitous** and is easily accessed everywhere. (adjectives, p. 161)

2. She was a **tenderhearted, good** soul. (adjectives, p. 161)

3. Our horse was **feisty** and **cantankerous.** (adjectives, p. 161)

4. The attorney considered the evidence **admissible** in court. (adjectives, p. 161)

5. We were asked for collateral to buy the **new** house. (adjectives, p. 161)

6. We went to the class **yesterday.** (adverbs, p. 163)

7. I **sometimes** take a different route to class. (adverbs, p. 163)

8. The children played **outside.** (adverbs, p. 163)

9. She has **already** been to the house. (adverbs, p. 163)

10. They ran the course **quickly** and **efficiently.** (adverbs, p. 163)

11. We found the remote control **in the living room.** (Adverbial phrase) (adjective and adverbial phrases, p. 168)

12. I found the magazine **while you were out.** (Adverbial phrase) (adjective and adverbial phrases, p. 168)

13. They were supposed to go **to the grocery store.** (Adverbial phrase) (adjective and adverbial phrases, p. 168)

14. Sue left **before I got there.** (Adverbial phrase) (adjective and adverbial phrases, p. 168)

15. **Even though she enjoyed her trip,** Elaine was **totally exhausted.** (Adverbial phrase) (adjective and adverbial phrases, p. 168)

16. He is the **kindliest** man I know. (comparatives and superlatives, p. 170)

17. She felt **worse** after taking the medicine. (comparatives and superlatives, p. 170)

18. The float was the **largest** I had ever seen. (comparatives and superlatives, p. 170)

19. Ethel was **prettier** than anyone had ever seen her. (comparatives and superlatives, p. 170)

20. Stacy was **the oldest** sibling in her family. (comparatives and superlatives, p. 170)

21. As I was getting out of the car, I saw that the mall was just up ahead. OR Getting out of the car, I saw the mall was just up ahead. (misplaced modifiers and dangling participles, p. 175)

22. While I was running back to the house, a car sped by. (misplaced modifiers and dangling participles, p. 175)

23. He served hot dogs on paper plates to the men. (misplaced modifiers and dangling participles, p. 175)

24. Having read the original work, I found the article fascinating. (misplaced modifiers and dangling participles, p. 175)

25. To change the paper's focus, I had to rewrite the paper. (misplaced modifiers and dangling participles, p. 175)

Chapter 7
Sentences

The simplest possible **sentence** consists of a **subject,** which controls the action of the verb, and a **predicate,** which includes the verb and any objects, modifiers, or complements. Written English sentences begin with a capital letter and end with a full-stop punctuation mark (period, exclamation point, or question mark).

Phrases and Clauses

Sentences commonly include a variety of phrases and clauses. A **phrase** is a closely related group of words that lacks both a subject and a verb. In sentences, phrases act as grammatical units, such as subjects, objects, or modifiers.

Unlike a phrase, a **clause** has both a subject and verb. An **independent clause** can stand on its own as a complete sentence. A **dependent clause** must be attached to an independent clause to make sense. Like phrases, clauses can act as subjects, objects, or modifiers.

By stringing phrases and clauses together, we can create a variety of sentence types. A **compound sentence** has at least two independent clauses joined by a conjunction. A **compound-complex** sentence has at least two independent clauses plus at least one dependent clause.

Sentences are also classified by **mood.** A **declarative** sentence makes a statement. An **interrogative** sentence asks a question. An **imperative** sentence gives a command. Sentences also have **voice** (**active** or **passive**), which determines whether the subject of the sentence is doing or receiving the action of the main verb.

Sentences are prone to a number of grammatical and stylistic problems. This chapter will cover some of the most common:

- ❑ **Run-on sentences**
- ❑ **Comma splices**
- ❑ **Sentence fragments**
- ❑ **Misplaced or "dangling" modifiers**
- ❑ **Restrictive and nonrestrictive elements**
- ❑ **Unclear antecedents**
- ❑ **Lack of agreement**
- ❑ **Lack of parallelism**
- ❑ **Inconsistent use of tenses or pronouns**

Subjects

Every English sentence must contain a **subject.** A subject is anything that governs the action of a verb.

>   **The dogs** barked at me.
>   **Stars** are twinkling overhead tonight.
>   **The gross national product of India** is greater than that of its neighboring countries.

Generally, the subject is the doer of the action expressed by the verb; however, in passive sentences, the subject actually receives the action of the verb.

>   **The ancient tree** was destroyed by tiny bacteria.

(For more about passive sentences, see voice, p. 107, and sentence types: passive and active voice, p. 204.)

Extremely simple sentences can consist of only a subject and verb.

>   **Subject | verb.**
>   Night | is falling.
>   He | called.

A verb agrees with its subject in number and person. (See simple present tense, p. 85, for examples of verb forms that vary for number and person.) If the subject is singular, the verb it controls must be singular; and if the subject is plural, the verb must be plural.

>   My hands **are** cold. (**my hands** = third person plural)
>   The mail **is** late today. (**the mail** = third person singular)
>   I **am** ready to leave. (**I** = first person singular)

Subjects are almost always specifically named. However, even a single-word command can qualify as a sentence because it has an implied subject: you. (For more about commands, see mood, p. 111, and sentence types: declarative, imperative, and interrogative moods, p. 202.)

>   Stay! (*You* stay.)
>   Look! (*You* look.)
>   March! (*You* march.)

Subjects are usually nouns or pronouns. From a grammatical point of view, all the words that modify, explain, or identify the noun/pronoun are included as part of the subject. In these sentences, the main noun of the subject is underlined, but the entire subject is in boldface.

>   **The <u>man</u> standing on the corner** is selling t-shirts.
>   **The <u>movie</u> that I was telling you about** will be on TV tomorrow.

Infinitives and gerunds, which are derived from verbs but act as nouns, can also be subjects, along with their phrases. (See gerunds, p. 120; infinitives, p. 122.)

>   **Going for a drive in this terrible snowstorm** would be a bad idea.
>   **To identify the murderer** is the police department's goal.

Subjects can be simple (meaning that there is only one subject) or compound (meaning that there is more than one subject). Compound subjects are joined by a coordinating conjunction (see coordinating conjunctions, p. 135).

> Later, **Lupe** *and* **all her friends** threw a party to celebrate.
>
> **Louis, Marisa,** *and* **Roxanne** have the flu.

Example Problems

Identify the subject of each sentence.

1. Lifting so much weight without a spotter is dangerous.

    Answer: **Lifting so much weight without a spotter.** The main noun within this phrase is the gerund **lifting.** All the other words modify or explain that noun.

2. This video game that I bought yesterday seems to be defective.

    Answer: **This video game that I bought yesterday.** The main noun within this phrase is **video game;** the entire subject is actually the noun plus a relative clause (*that I bought yesterday*) modifying it.

3. I told her that she should not be so negative.

    Answer: **I.** Although there is another clause within this sentence (*she should not be so negative*), **she** is only the subject of the clause, not of the entire sentence.

Work Problems

Draw a line under the subject of each sentence.

1. Bill and Joe are good friends.

2. Take this ball back to the gym.

3. Singing in the school choir, playing on the basketball team, and working at the coffeehouse keep her busy almost all the time.

4. The coffee table broke when Mike dropped a bowling ball on it.

5. Conditions are not expected to improve any time soon.

6. What are you trying to say?

Worked Solutions

1. <u>Bill and Joe</u> are good friends. This is a compound subject joined by the coordinating conjunction **and.**

2. <u>(You)</u> Take this ball back to the gym. Because this sentence gives an order, the subject is not actually stated in the sentence, but the implied subject of all orders is **you.**

3. <u>Singing in the school choir, playing on the basketball team, and working at the coffeehouse</u> keep her busy almost all the time. This sentence has a compound subject (actually three gerund phrases) joined by the coordinating conjunction **and.**

4. <u>The coffee table</u> broke when Mike dropped a bowling ball on it. Although this sentence contains another clause with its own subject (Mike), **the coffee table** is the subject of the entire sentence; everything else simply explains why the coffee table broke.

5. <u>Conditions</u> are not expected to improve any time soon. This is a passive sentence in which the doer of the verb's action is not even named. (Who expects things not to improve?) However, **conditions** is the noun that controls the action of the verb, even if it is not doing the action itself.

6. What are <u>you</u> trying to say? In a question, normal word order is reversed, so locating the subject can be tricky. To make the subject easier to identify, try rewriting the question as a statement: **You** are trying to say what.

Special Types of Subjects

While most subjects are nouns or pronouns, some special exceptions exist.

The construction **there is** frequently begins English sentences and clauses.

> **There is** someone waiting here to see you.
> **There are** many possible answers to this question.
> I told him that **there were** no more tickets available.

There is the subject, but it is not a noun or pronoun. In this kind of usage, **there** is an expletive. In grammatical terms, an **expletive** is a word that has a grammatical function in a sentence but has no meaning of its own. Other expletives are the **it** of the construction **it is,** discussed later, and the auxiliary **do** when it is used to form the negative or question form of a verb (see simple present tense, p. 85; simple past tense, p. 87, for examples).

By itself, **there** is neither singular nor plural, but it can be followed by the singular verb **is** or the plural verb **are.** The form of the verb is determined by the noun that follows **there.**

> There **are** some **pencils** (*plural*) in the drawer.
> There **is** a **letter** (*singular*) for you from the IRS.

Other possible combinations involve tense or mood: **there was/were** (*past*), **there will** (*future*), **there would** (*modal*), and so on.

The construction **it is** functions much like **there is.**

> **It is** difficult to explain why this sentence works.
> I do not want to go out because **it is** raining.
> **It will be** important for him to manage his time.

It is does not have a plural form, but can vary for tense or mood: **it was, it will, it would,** and so on.

The **it** of the construction **it is** is an expletive. This expletive **it** might look like a pronoun, but it is not because it does not replace or refer to a noun. The same is true of the **it** that appears as the subject of these sentences:

It appears that the recession is over.

It seems that he did not want to retire after all.

It does not matter what you do.

Example Problems

Identify the subject of each sentence.

1. It seems that there are never enough chairs to go around.

   Answer: **It.** The **there** of **there are** is the subject of a clause embedded in the sentence, not the entire sentence.

2. It is now seven o'clock.

   Answer: **It.** The **it is** construction is often used to express time or weather.

Work Problems

Supply the correct form of the verb *to be*.

1. There _____ several options in front of us.

2. There _____ six boxes here yesterday.

3. It _____ more fun when lots of people show up.

4. There _____ a broken desk in the back of the room.

5. It _____ a raccoon that tipped over our garbage can last night.

Worked Solutions

1. **Are** (The verb agrees with the plural noun **options.**)

2. **Were** (**Yesterday** requires past tense; the verb agrees with the plural noun **boxes.**)

3. **Is** (**It is** always followed by a singular verb form.)

4. **Is** (The verb agrees with the singular noun **desk.**)

5. **Was** (**It** always requires a singular verb; **last night** requires past tense.)

Predicates

In a sentence or a clause, the **predicate** includes the verb and any objects, modifiers, or complements. Basically, the predicate is anything other than the subject. In these sentences, the verb is underlined, but the entire predicate is in boldface.

Mr. O'Malley <u>**will coach**</u> **the soccer team next year.**

An unexpected winter storm <u>**damaged**</u> **citrus crops throughout Florida.**

Our softball team <u>**is trying**</u> **to raise money to buy new uniforms.**

When the subject is followed by a linking verb (linking verbs, p. 83), usually a form of the verb *to be*, the sentence has one of three special types of predicates: a **predicate noun,** a **predicate adjective,** or a **predicate preposition.**

A **predicate noun** is a noun that follows a linking verb and renames or identifies the subject. The predicate noun includes the noun and any words that modify it.

Dr. Tranh **is a dentist.**

Derek and Tim **are the best runners on the cross-country team.**

The *B Minor Mass* **was Bach's masterpiece.**

A **predicate adjective** is an adjective that follows a linking verb and describes the subject. The predicate adjective includes the adjective and any words that modify or explain it.

Chocolate **is delicious with raspberries.**

Adrian and his sister **are very talented.**

This assignment **is almost impossible to finish.**

Both predicate nouns and predicate adjectives are considered **subject complements.** Subject complements rename, describe, identify, or explain the subject.

A **predicate preposition** is a prepositional phrase following *to be* that tells where the subject is.

The hockey sticks **are in the closet down the hall.**

Araceli **is behind the door.**

Your glasses **were on the table where you left them.**

Example Problems

What is the predicate of each sentence?

1. My cell phone fell into the swimming pool.

    Answer: Fell into the swimming pool. **Fell** is the verb; the rest is a prepositional phrase telling where the phone fell.

2. I expect that we will need to make more than one trip.

    Answer: Expect that we will need to make more than one trip. **Expect** is the verb; the rest is a dependent clause explaining what I expect. Notice that even though the clause has its own subject and verb *(we will need to make)*, these are simply part of the predicate and do not control the sentence.

3. The necklace that she wore to the banquet was extremely valuable.

    Answer: Was extremely valuable. This is an example of a predicate adjective. The subject that it modifies is a noun *(necklace)* plus a relative clause *(that she wore)* with a prepositional phrase *(to the banquet).*

Work Problems

For each sentence, draw one line under the entire predicate. Draw two lines under the main verb within the predicate.

1. No one understands this problem better than I do.

2. The ugly old picture that used to hang in the hall turned out to be the work of a famous painter.

3. The hospitals were overwhelmed by patients injured during the earthquake.

4. Do you still have that old car your grandfather gave you?

5. Applications must be submitted to the selection committee by the end of the week.

Worked Solutions

The bolded section stands for the double-underline mentioned in the instructions for this section.

1. No one **understands** this problem better than I do.

    This predicate contains a verb, an object, and a modifying phrase.

2. The ugly old picture that used to hang in the hall **turned out** to be the work of a famous painter.

    Do not be fooled by subjects that include relative clauses, as this one does. The verb **used to hang** is not the main verb of the sentence. The main verb of the sentence will almost always follow the entire subject.

3. The hospitals **were overwhelmed** by patients injured during the earthquake.

    This is a passive sentence, so the predicate actually contains the doer of the action of the main verb: **Patients injured during the earthquake** overwhelmed the hospitals.

4. Do you still **have** that old car your grandfather gave you?

    It would not be wrong to include **do** as part of the predicate, but it really has no meaning; it is required to turn the sentence into a question. **Still** is an adverb modifying **have,** so it is not part of the verb itself.

5. Applications **must be submitted** to the selection committee by the end of the week.

    This is another passive sentence, but the predicate does not contain the doer of the action. Instead, the predicate is nothing but prepositional phrases strung together.

Objects

Except for the special predicates that follow the verb *to be*, most predicates contain at least one object. An **object** is anything that receives the action of the verb. In these sentences, the objects are underlined.

> Kentaro gave <u>me</u> <u>his notes</u>.
>
> They have been installing <u>new computers</u> in the lab.
>
> I wrote a <u>letter</u> to the <u>president.</u>

There are two types of objects: direct and indirect. (See transitive and intransitive verbs: direct objects, p. 79, and indirect objects, p. 81, for more information.)

A **direct object** tells *who* or *what* received the action of the verb. A direct object can be a person or a thing.

> The ancient Egyptians built **the pyramids.** (*What* did they build? The pyramids.)
>
> The noise scared **Anna.** (*Whom* did the noise scare? Anna.)
>
> The Tylers raise **chickens.** (*What* do they raise? Chickens.)

An **indirect object** tells *to whom* or *for whom* the action of the verb was done. An indirect object cannot appear in a predicate unless a direct object already exists. Indirect objects are usually people or living beings. In these sentences, the direct object has a line beneath it, while the indirect object is bolded.

> We gave **our teacher** <u>a birthday card</u>.
>
> The librarian read **the children** <u>a story</u>.
>
> Sarah bought **Steve** <u>some flowers</u>.

We can move the indirect object to the end of the sentence if we use *to* or *for*.

> We gave <u>a birthday card</u> *to* **our teacher.**
>
> The librarian read <u>a story</u> *to* **the children.**
>
> Sarah bought <u>some flowers</u> *for* **Steve.**

Notice these common English sentence patterns:

> **Subject | Verb.**
>
> **Subject | Verb | Direct Object.**
>
> **Subject | Verb | Indirect Object | Direct Object.**
>
> **Subject | Verb | Direct Object |** *to/for* **| Indirect Object.**

Like a subject, a direct object can have a complement. An **object complement** renames, describes, identifies, or explains a direct object. Do not confuse object complements with direct objects.

> This gloomy weather makes me tired.
>
> **me** = direct object
>
> **tired** = object complement

Her business sense earned her great wealth.

her = indirect object

wealth = direct object

(This sentence can be rephrased to pull out the indirect object: Her business sense earned great wealth *for* her.)

Example Problems

Identify any objects in these sentences.

1. Mrs. Robson made the cake for the picnic.

   Answer: **Cake** is a direct object. **Picnic** is not a direct object because it is not a person; instead it is the object of the preposition **for.**

2. The lions roared in their cages.

   Answer: No objects. Not every sentence has an object. The verb **roar** does not need anything to receive its action.

3. Evan's friends found him a new apartment.

   Answer: **New apartment** is a direct object (*What* did Evan's friends find? An apartment.) **Him** is an indirect object (For *whom* did they find it? For him.)

Work Problems

Draw one line under any direct objects. Draw two lines under any indirect objects:

1. Many students find indirect objects difficult to identify.

2. Grammatical principles determine the structure of a sentence.

3. I loaned Julie my new sandals.

4. Dave called Rick a coward.

5. We are planning a surprise for Mrs. Lao.

Worked Solutions

The bolded section stands for the double-underline mentioned in the instructions for this section.

1. Many students find <u>indirect objects</u> difficult to identify.

   What do students find? Indirect objects. **Difficult** is an object complement.

2. Grammatical principles determine <u>the structure of a sentence</u>.

   It would be acceptable to say that **structure** by itself is the direct object because it is the main noun of this phrase. However, the entire phrase functions as a direct object.

3. I loaned **Julie** <u>my new sandals</u>.

    What did I loan? My new sandals. To *whom* did I loan them? To Julie.

4. Dave called <u>Rick</u> a coward.

    Who did Dave call? Rick. **Coward** is an object complement, not a direct object. Try rewriting the sentence and the reason becomes clearer: Dave called a coward for Rick? Dave called a coward to Rick? Both options do not make sense.

5. We are planning <u>a surprise</u> for **Mrs. Lao.**

    The indirect object here is obvious because of the preposition **for.** *What* are we planning? A surprise. For *whom* are we planning it? For Mrs. Lao.

Phrases

When we talk about grammar, we usually talk about single words, but in reality, most grammar involves groups of words that function as a unit. A **phrase** is any collection of closely related words that lacks both a subject and a verb. In sentences, phrases serve a variety of functions, acting as nouns, verbs, modifiers, subjects, and objects.

A small black dog was sitting on the steps behind the building, looking hungry and tired.

In this sentence, there are several phrases, each made up of many smaller pieces.

1. A **noun phrase** (*a small black dog*) acts as the subject. This phrase consists of a noun (*dog*) and the two adjectives (*small, black*) that modify the noun. Finally, an article (*a*) identifies the noun.

2. Two **prepositional phrases** (*on the steps, behind the building*) act as adverbs; they tell where the dog was sitting. Each phrase consists of a preposition (*on, behind*) and the noun that is the object of the preposition (*steps, building*). Finally, each noun has an article (*the*) preceding it.

3. A **participial phrase** (*looking hungry and tired*) acts as an adjective; it describes the small black dog. This phrase consists of a participle (*looking*) and two adjectives (*tired, hungry*) joined by a coordinating conjunction (*and*).

As the example above shows, phrases are usually named according to the controlling or most important piece of the phrase: **noun phrase, prepositional phrase, participial phrase,** and so on.

A **noun phrase** includes a noun (types of nouns, p. 34) or pronoun and anything modifying it. The modifiers can be simple adjectives, participles, relative clauses, or prepositional phrases. Remember that gerunds (gerunds, p. 120) or infinitives (infinitives, p. 122) are nouns and can be part of a noun phrase. In these noun phrases, the noun is underlined.

Jeff won **an incredibly large stuffed <u>teddy bear</u>** at the carnival.
<u>**Swimming** in shark-infested waters</u> is a risky form of recreation.
Those classified <u>documents</u> lying on the desk could easily be stolen.

A **prepositional phrase** includes a preposition, the noun or pronoun object of the preposition, and any adjectives modifying that object (prepositional phrases, p. 154). Short prepositional phrases are often strung together and sometimes form parts of other types of phrases. In these prepositional phrases that follow, the preposition is underlined.

> Every year, salmon spawn <u>in</u> the Columbia River.
>
> I am going <u>to</u> the mall <u>with</u> Terry.
>
> Those classified documents lying <u>on</u> the desk could easily be stolen. (This prepositional phrase is part of a larger noun phrase.)

A **participial phrase** is usually introduced by a participle (participles, p. 124). Participial phrases act as adjectives, so they sometimes form part of a larger noun phrase. In the following participial phrases, the participle is underlined.

> <u>**Running**</u> **as fast as she could,** Miriam tried to catch the bus.
>
> The ancient castle, <u>**weathered**</u> **by time,** had a romantic look.
>
> Those classified documents <u>**lying on the desk**</u> could easily be stolen. (This participial phrase is part of a larger noun phrase.)

Example Problems

Identify the type of phrase underlined in each sentence.

1. <u>Fishing at Lake Warren</u> is my dad's favorite weekend activity.

   Answer: **Noun phrase. Fishing** is a gerund, and with its modifiers it forms the subject of the sentence. You might have noticed that this noun phrase contains a prepositional phrase ("at Lake Warren").

2. Jesse designed a mural <u>for the new courthouse</u>.

   Answer: **Prepositional phrase.** This phrase consists of the preposition **for** and its noun object, **courthouse.** The phrase tells where the mural is.

3. The snow, <u>drifted into white dunes</u>, covered the entire countryside.

   Answer: **Participial phrase.** This phrase, introduced by the participle **drifted,** is an adjective modifying the noun **snow.**

Work Problems

Identify the type of underlined phrase in each sentence.

1. I was unable to speak to <u>anyone who could answer my question</u>.

2. The concert <u>announced only yesterday</u> has already been canceled.

3. A solitary sunflower grew <u>in a corner of the garden</u>.

4. <u>That catalog from the art supply company</u> has everything I need.

5. We should put the rocking chair <u>by the lamp</u>.

Worked Solutions

1. **Noun phrase.** (The main noun is **anyone**; it is modified by a relative clause that begins with **who.**)

2. **Participial phrase.** (It modifies the noun **concert.**)

3. **Prepositional phrase.** (There are actually two prepositional phrases; the first begins with **in,** the second with **of.**)

4. **Noun phrase.** (This phrase consists of the noun **catalog** and a prepositional phrase introduced by **from.**)

5. **Prepositional phrase.** (This phrase tells where the chair should go.)

Special Types of Phrases

In the previous section, phrases were classified according to the words that control them. Sometimes phrases are classified according to their function in a sentence.

An **appositive phrase** is a noun phrase that renames or re-identifies a noun or noun phrase that precedes it. A simple appositive can contain only one word (a noun), but appositive phrases are common. Appositives are always set off by commas.

> That girl standing over there, **the blond,** looks just like my cousin.
>
> Mr. Takeshi, **a third-degree black belt,** won the karate championship.
>
> My favorite dessert, **chocolate raspberry torte,** takes a long time to prepare.
>
> Her act for the talent show, **walking across hot coals,** went down in flames.

An **absolute phrase** does not directly modify a specific noun or pronoun. Instead, it modifies the entire sentence, adding information that would not otherwise be known. An absolute phrase usually contains a noun or pronoun, a participle, and any other words modifying them. Absolute phrases are usually set off by commas. (It is rare, but possible, for absolute phrases to be set off by dashes.)

> **Their hope fading as the hours passed,** the rescuers searched the rubble for survivors.
>
> The children, **feet covered with mud,** waited on the doorstep.
>
> Carlito faced the angry crowd, **his eyes flashing.**

If the participle of the absolute phrase is any form of the verb *to be,* it is usually omitted.

> Carlito faced the angry crowd, **his expression grim.** (**his expression** *being* **grim**)

Example Problems

Identify the absolute or appositive phrase in each sentence.

1. Mrs. Ulrich, my piano teacher, just had a baby.

   Answer: **My piano teacher** is an appositive. It renames the subject **Mrs. Ulrich.**

2. The lion, its jaws stretched wide, roared ferociously.

   Answer: **Its jaws stretched wide** is an absolute phrase. It contains a noun (**jaws**), a participle (**stretched**), and their modifiers. It adds new information to the sentence.

Work Problems

Underline the absolute or appositive phrase in each sentence and make sure it is correctly punctuated.

1. I met Janet Michaels the new volleyball coach at practice yesterday.

2. Their confidence high after a winning streak the team easily won the championship.

3. The car flipped over and skidded against the wall its wheels spinning uselessly.

Worked Solutions

1. I met Janet Michaels, <u>the new volleyball coach,</u> at practice yesterday.

    This is an appositive phrase and must be set off by commas. Remember that appositives always immediately follow the nouns they rename.

2. <u>Their confidence high after a winning streak,</u> the team easily won the championship.

    This is an absolute phrase. Because it comes at the beginning of the sentence, it must be followed by a comma.

3. The car flipped over and skidded against the wall, <u>its wheels spinning uselessly</u>.

    This is an absolute phrase. Because it comes at the end of the sentence, it must be preceded by a comma.

Clauses

A **clause** is a closely related group of words that includes both a subject and a verb.

> **The work was difficult,** but **the results were worth it.**

Clauses contrast with phrases, which do not have subjects and verbs.

An **independent clause** expresses a complete thought and can stand on its own as a sentence:

> **Jack painted the fence.**
> **Jack painted the fence,** but with the wrong paint.

A **dependent clause** contains a subject and verb but does not express a complete thought and cannot stand on its own. A dependent clause relies on an independent clause to complete its meaning. In these examples, the independent clause is in boldface and the dependent clause is italicized.

> **The movers ruined the china cabinet** *that belonged to my great-grandmother.*
> **My best friend,** *who paints oils and watercolors,* **has a show at the art gallery.**

Dependent clauses are often introduced by either a subordinating conjunction (subordinating conjunctions, p. 138) or a relative pronoun (relative pronouns p. 57). Dependent clauses introduced by a subordinating conjunction are called **subordinate clauses,** and those introduced by relative pronouns are called **relative clauses.**

> The parade, **which** *had been planned for months*, had to be moved. (relative pronoun)
>
> I thought it was a good deal **until** *I heard the price*. (subordinating conjunction)

Like phrases, clauses serve a variety of functions in a sentence. They can act as nouns (subjects or objects), adjectives, or adverbs.

Example Problems

How many clauses are in each sentence?

1. The voters no longer believed that the government could solve their problems.

    Answer: **Two.** The two clauses are separated by the relative pronoun **that.**

2. Valentine's Day is a popular time to buy chocolates.

    Answer: **One.** This sentence contains a single subject and a single verb.

3. The directions she gave me were incomplete, but I found her house anyway.

    Answer: **Three.** They are an independent clause (**the directions were incomplete**), a dependent clause (**she gave me**) modifying **directions** from which the relative pronoun **that** has been omitted, and another independent clause (**I found her house anyway**) joined to the first one by the coordinating conjunction **but.**

Work Problems

Draw one line under any independent clauses and two lines under any dependent clauses.

1. The movie was not successful when it was first released.

2. Teresa carefully took the figurine from the shelf.

3. The Smiths, who bought the house next to mine, have three children.

4. While Irene worked at the front counter, Abby cooked in the kitchen.

5. Ernesto wrote a book that won several awards.

Worked Solutions

The bolded section stands for the double-underline mentioned in the instructions for these questions.

1. <u>The movie was not successful</u> **when it was first released.**

    When is a subordinating conjunction.

2. <u>Teresa carefully took the figurine from the shelf.</u>

   This entire sentence is a single independent clause.

3. <u>The Smiths</u>, **who bought the house next to mine,** <u>have three children.</u>

   Who is a relative pronoun referring to **the Smiths.**

4. **While Irene worked at the front counter,** <u>Abby cooked in the kitchen.</u>

   While is a subordinating conjunction.

5. <u>Ernesto wrote a book</u> **that won several awards.**

   That is a relative pronoun referring to the noun **book.**

Special Types of Clauses: "That" Clauses

Clauses beginning with **that** are common in English. There are two distinct types of "that" clauses.

In the first type, **that** is a relative pronoun (relative pronouns, p. 57). In relative clauses, **that** refers to a noun antecedent. The entire "that" relative clause is an adjective describing the noun antecedent.

> Those flowers *that she gave you* smell wonderful. (antecedent = **flowers**)
> The trees *that grow in this forest* are thousands of years old. (antecedent = **trees**)

In the second type of "that" clause, **that** is not a relative pronoun because it does not replace a noun. Instead, the entire "that" clause itself is a noun. Typically, these "that" noun clauses follow verbs of communication, such as *tell, say,* and *report,* and verbs of thought or emotion, such as *forget, remember, think, learn, know, discover, hope, fear,* and *believe.*

> She said *that she would be late.*
> Lori forgot *that the meeting had been canceled.*
> The engineers believed *that they could design a better car.*

Whenever **that** is not the subject of a clause, it can be omitted.

> The engineers believed *they could design a better car.*

In the examples above, the "that" noun clause is the object of the verb. "That" noun clauses can also be subjects.

> *That he expressed no remorse for his crimes* turned the jury against him.
> *That they were able to accomplish so much* surprised their critics.

Example Problems

Is the "that" clause a relative clause or a noun clause?

1. Officials hope that opening a new school will relieve overcrowding.

   Answer: **Noun clause,** object of the verb **hope.** Here, **that** is not a pronoun.

2. Chuck uses a fishing lure that trout cannot resist.

   Answer: **Relative clause,** modifying the noun **fishing lure,** which is the antecedent of the pronoun **that.**

Work Problems

Underline the "that" clause in each sentence and determine whether is it is a relative or noun clause:

1. Sheila remembered that blue is your favorite color.

2. Connor hates the shoes that his mother bought for him.

3. The rental company assures us that they have all the chairs we need.

Worked Solutions

1. Sheila remembered <u>that blue is your favorite color</u>. Noun clause, acting as the object of the verb **remembered.**

2. Connor hates the shoes <u>that his mother bought for him</u>. Relative clause, modifying the noun **shoes.**

3. The rental company assures us <u>that they have all the chairs we need</u>. Noun clause, acting as the object of the verb **assures.**

Special Types of Clauses: "If" Clauses

The **"if" clause** (also called a **conditional clause**) is a common structure in English sentences. An "if" clause indicates that if a certain condition is fulfilled, some other action will occur. **If** is sometimes paired with **then**. (**If** x, **then** y.) But even when **then** is not stated, the cause-effect relationship is understood.

> **If** you had listened to me, **then** you would have known what to do.
> **If** it keeps raining, we will postpone the game.
> **If** I had been there, I could have helped you.

Sentences with "if" clauses often include **modal auxiliaries** (modal auxiliaries, p. 116), such as *would, could,* or *might,* or **subjunctive verbs** (mood, p. 111).

> If I **were** *(subjunctive)* a movie star, I **would** *(modal)* live in Beverly Hills.

The tense of the verb in the "if" clause affects the tense of the verb in the clause that follows it. Common patterns are:

> "if" clause = **simple present**
> "then" clause = **simple present**
> If you **make** a nice sauce for it, yak **is** delicious.

"if" clause = **simple present**

"then" clause = **simple future**

If you **study,** you **will pass** the exam.

"if" clause = **simple past**

"then" clause = **modal auxiliary + base form**

If a teacher **discovered** their cheating, they **could be** suspended.

"if" clause = **past perfect**

"then" clause = **modal auxiliary + have + past participle**

If Jill **had been** there, everything **might have been** different.

"if" clause = **subjunctive**

"then" clause = **modal auxiliary + base form**

If she **were** smart, she **would start** her research right now.

Sentences with "if" clauses can also issue commands.

"if" clause = **simple present**

"then" clause = **imperative**

If you **go** to the store, **buy** an extra gallon of milk.

Example Problems

Supply the correct form of the verb indicated.

1. If my VCR (break, not), I could have taped the show for you.

    Answer: **had not broken.** Past perfect "if" clauses are usually paired with **modal + have + past participle** "then" clauses.

2. If you (want) better grades, then (pay) more attention in class.

    Answer: **want, pay.** The first clause is in present tense, and the second clause is imperative, giving a command.

Work Problems

Supply the correct form of the verb indicated.

1. If Marcia had seen the road sign, she (get, not) lost.

2. If the drought continues, some farmers (lose) their crops.

3. If the boss came in right now, he (tell) us to go back to work.

4. If we had understood the consequences, we (made) better decisions.

5. If you want pancakes for breakfast, then I (make) some for you.

Worked Solutions

1. **Would not have gotten.** The "if" clause verb is in past-perfect tense, so use **modal + have + past participle** in the "then" clause.

2. **Will lose** (also acceptable: **may, might,** or **could lose**). The proper modal to use in this case depends on the degree of certainty of the statement.

3. **Would tell.** The "if" clause verb is in simple past tense, so use a modal in the "then" clause.

4. **Would have made.** The "if" clause verb is in past perfect tense, so use **modal + have + past participle** in the "then" clause.

5. **Will make.** The "if" clause verb is in simple present tense, so use simple future tense in the "then" clause. It would also be acceptable to say **can** or **could make,** although this would change the meaning slightly, indicating more of a polite offer on the part of the speaker.

Sentence Types: Compound and Complex

A simple sentence contains a single clause. If a sentence contains at least two independent clauses, it is called a **compound sentence.** The clauses in compound sentences are joined by a coordinating conjunction (*and, but, or, for, so;* see coordinating conjunctions p. 135). The independent clauses could stand alone as sentences, but joining them implies a relationship between them.

> **I studied for days,** but **I barely passed the test.**
> **Last summer was hot and dry,** and **the risk of wildfires was severe.**

If a sentence contains one independent clause and one dependent clause, it is called a **complex sentence.**

> **I remember the lessons** *that you taught me.*
> **The shirt was ruined** *because I spilled grape juice on it.*

If a sentence contains at least two independent clauses plus at least one dependent clause, it is called a **compound-complex sentence.**

> *Although the forecast predicted rain,* **the fair was held as planned,** and **attendance was good.**

Punctuating Clauses within Sentences

If two independent clauses are joined by a coordinating conjunction, use a comma before the coordinating conjunction (see commas, p. 229).

> The surgery was successful, **and** the patient recovered fully.
> The road is blocked, **so** we must take an alternate route.

Two independent clauses can also be joined without a coordinating conjunction; use a semicolon to separate the clauses. (The semicolon can also be followed by a **conjunctive adverb** and a comma; commas p. 229; semicolons, p. 233.)

> The surgery was successful; the patient recovered fully. (*semicolon only*)
> The road is blocked; **therefore,** we must take an alternate route. (*conjunctive adverb*)

If an independent clause is followed by a subordinate clause, usually no punctuation is required at the join. But if the subordinate clause comes before the independent clause, use a comma at the end of the subordinate clause.

> I went to work even though I was feeling ill. *(no punctuation needed)*
>
> Even though I was feeling ill, I went to work. *(subordinate clause comes first; follow with a comma)*

Example Problems

Is this sentence simple, compound, complex, or compound complex?

1. We enjoyed the movie even though it was silly and sentimental.

    Answer: **Complex.** The dependent clause is introduced by the subordinating conjunction **even though.**

2. Michelle picked up her son from school and took him to soccer practice.

    Answer: **Simple.** This sentence has only one clause, although it has two verbs (**picked up** and **took**). Do not confuse compound subjects or compound verbs with compound clauses.

3. Karl applied to five colleges, and one offered him a scholarship.

    Answer: **Compound.** The two independent clauses are joined by **and.**

4. Because the traffic was so heavy, the drive took longer than we expected, and we almost missed the meeting.

    Answer: **Compound-complex.** The two independent clauses are joined by **and.** The subordinate clause is introduced by **because.**

Work Problems

Is this sentence simple, compound, complex, or compound complex?

1. Lola, Amanda, and Greg took down the chairs, swept the floor, and locked the room.

2. The wind blew, and the old tree shook, but it did not fall.

3. Although the snow was blinding, the hikers stayed on the trail, and eventually they found their way back to the cabin.

Worked Solutions

1. **Simple.** Even though this clause has three subjects and three verbs, it is still a single clause because all three subjects did all three actions. It may be easier to think of the **Lola, Amanda, and Greg** as the subject and **took down, swept, and locked** as the predicate of this large clause. If the sentence said, "Lola took down the chairs, Amanda swept the floor, and Greg locked the room," then it would be compound, because it would contain three separate clauses, each with its own subject and predicate.

2. **Compound.** This sentence has three clauses, linked by the coordinating conjunctions **and** and **but**.

3. **Compound complex.** The dependent clause is introduced by the subordinating conjunction **although,** and the two independent clauses are linked by the coordinating conjunction **and.**

Sentence Types: Declarative, Imperative, and Interrogative Moods

English sentences are sometimes classified according to the mood of their verbs (mood, p. 111). A sentence whose main verb is indicative is called a **declarative sentence.** Most English sentences are declarative; they simply make statements. A sentence whose main verb gives a command is an **imperative sentence.**

> **Listen** carefully to what he says.
> **Cut** a slice of pie for your grandmother.

An **interrogative sentence** asks a question. Interrogatives always end in a question mark (**?**) (question marks, p. 238). Technically, "interrogative" is not a verb mood, although one common way of asking a question involves **inversion,** that is, placing the verb in front of the subject. (See verb tenses, p. 84, for examples of how to invert verbs to ask questions.) Simple present- and past-tense verbs require the addition of the auxiliary verb **do** for inversion.

> *Declarative:* Tom **is going** to the store.
> *Interrogative:* **Is** Tom **going** to the store?
> *Declarative:* Nikita **loves** pineapple cake.
> *Interrogative:* **Does** Nikita **love** pineapple cake?

Inverted questions typically require a yes or no answer.

Another way of asking a question involves **wh- words** (*who, whom, whose, what, which, where, why, when,* and *how*). The wh- word comes in front of the inverted verb. Wh-word questions require a specific piece of information as an answer:

> **How** do you feel?
> **What** are you making for dinner?
> **Why** did you call him?
> **Where** is the movie playing?

Another way of asking a question involves **tag questions.** A tag question comes at the end of an otherwise declarative sentence. Tag questions have inverted verbs, but they use only the auxiliary, not the main verb of the sentence.

> You know Sasha.
> You know Sasha, **don't you?**

Tag questions expect confirmation of what the declarative sentence says. If the declarative sentence is positive, the tag question is negative. If the declarative sentence is negative, the tag question is positive.

> Giulio is going to the show, **isn't he?**
> Giulio isn't going to the show, **is he?**

Tag questions, which are common in spoken English, usually involve a contracted form of a negative (*isn't, aren't, don't, doesn't, can't, won't,* and so on).

In spoken English, speakers can turn any declarative or imperative sentence into a question using **rising intonation.** The pitch of the speaker's voice rises at the end of the sentence. The only way to note this difference in print is to place a question mark at the end of the sentence.

> Take the boxes to the attic. *(The pitch is level.)*
> Take the boxes to the attic? *(The pitch rises at the end of the sentence.)*

Finally, declarative sentences can contain **indirect questions.** These are usually second-hand reports of questions, not questions themselves. A sentence with an indirect question does not end with a question mark.

> Your mom asked me whether you would be going with us.
> Tara wondered what Amy thought of their plan.

Example Problems

Is this sentence declarative, imperative, or interrogative?

1. Stop here and let me out of the car.

    Answer: **Imperative.** There are actually two commands here: **stop** and **let me out.**

2. Tomorrow should be a beautiful day for sailing.

    Answer: **Declarative.** The sentence simply makes a statement; it does not ask a question or give a command.

3. When will you leave for work?

    Answer: **Interrogative.** This is an example of a question using a wh- word to ask for a specific piece of information.

Work Problems

Change the following declarative sentences into questions using the method indicated.

1. She dyes her hair. (inversion)

2. You could help me. (inversion)

3. Ben bought a car. (tag question)

4. The teacher told the class. ("what"question)

5. You will come. ("when" question)

Worked Solutions

1. Does she dye her hair?

   Simple present tense verbs require the addition of the auxiliary verb **do** to create inversion. "Dyes she her hair?" is not a pattern that appears in modern English.

2. Could you help me?

   Could is actually an auxiliary verb supporting the main verb, **help.** Move the auxiliary before the subject to invert the verb.

3. Ben bought a car, didn't he?

   Because the main verb is positive, the tag question is negative. The tag requires the use of the auxiliary verb **do** to form the question.

4. What did the teacher tell the class?

   As with simple inverted questions, in wh-word questions the auxiliary verb moves before the subject. (Verbs in simple-past tense, like **told,** require the addition of the auxiliary verb **did** for inversion.) The wh- word then comes before the auxiliary.

5. When will you come?

   Simple future tense moves the **will** auxiliary before the subject. The wh- word then comes before the auxiliary.

Sentence Types: Passive and Active Voice

Voice indicates whether the subject is doing the action of the verb or receiving the action of the verb. If the subject does the action, the sentence is in **active voice.** If the subject receives the action, the sentence is in **passive voice.**

> *Active:* Chris ate all the cookies.
> *Passive:* All the cookies were eaten by Chris.
> *Active:* The snow covers the cars.
> *Passive:* The cars are covered by the snow.

Notice that in each case, the subject and the direct object trade places. Passive sentences that name the doer of the action typically use the preposition **by** when they name the doer. (See voice, p. 107, for more about active and passive voice.)

Example Problems

Is this sentence active or passive?

1. Our class worked on the project together.

    Answer: **Active.** The subject **class** is doing the action of the verb **worked.**

2. Smoking is prohibited on campus.

    Answer: **Passive.** The subject, the gerund **smoking,** is receiving the action of the verb **prohibited;** the sentence does not say who or what is responsible for the prohibition.

Work Problems

Change the sentence from active to passive, or from passive to active.

1. Ilena coordinated the preparations for the awards banquet.

2. The earthquake had been predicted by geologists.

3. The mansion was built by an eccentric millionaire.

Worked Solutions

1. The preparations for the awards banquet were coordinated by Ilena. (active to passive)

2. Geologists had predicted the earthquake. (passive to active)

3. An eccentric millionaire built the mansion. (passive to active)

Common Pitfall: Frequently Encountered Sentence Problems

Strictly speaking, many of the common problems that plague English sentences are matters of style, rather than matters of grammar. However, stylistic problems can obscure a writer's meaning just as much as grammatical problems can, so students of grammar should be aware of these pitfalls. Much of this discussion applies only to written English, but learning to express your thoughts clearly in writing can also be helpful in situations where formal speaking is required.

Run-on Sentences

A **run-on sentence** contains at least two independent clauses that have been joined without proper punctuation or conjunctions.

>   **Run-on:** I asked her to bring soft drinks she did not.

There are three possible cures:

1. Separate the run-on into two sentences with a period.

    I asked her to bring soft drinks. She did not.

2. Separate the clauses with a comma and coordinating conjunction.

   I asked her to bring soft drinks**, but** she did not.

3. Separate the clauses with a semicolon.

   I asked her to bring soft drinks; she did not.

Example Problems

Is this sentence a run-on?

1. The bookcase is full we need another one.

   Answer: **Yes.** This sentence has two independent clauses without a proper join.

2. The monkeys in the primate house at the zoo have learned that they can manipulate zoo visitors into giving them carrots.

   Answer: **No.** Length does not determine whether a sentence is a run-on. This sentence has only one independent clause. The subject is **monkeys;** the verb is **have learned.**

Work Problems

Correct any sentence that is a run-on.

1. A thunderstorm is coming and it might have lightning we should go inside.

2. Medieval cathedrals often used stained glass windows to tell stories to those who could not read.

3. An octopus swam through the water coral reefs were all around.

Worked Solutions

1. A thunderstorm is coming, and it might have lightning, **so** we should go inside.

   A thunderstorm is coming, and it might have lightning. **W**e should go inside.

   A thunderstorm is coming, and it might have lightning; we should go inside.

   Notice that the first two independent clauses should have a comma between them, even though they are joined by **and.**

2. This is not a run-on sentence. It has one independent clause with one subject, **cathedrals,** with its verb, **used. Who could not read** is a relative clause modifying **those,** the object of a preposition.

3. An octopus swam through the water. **C**oral reefs were all around.

   An octopus swam through the water; coral reefs were all around.

   This particular run-on is probably not a good candidate to receive a conjunction because the two clauses are not closely related.

Comma Splices

A comma splice is a sentence containing at least two independent clauses joined by only a comma.

> *Comma splice:* Take your umbrella, it is raining.
> *Comma splice:* She did not know what to do, the situation was terrible.

The two cures are the same as for run-ons:

1. Separate the comma splice into two sentences with a period

   Take your umbrella**.** **It** is raining.

2. Separate the clauses with a semicolon.

   She did not know what to do**;** the situation was terrible.

Example Problems

Is this sentence a comma splice?

1. This restaurant makes the best French fries, smothered in garlic and Parmesan cheese.

   Answer: **No. Smothered** is not part of a clause; it introduces a participial phrase that describes the fries.

2. Steven Spielberg is famous for his movies, he is known all around the world.

   Answer: **Yes.** This sentence has two independent clauses joined by only a comma.

Work Problems

Correct any sentence that is a comma splice.

1. The Renaissance was fueled in part by the printing press, a technology known in Asia for centuries.

2. Many people believe that dreams can predict the future, dreams are often symbolic.

3. No one believed he would go through with it, the odds were against him.

Worked Solutions

1. This is not a comma splice. The noun phrase **a technology known in Asia for centuries** is actually an appositive renaming the noun **printing press.**

2. Many people believe that dreams can predict the future. **D**reams are often symbolic.

   It would also be acceptable to say:

   Many people believe that dreams can predict the future **or that** dreams are often symbolic. This changes the second independent clause into a relative clause, which is the object of the verb **believe.**

3. No one believed he would go through with it **because** the odds were against him.

   No one believed he would go through with it**. T**he odds were against him.

Sentence Fragments

A sentence fragment is either a phrase or a dependent clause masquerading as a sentence. Remember that a complete sentence must meet two criteria: It must have both a subject and verb, and it must express a complete thought. Here are some examples of sentence fragments.

> We went for a drive. After the game was over.
> Many activities are available at the camp. *Such as swimming, fishing, and hiking.*
> We went to the beach. *Too cold to swim. Built a sandcastle.*

To correct sentence fragments, make sure they contain both a subject and a verb. Often, a fragment can be joined to a related sentence that already expresses a complete thought:

> We went for a drive *after the game was over.*
> Many activities are available at the camp, **s**uch as swimming, fishing, and hiking.
> We went to the beach, **but it was** *too cold to swim,* **so we** *built a sandcastle.*

Example Problems

Identify the sentence fragment.

1. Using the VCR. I am taping my favorite TV show right now.

   Answer: **Using the VCR.** The fragment has no subject, and although it has a word that looks like a verb (**using**), the verb is incomplete.

2. Soon Lee wants to be a fashion designer. Because of the beautiful dresses.

   Answer: **Because of the beautiful dresses.** This fragment could easily be joined to the sentence that precedes it.

Work Problems

Correct the sentence fragments.

1. The Louvre Museum is full of art treasures. From many countries and time periods.

2. Since the recession. The school's budget has been severely cut.

3. His eyes wide. The little boy watched the circus acrobats.

Worked Solutions

1. The Louvre Museum is full of art treasures **f**rom many countries and time periods.

   The sentence fragment is now a prepositional phrase.

2. Since the recession, **t**he school's budget has been severely cut.

   The school's budget has been severely cut **s**ince the recession.

   The sentence fragment is now an adverbial phrase.

3. His eyes wide, **t**he little boy watched the circus acrobats.

   The little boy watched the circus acrobats, **h**is eyes wide.

   The sentence fragment is now an absolute phrase.

Misplaced or "Dangling" Modifiers

Because word order affects the meaning of English so much, modifiers need to stay close to the words they modify. (See misplaced modifiers and dangling participles, p. 175.) In sentences, phrases that act as modifiers also need to stay close to the things they modify.

The classic misplaced modifying phrase is the **dangling participle,** a participial phrase that usually appears at the beginning of a sentence, where it tries to modify the subject.

   Dangling Participle: Filled with flowers, my mother has a beautiful garden.

This phrase looks as if it modifies **my mother,** the noun following it. But the effect is comical: Is my mother filled with flowers? (She must have been hungry!) To correct the problem, make sure the phrase stays close to the noun it really modifies:

   Correction: My mother has a beautiful garden filled with flowers.
   Correction: Filled with flowers, my mother's garden is beautiful.

(See participles, p. 124, for more information.)

Do not confuse absolute phrases with dangling participles. Absolute phrases always include a noun; participial phrases do not. Absolute phrases do not modify a specific noun; participial phrases do.

   Absolute phrase:
   The train speeding away from him, Enrique realized he had just missed his ride home.

   Dangling participle, appears to modify **Enrique:**
   Speeding away from him, Enrique realized he had just missed the train.

   Corrected participle, modifies **train:**
   Enrique realized he had just missed the train speeding away from him.

Example Problems

Move the dangling participle to its correct position.

1. The porcelain statue was still in the curio case broken in the middle.

   Answer: The porcelain statue, broken in the middle, was still in the curio case. **Broken** needs to stay close to **statue,** the noun it modifies.

2. A woman was struck by a car bicycling to work.

   Answer: A woman bicycling to work was struck by a car. **Bicycling** needs to stay close to **woman,** the noun it modifies.

Work Problems

Correct any sentences with misplaced modifiers.

1. Driving in the storm, a large branch fell on my car.

2. When reading the play, it must be remembered that Shakespeare knew nothing about modern psychology.

3. Without a tutor to help him, calculus proved too difficult for Larry.

4. Worried about his sister, Mario could not concentrate on the lecture.

5. At the age of six, my mother gave me a violin.

Worked Solutions

(Please note that many acceptable corrections exist; these answers are only examples.)

1. While I was driving in the storm, a large branch fell on my car.

   Driving in the storm, I was shocked when a large branch fell on my car.

   The **branch** was not driving. The modifier needs to involve the subject of the sentence (the speaker).

2. When reading the play, you (or *one, students,* and so on) must remember that Shakespeare knew nothing about modern psychology.

   The original sentence has both a misplaced modifier and an unnecessary use of passive voice. Changing the sentence from passive to active clears up the modification problem.

3. Calculus proved too difficult for Larry without a tutor to help him.

   Without a tutor to help him, Larry could not master calculus.

   In the original sentence, the adverbial phrase is too close to the noun **calculus. Larry** is the one who lacks a tutor.

4. Correct as written. **Mario,** the subject, is the one who is worried.

5. My mother gave me a violin at the age of six. (still somewhat awkward)

    When I was six years old, my mother gave me a violin. (better)

    Modifiers involving age are frequently subject to misinterpretation. The original sentence implies that my mother was only six when she gave me the violin.

Restrictive and Nonrestrictive Elements

Depending on their purpose, phrases and clauses that act as modifiers might or might not require commas. A **restrictive element** introduces essential information into a sentence. Without it, the meaning of the sentence would be completely different. Restrictive elements are not set off from the rest of the sentence by commas:

> Police hope to find a jogger **who might have been a witness to the crime.** (This restrictive element identifies the specific jogger that police hope to find.)
>
> The information **released to the press** omitted several important facts. (This restrictive element tells which information omitted facts.)

A **nonrestrictive element** introduces extra information that does not affect the basic meaning of the sentence. Nonrestrictive elements are always set off by commas.

> The Palms Hotel, **built in 1905,** has a magnificent skylight in the lobby.
>
> Crocodiles and alligators, **which are both reptiles,** live in different parts of the world.

These nonrestrictive elements add interesting facts to each sentence without changing the meaning.

To help you decide whether an element is restrictive or nonrestrictive, try removing it from the sentence. If the sentence no longer makes sense or its basic meaning changes, the element is restrictive.

Traditionally, the relative pronoun **that** introduced only restrictive relative clauses and the relative pronoun **which** introduced only nonrestrictive relative clauses. (For a discussion of this issue, see gray area: restrictive "that" versus nonrestrictive "which," p. 57.)

Although many writers and speakers use either which or that for restrictive clauses, some teachers and editors prefer to use **which** only for nonrestrictive clauses. Students, therefore, should be aware of the **that/which** distinction.

That can never introduce a nonrestrictive clause. **Who, whom, whoever,** or **whomever** are appropriate choices when the clause refers to a person, regardless of whether the clause is restrictive or nonrestrictive.

Example Problems

Is this element restrictive or nonrestrictive?

1. The sunglasses **with the purple frames** are mine.

    Answer: **Restrictive.** These specific sunglasses are mine. To remove the element would change the meaning because sunglasses of different colors are not mine.

2. The city of New Orleans, **once governed by France,** is a popular vacation spot.

   Answer: **Nonrestrictive.** The basic statement of the sentence, **New Orleans is a popular vacation spot,** is not affected by the fact that France once governed the city.

Work Problems
Correctly punctuate the restrictive or nonrestrictive elements.

1. Fortunately, the dog, that bit Ralph, did not have rabies.

2. The telephone invented in 1876 changed modern society.

3. Does the scarf lying on the floor belong to you?

4. Margaret who is an aerospace engineer works for NASA.

5. The amendment, introduced by Senator Kerry, did not pass.

Worked Solutions

1. Fortunately, the dog that bit Ralph did not have rabies. (restrictive, no commas)

2. The telephone, invented in 1876, changed modern society. (nonrestrictive, set off by commas)

3. Correct as written. The participial phrase **lying on the floor** is restrictive, so no commas are used.

4. Margaret, who is an aerospace engineer, works for NASA.

   This is a nonrestrictive clause so it should be set off by commas. Theoretically, if I knew two Margarets, and only one Margaret was an engineer, the clause might become restrictive. Margaret who is an aerospace engineer works for NASA, but Margaret who is a nurse works for the Veterans Administration.

5. This sentence is even more ambiguous than sentence 4 because we do not know the context. Two possibilities exist:

   The amendment, introduced by Senator Kerry, did not pass. (Correct as is, nonrestrictive: There was only one amendment, and it did not pass; Senator Kerry just happened to have introduced it.)

   The amendment introduced by Senator Kerry did not pass. (Restrictive: There were many amendments, but the specific amendment introduced by Senator Kerry did not pass.)

Unclear Antecedents

The problem of **unclear antecedents** occurs when English pronouns become too far separated from the nouns to which they refer.

> The movie tells the story of the son of a crime lord and the rival gang leader who kills **his** father.

Whose father was killed? The son's, the crime lord's, or the gang leader's? **His** has three possible antecedents, the closest one being **gang leader.** Often the best way to correct such problems is to rewrite the sentence.

> The movie tells the story of a young man whose crime-lord father is killed by a rival gang leader.

Other antecedent problems occur when a pronoun refers to an abstract idea, a set of circumstances, or an unidentified group of people:

> *Unclear:* They created the situation and then tried to fix it, **which** was intolerable.
> (What was intolerable? Creating the situation, fixing it, or both?)
> *Correct:* They created the situation, **which** was intolerable, and then tried to fix it.

> *Unclear:* Carrie quit her job at the law firm because **they** constantly criticized her.
> (Who criticized her? The law firm?)
> *Correct:* Carrie quit her job at the law firm because **the senior partners** constantly criticized her.

Example Problems
What is the antecedent of the pronoun in boldface?

1. Before Eva met Cynthia, **she** had been timid and shy.

   Answer: **Unknown. She** could mean either girl. To avoid ambiguity, state explicitly: Before Eva met Cynthia, **Eva** had been timid and shy.

2. Steve said he is meeting with Shaun, and **he** will set up the new network hub.

   Answer: **Unknown.** The first **he** clearly refers to Steve. Does the second **he** also refer to Steve? Or does it refer to Shaun, the closest antecedent? Use a name to make the meaning clear: **Shaun** will set up the new network hub.

Work Problems
Correct any unclear antecedents.

1. Dave was singled out for punishment and blamed me, which was unfair.

2. Yvonne gave Jeanette her grandmother's wedding ring.

3. That chair belonged to Martin's father or his friend.

Worked Solutions

1. Dave was singled out for punishment, which was unfair, and blamed me.

    OR

    Dave was singled out for punishment and unfairly blamed me.

    The antecedent of **which** was unclear in the original.

2. Yvonne gave Jeanette the wedding ring that had belonged to Jeanette's grandmother.

    OR

    Yvonne gave Jeanette the wedding ring that had belonged to Yvonne's grandmother.

    The antecedent of **her** was unclear in the original.

3. That chair belonged to Martin's father or his father's friend.

    OR

    That chair belonged to Martin's father or Martin's friend.

    The antecedent of **his** was unclear in the original. (The first option is still slightly ambiguous in its use of the pronoun.)

Lack of Agreement

Verbs must agree with their subjects in person and number. Pronouns must agree with their antecedents in person, number, and gender.

Verbs agree with their subjects, not with modifiers. Do not be distracted by modifiers that come between the noun and the verb.

>   *Incorrect:* A crowd of **people are** waiting. (**People** is not the subject; it is part of a modifier.)
>   *Correct:* A **crowd** of people **is** waiting. (The singular noun **crowd** is the subject.)

Singular subjects joined by **and** take a plural verb form and a plural pronoun. Singular subjects joined by **or** take a singular verb form and a singular pronoun. If you must join mixed subjects (singular/plural, male/female) with **or,** the verb and pronoun agree with the nearest subject. However, this is extremely awkward and should be avoided (agreement of pronouns with antecedents, p. 55).

>   Bill **and** Ted **are** going on **their** trip soon.
>   Denise **or** Amy **is** going to loan you **her** racket.
>   *Awkward:* The Jones brothers or Samantha **is** going to contribute **her** best recipe.

Collective nouns (collective nouns, p. 35), such as **team, jury, group, bunch,** and **crowd,** can be either singular or plural depending on the context.

>   **The team is** going to the championship. (*thinking of the team as one unit*)
>   **They are** giving **their** best effort. (*thinking of all the team members*)

Most indefinite pronouns are singular, but **both, many, few, all, some,** and **others** are usually plural (indefinite pronouns, p. 67).

> Everybody **is** happy to hear the news.
> No one **is** absent today.
> Some **are** absent today.

Some people object to the use of plural pronouns to refer to singular indefinite antecedents, but most writers and editors now find it acceptable. In fact, a safe alternative to potentially sexist language is to use a plural antecedent (gray area: sexist language and indefinite pronouns, p. 69).

> *Avoid:* **Everyone** brought **his** paper.
> *Usually Acceptable:* **Everyone** brought **their** paper.
> *Acceptable:* **Everyone** brought **his or her** paper.
> *Acceptable:* **All students** brought **their papers.**

Example Problems

In the first blank, put the correct form of the verb *to be*. In the second blank, put the correct pronoun.

1. Raquel and Olga _____ leaving _____ shoes in the laundry room.

   Answer: **Are, their.** Subjects joined by **and** are plural.

2. Either Tatiana or Stella _____ taking _____ camcorder on the trip.

   Answer: **Is, her.** Subjects joined by **or** are singular.

Work Problems

Correct any agreement problems.

1. A container of tongue depressors are on the counter.

2. I asked Leo or Steve to bring their guitar.

3. A flock of birds and a solitary cloud is moving across the sky.

4. Everybody need an opportunity to prove themselves.

5. Dehydration or heatstroke are real dangers for desert hikers.

Worked Solutions

1. A container of tongue depressors **is** on the counter.

   OR

   The tongue depressors **are** on the counter.

   (Remember that the verb agrees with the noun of the subject, not with the noun's modifiers.)

2. I asked Leo or Steve to bring **his** guitar.

   I asked Leo **and** Steve to bring **their guitars.**

   (Nouns joined by **or** require a singular pronoun.)

3. A flock of birds and a solitary cloud **are** moving across the sky.

   Despite the fact that the subject closest to the verb is singular, this sentence has two subjects joined by **and,** so it requires a plural verb.

4. Everybody **needs** an opportunity to prove themselves.

   Most writers would not object to the use of the plural pronoun **themselves** in this case because it avoids the sexist pronoun **he** and the wordy **himself or herself.** However, to duck the issue, we could say, "**We all need** an opportunity to prove **ourselves.**"

5. Dehydration or heatstroke **is a real danger** for desert hikers.

   OR

   Dehydration **and** heatstroke are real dangers for desert hikers.

   The second option actually makes more sense because both conditions are dangers.

Lack of Parallelism

Parallelism is a rule of style stating that parts of a sentence that have the same grammatical function or weight should have the same grammatical form. Lack of parallelism commonly affects grammatical units joined by conjunctions.

> *Lack of parallelism:* Mondo Resort guests can enjoy walks through the resort's beautiful grounds, a swim in the pool, and eating in our four-star restaurant.

This sentence has three objects, but they are all stated differently. Compare these sentences:

> *Parallel:* Mondo Resort guests can enjoy **walking** through our grounds, **swimming** in our pool, and **eating** in our four-star restaurant.
>
> *Parallel:* Mondo Resort guests can enjoy **a walk** through the grounds, **a swim** in the pool, and **a meal** in the four-star restaurant.

In the parallel sentences, the three objects have the same grammatical form (gerunds or singular nouns), and they are described similarly. These sentences flow more smoothly because they are parallel.

Example Problems

Is this sentence parallel?

1. I need to do the laundry, walk the dog, and my mother wants me to mail a package.

   Answer: **No.** The first two items on the list are infinitives (**to do, to walk**), but the third item introduces a new clause. A parallel option might say, "I need to do the laundry, walk the dog, and mail a package."

2. To fix the problem, press the reset button, wait five seconds, and restart the computer.

    Answer: **Yes.** This list offers three imperatives (**press, wait,** and **restart**), all similarly phrased.

Work Problems

Correct any lack of parallelism.

1. The governor has the will, the means, and needs to act now to pass the legislation.

2. Divers found bottles of wine, gold bars, and boxes of treasure on the sunken ship.

3. The Central High team did well, but the team from East High lost in the first round.

Worked Solutions

1. The governor has the will and the means to pass the legislation, but he needs to act now.

    The original looks as if it will list three items the governor has, but it introduces a new verb as the third item in the series. The three are not alike, so the only solution is to separate them.

2. Divers found wine bottles, treasure boxes, and gold bars on the sunken ship.

    Bars of gold is another possible solution, but this option is less wordy.

3. The Central High team did well, but the East High team lost in the first round.

    Besides being parallel in the way it describes the two teams, this sentence is less wordy than the original.

Inconsistent Use of Tenses or Pronouns

Like parallelism, consistent use of tenses and pronouns is just a way of keeping written passages smooth and clean. Inexperienced writers tend to shift back and forth between tenses and pronouns. This is acceptable in spoken English, but not in written English.

Inconsistent: We went to practice, and the coach tells us that you need to learn a new drill. (This shifts from past to present and from **we** to **you.**)

Consistent: We went to practice, and the coach **told** us that **we needed** to learn a new drill. (This example consistently uses past tense and **we.**)

Inconsistent: Many people enjoy winter sports at Big Bear Mountain. You could go skiing, snowboarding, or skating. One did not have to be a good skier to have fun in the snow. (This shifts from present to conditional/past and from **people** to **you** to **one.**)

Consistent: Many people enjoy winter sports at Big Bear Mountain. **They can** go skiing, snowboarding, or skating. **They do** not have to be good **skiers** to have fun in the snow.

Example Problems

Do the following sentences show inconsistent use of tenses or pronouns?

1.   I gave the children some ice cream. They had just gotten back from the park, and they were hungry.

     Answer: **No.** This sentence is consistently in past tense, and correctly uses simple past and past-perfect tense to indicate the sequence of events.

2.   When you first read a Jane Austen novel, you might be surprised by the lack of description. The author focuses one's attention on the characters' actions, not their appearance.

     Answer: **Yes. You,** used in a general, impersonal sense, gets changed to the impersonal **one** in the second sentence. While there is nothing wrong with an impersonal **you,** it is easily overused. One way to avoid using impersonal elements is to substitute an imaginary person or persons: **A reader** approaching a Jane Austen novel might be surprised by the lack of description. The author focuses **the reader's** attention on the characters' actions.

Work Problems

Correct any inconsistent uses of tense or pronouns.

1.   The first two proposals are reasonable, but the third required more resources than we have.

2.   Upon entering the museum, you are impressed by the marble columns and the high dome. One might think you entered a palace rather than a museum.

3.   He sees us, and then he turned away, as if he thinks that would fool you.

Worked Solutions

1.   The first two proposals are reasonable, but the third **requires** more resources than we have. (Another solution is to use past tense throughout.)

2.   Upon entering the museum, you are impressed by the marble columns and the high dome. **You** might think **you are entering** a palace rather than a museum. (Another solution is to use **one** instead of **you** throughout.)

3.   He **saw** us, and then he turned away, as if he **thought** that would fool **us.** (Another solution is to use present tense throughout.)

Chapter Problems

Problems

Draw one line under the subject of the sentence and two lines under the predicate.

1. The laundry basket and the soap are in the utility room.

2. I put the pizza in the oven.

3. Roses are red, but violets are blue.

4. Those thin, square peppermint patties are my favorite candies.

5. Whenever he can, my dad likes to go golfing with his buddies.

Draw one line under any direct objects and two lines under any indirect objects.

6. Suzanne and her sister Marcia cannot eat sweets.

7. Lucy loves Linus' piano playing.

8. Give Sylvia my best wishes.

9. Tony offered Tao a spot on the team.

Identify the type of underlined phrase or clause (participial, noun, prepositional, absolute, independent, relative, and so on).

10. Lying in the middle of the road, the large rock was a traffic hazard.

11. We are delivering the shipment to their warehouse in Texas.

12. Today we learned that whales are actually mammals, not fish.

13. His hands trembling with fear, Wesley slowly opened the door.

14. I enjoyed the play even though I had a terrible cold.

15. Spending the day in the mountains is a wonderful way to relax.

16. This restaurant has excellent food, but the service is terrible.

17. The new fan belt that we installed in the furnace should fix the problem.

18. Our new teacher, a professional potter, showed us how to use a pottery wheel.

19. If no one else objects, we can begin work tomorrow.

Turn the following statements into questions using the method indicated.

20. The mail arrived. (when)

21. You went to the doctor. (inversion)

22. They did not tell anyone what happened. (tag question)

Correct any problems in the following sentences.

23. Irene told Rosa that she could babysit for her.

24. Mr. Cohen who owns a bakery will finish his MBA degree this fall.

25. The plan was overly ambitious. Which doomed it to failure.

26. No one could believe the news, it seemed too good to be true.

27. A box of chocolates are on the counter.

28. Believing their cause was just, the civil rights movement refused to be stopped.

29. I lost the bracelet, that had all my gold charms attached.

30. The owners want to acquire new players, keep the best of this year's team, and a new stadium.

31. Neither patience nor perseverance were enough to solve the problem.

32. Everyone wants to succeed definitions of personal success differ however.

Answers and Solutions

The bolded section stands for the double-underline mentioned in the instructions for this section.

1. The laundry basket and the soap **are in the utility room.** This sentence has a compound subject. The predicate in this case is a predicate preposition.

2. I **put the pizza in the oven.** Subjects can be a single word, such as I.

3. Roses **are red,** but violets **are blue.** This sentence is made up of two independent clauses, so each one has its own subject and its own predicate. Both of the predicates are predicate adjectives.

4. Those thin, square peppermint patties **are my favorite candies.** This sentence has a noun phrase as the subject, the main noun of which is **patties.** The predicate in this case is a predicate noun.

5. **Whenever he can,** my dad **likes to go golfing with his buddies.** The subject of this sentence does not come at the beginning because an adverbial clause introduces the sentence. (Technically, the adverbial clause has its own subject, **he,** and a predicate, **can,** but these are not the subject and predicate of the entire sentence.)

6. Suzanne and her sister Marcia cannot eat sweets. Note that **Marcia** is not an indirect object; it is part of a compound subject.

7. Lucy loves <u>Linus' piano playing</u>. **Linus** is not an indirect object. Linus' name is a possessive modifying the gerund **playing.**

8. Give **Sylvia** <u>my best wishes</u>. Although this sentence is imperative, that does not affect its basic pattern: (implied subject **you**) + verb + indirect object + direct object.

9. Tony offered **Tao** <u>a spot on the team</u>. *What* did Tony offer? A spot on the team (direct object). To *whom* did he offer it? To Tao (indirect object).

10. <u>Lying in the middle of the road</u> = participial phrase, modifying the noun **rock**

11. <u>To their warehouse in Texas</u> = prepositional phrase

12. <u>That whales are actually mammals, not fish</u> = noun clause, acting as the object of the verb **learned**

13. <u>His hands trembling with fear</u> = absolute phrase

14. <u>Even though I had a terrible cold</u> = subordinate clause (a dependent clause, introduced by the subordinating conjunction **even though**)

15. <u>Spending the day in the mountains</u> = noun phrase (specifically a gerund phrase, acting as the subject of the sentence)

16. <u>This restaurant has excellent food</u> = independent clause; <u>the service is terrible</u> = independent clause. The two clauses joined by the coordinating conjunction **but** form a compound sentence.

17. <u>That we installed in the furnace</u> = relative clause (a dependent clause, introduced by the relative pronoun **that**), modifying the noun **belt**. Bonus points if you said it was restrictive!

18. <u>A professional potter</u> = appositive (a noun phrase)

19. <u>If no one else objects</u> = "if" clause or conditional

20. When did the mail arrive? (For wh- questions, invert the verb and place the wh- word in front of it. Verbs in simple-past tense require the auxiliary **did** for inversion.)

21. Did you go to the doctor? (For inverted questions, move the verb in front of the subject. Verbs in simple-past tense require the auxiliary **did** for inversion.)

22. They did not tell anyone what happened, did they? (For tag questions, if the main sentence is positive, the tag must be negative. The verb of the tag question is inverted.)

23. Irene offered to babysit for Rosa.

    OR

    Rosa offered to babysit for Irene. (In the original, the antecedents of the pronouns are impossible to determine.)

24. Mr. Cohen, who owns a bakery, will finish his MBA degree this fall. (Nonrestrictive elements must be set off with commas.)

25. The plan was overly ambitious, which doomed it to failure. (The sentence fragment should be joined to the sentence before it.)

26. No one could believe the news because it seemed too good to be true.

    OR

    No one could believe the news. It seemed too good to be true.

    (The two independent clauses in this comma splice can either become two sentences or remain as one with the addition of a comma and a subordinating conjunction.)

27. A box of chocolates is on the counter. (**Box** is singular, not plural, even though it is followed by the plural noun **chocolates.**)

28. Believing their cause was just, the leaders of the civil rights movement refused to be stopped. (The dangling participle had nothing to modify; the civil rights movement is an "it," not a "they." Adding **the leaders** as a subject provides something for the participle to modify.)

29. I lost the bracelet that had all my gold charms attached. (Restrictive elements do not use commas.)

30. The owners want to acquire new players, keep the best of this year's team, and build a new stadium. (The third item was a noun, not a verb, so the list was not parallel.)

31. Neither patience nor perseverance was enough to solve the problem. (Subjects joined by **neither . . . nor** take a singular verb.)

32. Everyone wants to succeed; however, definitions of personal success differ.

    OR

    Everyone wants to succeed. However, definitions of personal success differ.

    (This sentence was a run-on. The independent clauses can either become separate sentences or receive a proper join with punctuation and a conjunction.)

Supplemental Chapter Problems

Problems

Draw a line under the main noun of the subject. Is the predicate a predicate noun, predicate adjective, or predicate preposition?

1. The moon and the stars are especially bright tonight.

2. Believing in your own abilities is a requirement for success.

3. An old, broken-down jalopy is in their garage.

Draw one line under any direct objects and two lines under any indirect objects.

4. The gooey green space aliens brought a message of peace to the inhabitants of planet Earth.

5. I inherited all my grandfather's old cameras.

6. I suddenly remembered what she had asked me to do.

7. Anyone can contribute a story to the literary magazine.

8. The eccentric millionaire left his estate to his cat.

Identify the type of underlined phrase or clause (participial, noun, prepositional, absolute, independent, relative, and so on).

9. Thinking he would be punished, the little boy lied about breaking the window.

10. The cat is sleeping on top of the television set.

11. The big oak swayed in the heavy wind, its branches creaking.

12. I would gladly give you a ride, but my car is being repaired.

13. If California were a country, it would be one of the largest economies in the world.

14. This mural, one of the best examples of Roman fresco, is from the ruins of Pompeii.

15. The woman who was here earlier said that the store had gone bankrupt.

16. The Strawberry Festival, which had poor attendance last year, was canceled.

17. Everyone likes Sharon because she is so kind and generous.

18. Reading to young children can help them improve their language skills.

Change each sentence into the form indicated.

19. (Imperative) You are putting down the box.

20. (Active) Thai food is enjoyed by people of all nationalities.

21. (Question, why) He brought lemons instead of oranges.

22. (Declarative) Does Roberto like to dance?

23. (Passive) Health officials condemned the building.

Correct any problems in the following sentences.

24. William and Steve opened his new business on Monday.

25. The house, at the end of the street, is for sale.

26. To go to Paris, studying art, and become a great artist were his secret ambitions.

27. The gym has facilities for many activities. Such as racquetball, basketball, and swimming.

28. Andy Mitchell who uses a wheelchair just became the president of the freshman class.

29. Looking over her shoulder, the answers on her test could be seen.

30. The German autobahn is similar to the American interstate system both are controlled access, multilane roads.

31. The vase of flowers are on the table in the kitchen.

32. Ivan brought Gunter his football gear.

33. I could not tell if the sign says Main Street or March Street.

Answers

1. The <u>moon</u> and the <u>stars</u> are especially bright tonight. Predicate adjective (subjects, p. 184; predicates, p. 188)

2. <u>Believing</u> in your own abilities is a requirement for success. Predicate noun (subjects, p. 184; predicates, p. 188)

3. An old, broken-down <u>jalopy</u> is in their garage. Predicate preposition (subjects, p. 184; predicates, p. 188)

The bolded section below equals the double-underline mentioned in the instructions for this set of problems.

4. The gooey green space aliens brought <u>a message of peace</u> to **the inhabitants of planet Earth.** (objects, p. 190)

5. I inherited <u>all my grandfather's old cameras.</u> (objects, p. 190)

6. I suddenly remembered <u>what she had asked me to do.</u> (objects, p. 190)

7. Anyone can contribute <u>a story</u> to the literary magazine. (objects, p. 190)

8. The eccentric millionaire left <u>his estate</u> to **his cat.** (objects, p. 190)

9. <u>Thinking he would be punished</u> = participial phrase (phrases, p. 192)

10. <u>On top of the television set</u> = prepositional phrase (phrases, p. 192)

11. <u>Its branches creaking</u> = absolute phrase (special types of phrases, p. 194)

12. <u>I would gladly give you a ride</u> = independent clause; <u>my car is being repaired</u> = independent clause (clauses, p. 195)

13. <u>If California were a country</u> = "if" clause (special types of clauses: "if" clauses, p. 198)

14.   <u>One of the best examples of Roman fresco</u> = noun phrase; appositive (special types of phrases, p. 194)

15.   <u>Who was here earlier</u> = relative clause; restrictive (clauses, p. 197); <u>that the store had gone bankrupt</u> = noun clause (special types of clauses: "that" clauses, p. 197)

16.   <u>Which had poor attendance last year</u> = relative clause; nonrestrictive (clauses, p. 195)

17.   <u>Because she is so kind and generous</u> = subordinate clause (clauses, p. 195)

18.   <u>Reading to young children</u> = noun phrase (phrases, p. 192)

19.   Put down the box. (sentence types: declarative, imperative, and interrogative moods, p. 202)

20.   People of all nationalities enjoy Thai food. (sentence types: passive and active voice, p. 204)

21.   Why did he bring lemons instead of oranges? (sentence types: declarative, imperative, and interrogative moods, p. 202)

22.   Roberto likes to dance. (sentence types: declarative, imperative, and interrogative moods, p. 202)

23.   The building was condemned by health officials. (sentence types: passive and active voice, p. 204)

24.   William and Steve opened **their** new business on Monday. (lack of agreement, p. 214)

25.   The house **at the end of the street** is for sale. (restrictive and nonrestrictive elements, p. 211)

26.   To go to Paris, **study** art, and become a great artist were his secret ambitions. (lack of parallelism, p. 216)

27.   The gym has facilities for many activities, **such** as racquetball, basketball, and swimming. (sentence fragments, p. 208)

28.   Andy Mitchell, **who uses a wheelchair,** just became the president of the freshman class. (restrictive and nonrestrictive elements, p. 211)

29.   Looking over her shoulder, **he could see the answers on her test.** (misplaced or "dangling" modifiers, p. 209)

30.   The German autobahn is similar to the American interstate system. **B**oth are controlled access, multilane roads.

      OR

      The German autobahn is similar to the American interstate system; **both** are controlled-access, multilane roads. (run-on sentences, p. 205)

31.   The vase of flowers **is** on the table in the kitchen. (lack of agreement, p. 214)

32. Ivan brought **Gunter's** football gear.

    OR

    Ivan brought his football gear for Gunter. (unclear antecedents, p. 213)

33. I could not tell if the sign **said** Main Street or March Street.

    OR

    I **cannot** tell if the sign says Main Street or March Street. (inconsistent use of tenses or pronouns, p. 217)

Chapter 8
Punctuation, Capitalization, and Other Issues

Punctuation marks are a set of standardized symbols including periods, commas, apostrophes, semicolons, and colons. Punctuation is used to make text easier to read and to convey specific meaning. Its proper use is governed by a unique combination of grammatical rules and stylistic guidelines. Punctuation is used to divide words into grammatical units, such as sentences, phrases, and clauses in sentences. Related issues involve the use of capital letters, the use of abbreviations and acronyms, the use of numerals, and the use of italics and underlining. Knowing a few simple rules and following a set of guidelines can make a writing experience, in any situation, easier to manage.

The rules for all these forms of grammar have evolved over hundreds of years of use. Punctuation marks give visual cues through a set of standardized markings to give variety to writing that might be expected from facial expressions in a person-to-person conversation. Capital letters give the needed and emphasized focus to set off differences between organizations or groups. Abbreviations aid in recognizing a common set of standard and accepted shortened versions of proper names or frequently used words that can be shortened without confusing the reader. Acronyms indicate that specific groups are being referred to without having to repeat their sometimes lengthy titles. Numerals are always effective tools to communicate ideas that either cannot be expressed in written form or to emphasize numerically some rather large expressions. Italics and underlining are useful to denote proper titles, foreign words, or emphasized words.

No matter how these skills are employed, proper punctuation and capitalization will always improve writing. Knowing how to use these rules can increase confidence and skill.

Periods

Periods are the most basic of punctuation marks. A period is used to end a declarative sentence (a sentence that makes a statement or answers a question).

> He is going to the store.
> Sam just left.

A period is used to end an imperative sentence (a sentence that gives an order) when no special urgency is being communicated.

> Hand me the remote control, please.
> Finish your homework so we can go to the movies.

Periods are used within quotations marks (quotation marks, p. 243). If a sentence ends with an abbreviation or acronym, do not add a second period (abbreviations and acronyms, p. 255).

> He said, "I am not going with you to town."
> He was set to arrive at 8 p.m.

Periods are also used after titles and as part of an abbreviation (abbreviations and acronyms, p. 255).

Mr.	Dr.	Gov.	Gen.	a.m.
Mrs.	Ph.D.	Hon.	Col.	p.m.
Ms.	Fr.	Maj.	Sgt.	Jan.

Example Problems

Add periods where necessary in the following sentences.

1. The committee petitioned Gov Janet Scott to dedicate more state funds to education

   Answer: The committee petitioned Gov. Janet Scott to dedicate more state funds to education. A period is used after the governor's abbreviated title, and a period is used at the end of a declarative sentence.

2. Meet me at Wendy's for lunch

   Answer: Meet me at Wendy's for lunch. A period is used at the end of an imperative sentence when no special urgency is being communicated.

3. Paula said to her teacher, "This homework assignment is very difficult"

   Answer: Paula said to her teacher, "This homework assignment is very difficult." A period is used at the end of a declarative sentence, and the period is located inside the quotation marks.

Work Problems

Insert periods in the sentences where needed.

1. Dr David Jones was called to the emergency room

2. We gave a present to Mrs Wilson for teaching our class

3. Paula said to her friend, "I can't be ready to leave by 6:30 am"

Worked Solutions

1. Dr. David Jones was called to the emergency room. (Insert a period after the abbreviated title and at the end of a declarative sentence.)

2. We gave a present to Mrs. Wilson for teaching our class. (Insert a period after the abbreviated title and at the end of a declarative sentence.)

3. Paula said to her friend, "I can't be ready to leave by 6:30 a.m." Periods are used to abbreviate the time; because the last period in the abbreviation ends a declarative sentence, no additional period is needed. Also note that the quotation (the words Paula said) ends the sentence, so the period is placed inside the quotation marks.

Commas

Commas are, perhaps, the most misunderstood and misused type of punctuation. Their use is governed by a unique mix of strict grammar rules and style guidelines.

❏ When two independent clauses are joined by one of the coordinating conjunctions *and*, *but*, *for*, *nor*, and *or*, use a comma before the coordinating conjunction.

   Example: The airplanes were built for acrobatics, and the pilots were highly skilled.

   Example: We were told to board the ship at 11 a.m., and we arrived at the docks early, but the ship had already departed.

❏ Commas are used to separate an introductory element from the main clause of a sentence. One of the most common introductory elements is a participial phrase (phrases, p. 192).

   Example: Driving as quickly as they could, Bill and Kathy arrived just in time to pick me up.

   Example: Wailing like a banshee, Chris ran past us and disappeared into the night

❏ Commas are used to set off a dependent clause that comes before the main clause of a sentence.

   Example: Even though the movie was boring, we stayed until the end.

   Example: If you keep criticizing me, I will ignore you.

❏ Commas are used to set off a variety of introductory words, including *yes, no, oh, ah,* and adverbs such as *well,* at the beginning of a sentence.

   Example: No, I can't imagine why Stacy did that to us.

   Example: Well, you may have another piece of candy if you will brush your teeth afterward.

❏ Commas are used to set off declarative elements of a sentence from a tag question (Sentences: sentence types: declarative, imperative, and interrogative moods, p. 202).

   Example: You are counting on me, aren't you?

   Example: That concert was incredible, don't you think?

❏ Commas are used to set off a nonrestrictive sentence element from the remainder of the sentence (restrictive and nonrestrictive elements, p 211).

   Example: I like these jeans, which I bought at the Gap, because they fit really well.

   Example: The new James Bond movie kept us entertained, even though it was too long, because the special effects were so good.

❏ Commas are used to set off an appositive phrase from the remainder of the sentence (special types of phrases, p. 194).

   Example: I saw Mrs. Gruber, the woman in the blue jacket, the last time we were here.

   Example: My cell phone, a Samsung, gets great reception.

❑ Commas are used to set off interrupter elements from the remainder of a sentence. These interrupters appear as words, phrases, and clauses in the middle of a sentence, interrupting the main thought or idea of the sentence (special types of phrases, p 194).

Example: If Paul scores twenty points in the game tonight, and I really doubt that he will, he will be this year's most valuable player.

Example: Brenda, not Paula, was the one who really should be thanked.

❑ Commas are used between sets of numbers to avoid confusion and make them easier to read. Commas are used to set off the main elements of a street address. They are also used in dates to separate the day of the month from the year.

Example: World War II started on September 1, 1939. (*Note:* The word *September* and the number *1* are not easily confused; therefore, a comma is not needed.)

Example: I lived at 125 Division Street, Lake Charles, Louisiana, for about three years.

❑ If the month and season are given (or the season and the year), but not the day, there is no need for a comma.

Example: I left France in June 1980.

Example: We were supposed to leave by Summer 1990.

❑ No comma is used, however, in the European style of writing dates.

Example: World War II started on 1 September 1939.

❑ Commas are used following a greeting at the beginning of a personal letter and following the salutation at the end of a letter.

Example: Dear Mr. Dawes,

Best regards,

Sincerely,

❑ Commas are used when necessary to avoid confusion and preserve the meaning of a sentence.

Example: We asked Mrs. Brown who flunked, and laughed.

❑ Commas are used to in numbers containing four or more digits (some newspapers and other publications only use commas with numbers that have five or more digits). For larger numbers, commas are used to arrange digits into groups of three. Years do not use commas in order to avoid confusion with four-digit numbers.

Example: The class of 2003 raised some $8,346 for local charities.

Example: Paul McCartney made more than $70,500,000 in 2002.

❑ Commas are used to separate names, when the name is inverted (as in a biography, catalog, or index).

Example: Sherman, William Tecumseh

Example: Cuba, the Culture of

Example: Pen, ball point

❑ Commas are used to set off direct quotations from the rest of the sentence.

Example: He said to me, "There are many things that you need to know."

Example: My mother always tells me that "to err is human, to forgive divine."

Gray Area: The Serial Comma

Commas are used to separate phrases, clauses, and items in a list or series. The comma is placed after each element in the series or list; a final comma (called the serial comma) is placed before the conjunction. Some newspapers and other publications do not use the serial comma before the conjunction.

> *With Serial Comma:* The first time we went, there were several new cars, trucks, and SUVs to choose from.
> *Without Serial Comma:* The first time we went, there were several new cars, trucks and SUVs to choose from.

> *With Serial Comma:* Heidi likes to bring her own food, eat dinner at her desk, and work late.
> *Without Serial Comma:* Heidi likes to bring her own food, eat dinner at her desk and work late.

Similarly, commas are used to separate coordinating adjectives that modify a noun.

> I couldn't help noticing her bright, mischievous, and classic smile.

OR

> I couldn't help noticing her bright, mischievous and classic smile.

In this case the words *bright, mischievous,* and *classic* modify the word *smile.*

Example Problems

Explain why each comma is used in the following sentences.

1. Although both teams were on time, the game started late.

   Answer: A comma is used to separate a dependent clause (**Although both teams are on time**) from the main clause of the sentence (**the game started late**).

2. We went to the football game, but we forgot our tickets.

   Answer: A comma comes after **game** because **but** is a coordinating conjunction that joins two independent clauses.

3. I had lived at 901 East Elm Street, Goldsboro, North Carolina, since February 17, 1997.

   Answer: The commas are inserted after the address elements in this sentence: the street, the city, and the state. Also, commas are used to separate the day of the month from the year.

4. The ABC Corporation gave $1,543,978 to the political action committee.

   Answer: Commas are used to separate large numbers into groups of three digits.

5. Christine was punctual, thankfully, and should not be penalized.

   Answer: Commas are used in this sentence to set off the interrupting word **thankfully.**

6. Dear Mr. and Mrs. Davis,

    Answer: A comma is used after the salutation in a personal letter.

7. Carter, James Earl

    Answer: A comma is used after an inverted name in an index or bibliography.

8. I was dazzled by her big, bright, deep blue eyes.

    Answer: Commas are used after coordinating adjectives (**big, bright, deep blue**) before a noun (**eyes**).

Work Problems

Insert commas in the following sentences where needed.

1. I had intended to get out more but I have decided instead to stay indoors.

2. If I had a nickel for every time he said that I'd be a millionaire.

3. No there isn't enough time to go there and get back.

4. You will be there won't you?

5. If you've never been there will be big medium and small airplanes.

6. Joe not Matthew will come by to fix your computer.

7. The Nelsens, Ryans, and Pearsons are all getting together for a picnic.

8. We were so excited by the race, which at times was fast and furious, that we hardly noticed the day had gone by.

9. World War I officially ended on November 11 1918.

10. Dear Mr. Darcy

11. Our employee campaign raised $1178453 this year.

12. Taft William Howard

13. She asked "How are we supposed to get there?"

Worked Solutions

1. I had intended to get out more, but I have decided instead to stay indoors. (Insert a comma before the coordinating conjunction **but** because it is separating two independent clauses.)

2. If I had a nickel for every time he said that, I'd be a millionaire. (Insert a comma after the introductory element of the sentence.)

3. No, there isn't enough time to go there and get back. (Insert a comma after **no** at the beginning of the sentence.)

4. You will be there, won't you? (Insert a comma between the declarative element of a sentence and a tag question.)

5. If you've never been, there will be big, medium, and small airplanes. (Insert a comma after the introductory element, and after the items in a series.)

6. Joe, not Matthew, will come by to fix your computer. (Insert commas to set off the interrupter element **not Matthew** from the remainder of the sentence.)

7. The Nelsens, Ryans, and Pearsons are all getting together for a picnic. (Commas are inserted after items in a list and before the conjunction **and.**)

8. We were so excited by the race, which at times was fast and furious, that we hardly noticed the day had gone by. (Use commas to set off a nonrestrictive clause from the remainder of the sentence.)

9. World War I officially ended on November 11, 1918. (Use a comma between the day of the month and the year.)

10. Dear Mr. Darcy, (Use a comma after the salutation in a personal letter.)

11. Our employee campaign raised $1,178,453 this year. (Use commas in a figure with more than four digits.)

12. Taft, William Howard (Use a comma when a name is inverted in an index or bibliography.)

13. She asked, "How are we supposed to get there?" (Use a comma before a direct quote.)

Semicolons

Semicolons are used to designate a break in a sentence that is more pronounced than a comma break. Semicolons are used to separate independent clauses (phrases, p. 192; clauses, p. 195) where the clauses are closely related.

Example: I have asked him for help several times; he has always been very helpful.

Semicolons are used to join two or more independent clauses joined by coordinating conjunctions *and, but, for, nor, or, so,* and *yet* when the clauses themselves contain commas. Do not join clauses of unequal rank, such as independent and dependent clauses, with a semicolon. Longer sentences, not short, clipped ones, usually take a semicolon.

It was time for Mary to close her office, pack her bags, and visit all her clients; but there were so many of them, and they were so scattered across the country, that she would be on the road for weeks.

Semicolons also are used before conjunctive adverbs (conjunctive adverbs, p. 143) and transitional phrases that join independent clauses.

Conjunctive adverbs		
also	however	next
anyhow	incidentally	nonetheless
anyway	indeed	otherwise
besides	instead	similarly
consequently	likewise	still
finally	meanwhile	then
furthermore	moreover	therefore
hence	nevertheless	thus

Transitional phrases		
as a result	even so	in the second place
at any rate	in addition	in addition to
at the same time	in fact	on the contrary
by the way	in other words	in so far as

The writer worked on the project for several months, to the frustration of his editor; still, that same editor was pleased when the final product came in.

We had been riding around the town for hours, looking for a particular address; at the same time, we did get to know the area quite well.

Semicolons are used to separate a series of sentence elements (phrases and clauses) when the elements themselves are long and contain commas.

In his research paper, Jeff worked diligently to include as much information as possible about Herman Melville, the acknowledged master of the sea novel; Nathaniel Hawthorne, Melville's friend and fellow writer; and Mark Twain, the celebrated "dean" of American humorist authors.

Semicolons are placed outside of quotation marks.

Example: Dr. Thompson told me, "You will probably feel drowsy after taking this medicine"; however, I haven't had any side effects.

Example Problems

Explain why semicolons are used in the following sentences.

1. Sarah was the first one who ran down the street; however, Sam was the one who came up with the prize.

   Answer: These two independent clauses are joined by the conjunctive adverb **however,** so a semicolon is used.

2. Hugh was amazed by the depth of the opposing team's bench strength; at the same time, he knew his team could win the basketball game.

    Answer: These two independent clauses are joined by the transitional phrase **at the same time,** so a semicolon is used.

3. The computers in our library have flat screen monitors, DVD players, CD burners, and other sophisticated hardware; are loaded with the newest software, utilities, and applications; and have three types of security built in.

    Answer: Semicolons are used to separate a series of long phrases that contain commas.

Work Problems

Insert semicolons where needed.

1. There were times when we needed to stop and assess our situation likewise, there were times when we moved forward without stopping.

2. Each of us had enough time for sightseeing nevertheless we were all there for business in North Carolina.

3. Chad has been searching for our baggage for a few minutes at the same time, he was looking for a taxi and trying to find an umbrella.

4. Abraham Lincoln said, "Work, work, work is the main thing" Kay Stepkin said, "Work is an essential part of being alive" and Mencius said, "Those who work their minds rule; those who work with their backs are ruled."

Worked Solutions

1. There were times when we needed to stop and assess our situation; likewise, there were times when we moved forward without stopping. (Use a semicolon when two independent clauses are joined by the conjunctive adverb **likewise.**)

2. Each of us had enough time for sightseeing; nevertheless, we were all there for business in North Carolina. (Use a semicolon to separate the two independent clauses at the conjunctive adverb **nevertheless.**)

3. Chad has been searching for our baggage for a few minutes; at the same time, he was looking for a taxi and trying to find an umbrella. (Use a semicolon to separate the two independent clauses at the transitional phrase **at the same time.**)

4. Abraham Lincoln said, "Work, work, work is the main thing"; Kay Stepkin said, "Work is an essential part of being alive"; and Mencius said, "Those who work their minds rule; those who work with their backs are ruled." (Use semicolons to separate a series of clauses when the clauses themselves are punctuated with commas. Note that when the semicolon is not part of the actual quote, it is placed outside of the quotation marks.)

Colons

Like semicolons, colons mark a distinct break in a sentence. The difference is that colons are used between clauses that are closely linked in topic. Where two clauses are connected by a colon, the second clause typically continues the thought of the first clause, or the second clause contains an elaboration or illustration of the topic discussed in the first clause.

> Sharon has fourteen trophies on her bookshelf: eight of them are from karate tournaments.
>
> The mayor was thrown out of office: his years of embezzlement were finally discovered.

If the colon introduces more than one complete sentence, then the word immediately following the colon should be capitalized.

> The dinners served on our cruise were rich and extravagant: At one meal we were served steak, lobster, and shrimp. At another meal we had rack of lamb, a tray of oysters and mussels, and six types of vegetables.

Colons are used to introduce formal statements and portions of a speech. Note that a formal statement or quote following the colon should begin with a capital letter.

> The attorney could not help himself when he began his closing arguments: "My client is a good man, a decent man, and should not be here on trial today."
>
> If you want an opinion, I will give it to you: Children riding in cars should always be required to wear seatbelts.

> Note that colons are used outside of quotation marks.

> Shakespeare said, "Love sought is good, but given unsought is better": love is more enjoyable when it is a gift.

Colons can also introduce long quotations from other works.

> One interpretation of John Keats' "Ode on a Grecian Urn," is that the urn is a symbol of permanence while generations of people come and go:

> Thou shalt remain, in midst of other woe
> Than ours, a friend to man, to whom thou say'st,
> "Beauty is truth, truth beauty,"—that is all
> Ye know on earth, and all ye need to know.

A colon is used at the end of an independent clause that introduces items in a series.

> The economic power of our country depends upon several factors: the output of our factories, the import and export of goods, and the purchasing power of consumers.

Colons can also follow salutations in business letters.

> Dear Madam or Sir:
> Dear Mr. President:

Colons can be found between numbers in time statements and Biblical citations.

> 12:15 p.m.
> 21:50
> Genesis 18:2
> John 3:16

Example Problems

Explain how colons are used in the following sentences.

1. The doctor made this statement during his lecture: "We have not yet begun to tackle the issue of curing the common cold in a serious manner."

   Answer: Use a colon after an independent clause that introduces a portions of a speech.

2. Job 42:2

   Answer: Use colons with Biblical references or citations.

3. The time is 2:37 p.m.

   Answer: Use a colon with a time statement.

4. Dear Mr. Vice President:

   Answer: Use a colon in the salutation of a business letter.

5. He listed the colors of the cats in order: black, brown, and white.

   Answer: Use a colon after an independent clause that introduces a series of items.

Work Problems

Insert colons where they are needed.

1. Dear Ms. Capolini

2. 445 a.m.

3. Jeremiah 430

4. There are three colors on the American flag red, white, and blue.

Worked Solutions

1. Dear Ms. Capolini: (Use a colon after the salutation in a business letter.)

2. 4:45 a.m. (Use a colon in time statements.)

3. Jeremiah 4:30 (Use a colon in Biblical references.)

4. There are three colors on the American flag: red, white, and blue. (Use a colon after an independent clause that introduces items in a series.)

Question Marks

Question marks are used at the end of a sentence to signal a direct question, an interrogative series, an interrogative question within a sentence, and to express editorial doubt.

❏ Direct question:

Where are you going in such a hurry?

❏ An interrogative series:

What do you think of the candidate's views on foreign policy? domestic policy? the economy?

❏ An interrogative question within a sentence (Note that if the sentence's primary clause precedes the question, then the first letter of the question is capitalized):

How soon would it happen? she wondered.

Linda wrung her hands with despair as she asked herself, What if I caused the accident?

❏ To express editorial doubt:

Although Chaucer was born in 1340 (?), we do not know his exact date of birth.

Exclamation Points

Exclamation points are used to signal interjections most commonly associated with fear, surprise, excitement, shock, and disbelief. An exclamation point can be used in place of a question mark to indicate that the overall emotion of the sentence is surprise rather than questioning.

Wow!
Super!
He hit that ball out of here!
Do you really think I'm that stupid!

Example Problems

Explain how question marks or exclamation points are used in the following sentences.

1. Get out of here!

    Answer: Use an exclamation point with interjections to show shock.

2. Are you serious!

    Answer: You can use an exclamation point instead of a question mark to indicate that the main emotion of the sentence is surprise.

3. What are the teacher's rules for homework? for make-up work? for missed tests? for grading papers?

    Answer: Use question marks for an interrogative series in a sentence.

4. Quickly! What are you waiting for?

    Answer: Use an exclamation point for an interjection to show surprise. Also, use a question mark to ask a question in a sentence.

Work Problems

Insert question marks or exclamation points where they are needed in the following sentences.

1. Are you in a hurry

2. Great

3. When were you going to tell me

4. Cool

5. Do you think the boss will change his position on break times health care employee parking

Worked Solutions

1. Are you in a hurry? (Use a question mark after a direct question.)

2. Great! (Use an exclamation point after a surprised expression.)

3. When were you going to tell me! (You can use an exclamation point instead of a question mark to indicate that the main emotion of the sentence is surprise.)

4. Cool! (Use an exclamation point after an expression of excitement.)

5. Do you think the boss will change his position on break times? health care? employee parking? (Use question marks after items in an interrogative series.)

Apostrophes

Apostrophes are used for two primary purposes: to show possession and to indicate shortened versions of words, known as contractions.

Contractions use apostrophes to show that letters have been omitted from a word or phrase. The same is true of numbers that have been left out.

> Can't (for *cannot*)
> Don't (for *do not*)
> It's (for *it is*)
> Who's (for *who is*)
> What's (for *what is*)
> '80 (for 1980)
> '03 (for 2003)

An apostrophe is used to show possession of an object.

> Tom's house is beautiful. (Tom owns the house.)
> Calvin's plush tiger is orange. (Calvin owns the tiger.)
> The skis are Susan's. (Susan owns the skis.)

An apostrophe is used to show possession by joint ownership.

> My mother and father's car is in the garage. (The mother and father both own the same car.)
>
> My brother and sister's lemonade stand is closed. (The brother and sister both own the same lemonade stand.)

An apostrophe is used to show ownership of two or more objects by two or more different entities, designating ownership by each.

> Cal and Vince's apartments. (Cal and Vince own jointly own more than one apartment.)
>
> Tom's and Sue's skateboards. (Tom and Sue each own their own separate skateboard.)

An apostrophe is used to form the possessive of a plural noun that ends in **–s.**

> The ladies' shoes are beautiful.
>
> The students' bookbags are brand new.

An apostrophe is used to form the possessive of a compound noun, by simply adding an apostrophe-s (**–'s**).

> The attorney general's decision is to let the insurance company sell insurance. (The attorney general has made a certain decision.)
>
> The color of paint was my sister-in-law's choice. (My sister-in-law made the choice.)

You can form the possessive of a plural compound noun by adding an apostrophe-s (**–'s**) to the end, but this results in an awkward construction. It is much better to rewrite the sentence.

> *Awkward:* My sisters-in-law's schedules are very hectic.
>
> *Better:* My sisters-in-law have very hectic schedules.

Gray Area: Handling 'S Situations

When the singular or collective form of a noun ends in **–s,** there are two ways to form the possessive. The preferred method is to add apostrophe-s (**–'s**). However, some publications add only the apostrophe.

> Paris's lights reflect beautifully off the Seine.
>
> The Jones's car is parked in the driveway.
>
> The class's attendance this year was excellent.

In most cases, apostrophes should not be used to form plurals. Some publications use apostrophes with dates, but this should be avoided if clarity can be preserved.

> We began the practice in the 1980s.
>
> He followed the four Cs when buying her diamond: color, clarity, cut, and cost.
>
> I have all of Aerosmith's CDs.
>
> There were three Cindys in my third-grade class.

However, some coined phrases do use apostrophes to indicate plurals (note that the apostrophe is necessary here to avoid confusion). Also, common abbreviations that have more than one period require the use of an apostrophe.

> I told my daughter to mind her *p*'s and *q*'s when she went to her friend's house.
> Elizabeth has earned three M.A.'s and two Ph.D.'s.

Use apostrophes with forms fashioned with verbs that are also abbreviations.

> O.K.'d
> O.K.'ing

Common Pitfall: "It's" versus "It is"

It is easy to confuse *it's* (meaning *it is*) with *its* (showing possession).

> It's the hardest thing I've ever had to do. (It is the hardest. . . .)
> Its windows had been destroyed after the storm. (The windows belonging to it were destroyed.)

Example Problems

In the following sentences, list the reason for each apostrophe and explain the meaning of the sentence.

1. Tom and Rene's house is painted a bright blue.

   Answer: Because Tom and Rene own the house as a couple or by joint ownership, the **–'s** is added after the second person's name.

2. The DVDs were sold by a company in Boston.

   Answer: In this sentence, **DVDs** is not a possessive; it is only a plural, so no apostrophe is needed.

3. Personal computers have been around since the 1980s.

   Answer: The **1980s** is a plural, not a possessive, so no apostrophe is used.

4. Jean's and Ethel's teaching styles are excellent.

   Answer: Because we are referring to the work of two individuals, and not their joint work, it is appropriate to use apostrophes after each named person.

5. It's time the dog had its bath.

   Answer: At the beginning of this sentence, **it's** is a contraction of **it is.** Later in the sentence, **its bath** refers to the dog having its own bath.

6. The Mavis's parakeet escaped out their front door.

   Answer: To form the plural of a noun that ends in **–s,** add an **–'s.**

Work Problems

Insert apostrophes when needed in the following sentences or expressions.

1. Whos pitching today?

2. The attorneys dotted the *i*s and crossed the *t*s.

3. There are times when the FAAs decisions save lives.

4. I loved the show about the 80s.

5. The sergeant majors house was the finest on post.

6. Your brothers and sisters gifts were under the tree.

7. The Grolshs cat wandered into our yard.

8. Beths new car is light brown.

9. By the late 1970s, large cars were not favored over small ones.

10. Our plane was O.K.d for take off.

Worked Solutions

1. Who's pitching today? (**Who's** is a contraction for **who is.**)

2. The attorneys dotted the *i*'s and crossed the *t*'s. (Coined phrases with plurals use apostrophes.)

3. There are times when the FAA's decisions save lives. (Abbreviations use an apostrophe to show possession.) (abbreviations and acronyms, p. 255)

4. I loved the show about the '80s. (An apostrophe is used to indicate some of the numbers have been omitted from a year.)

5. The sergeant major's house was the finest on post. (Add an –'s to the final word of a compound noun to indicate possession.)

6. Your brother's and sister's gifts were under the tree. (Use apostrophes to show possession by joint ownership.)

7. The Grolsh's cat wandered into our yard. (Add an –'s to a collective noun to form the possessive.)

8. Beth's new car is light brown. (Use an apostrophe to show possession or ownership.)

9. By the late 1970s, large cars were not favored over small ones. (No apostrophe is used to indicate the plural of a date.)

10. Our plane was O.K.'d for take off. (Use an apostrophe for a form fashioned with a verb.)

Quotation Marks

Quotation marks are used to indicate direct quotations, parts of larger works, and words given special emphasis. Two marks are used: one set opens the quote and the other set closes the quote.

❑ Quotation marks are used to surround direct quotations. These marks are to cite direct remarks from a speaker or words that come from another author.

>   *Example:* He said, "Here we go again," as a second wave of rain raced into town.

>   *Example:* After a few minutes he remarked, "Thank goodness the rain has stopped."

>   *Example:* In an article from the morning newspaper, I read that "an astounding three inches of rain fell in six hours in Greenville."

❑ Quotation marks are used for titles of shorter works and to indicate smaller sections of a larger work. These include periodical articles, essays, lectures, poems, sermons, short stories, chapters of books, songs, radio programs, and episodes of television shows.

>   **Article**   "At What Price Do We Cut Budgets to Save Dollars in Our Schools?" was an article that came from the newspaper.

>   **Sermon**   "Sinners in the Hands of an Angry God" is a popular sermon by Jonathan Edwards.

>   **Essay**   "On Behalf of the Insane Poor" is an essay by Dorthea Dix that attempted to move legislators to make reforms for the treatment of the poor and insane some 100 years ago.

>   **Poem**   "Mending Wall" is a short poem by Robert Frost. However, a long poem published as a complete work is italicized: *The Odyssey.*

>   **Short story**   Mark Twain's short story "The Notorious Jumping Frog of Calaveras County" launched his literary career.

>   **Song**   My favorite James Taylor song is "Fire and Rain." However, longer musical works, such as symphonies and operas, are given no special treatment: Mahler's 2nd Symphony.

>   **Radio program**   Garrison Keillor's "A Prairie Home Companion" comes on every Saturday night on the local public radio station.

>   **Television episode**   I had to laugh when I saw "The Trouble with Tribbles" from an old Star Trek episode.

❑ Quotation marks are used to give words special emphasis. Be careful not to use the marks on clichés.

>   *Example:* A few of her favorite words are "neat" and "classic."

❑ Another tricky situation is a quotation within a quotation. Standard quotation marks surround the larger quotation, and single quotation marks surround the embedded quote. In the example below, a segment of Rachael's presentation is a direct quote, so it is surrounded by standard quotation marks. As part of her presentation, Rachael directly quotes Joseph Campbell; his quote is surrounded by single quotes.

>   *Example:* In her presentation, Rachael reported the following: "Joseph Campbell encouraged people to study mythology. In his book, *The Power of Myth*, Campbell wrote that 'Myth helps you to put your mind in touch with this experience of being alive.'"

❑ Quotation marks can also be used to indicate irony. Be careful not to overuse them, though.

>   *Example:* Yes, that movie was so "riveting" that I slept right through it.

Example Problems

1. While Beth was looking the other way, he quickly asked her, "May I ask you out?"

    Answer: Use quotation marks around direct quotes taken from dialogue.

2. The newspaper headline "How could this have happened?" screamed to be read.

    Answer: Use quotation marks around the title of a newspaper article.

3. I read the poem "Tinturn Abbey" by Wordsworth and the famous essay "Preface to Lyrical Ballads" for our assignment last night.

    Answer: Poems and essays are short works of literature, and quotation marks are used around their titles.

4. The swing song "In the Mood" can be best described as "fun" and "one of the most well-known songs of the swing era."

    Answer: Songs, which are short works, are put inside quotation marks. Words that need special emphasis and phrases that are quoted from another source also use quotation marks.

5. The director encouraged the actress playing Laura by telling her, "You're doing a great job, but I want you to turn it up a notch. When the character Jim says to you, 'Somebody ought to—ought to—*kiss* you, Laura!' I want to see you turn your head and blush!"

    Answer: In this quote within a quote, the director's words to the actress are a direct quote, so standard quote marks surround them. Part of what the director says, however, is a direct quote that the character Jim says in the play. Jim's words are surrounded by single quotes because they are embedded within the larger direct quote from the director. Also, the punctuation marks in Jim's quote are reproduced exactly from the play, verbatim.

Work Problems

Insert quotation marks in the following sentences or expressions when needed

1. Her mother asked her, What time did you drop the dog off at the vet?

2. The newspaper mentioned that we could see several inches of snow with possible drifts.

3. What do you think of that Elvis tune, I Can't Help Falling in Love?

4. I read The Rime of the Ancient Mariner and was amazed at the tone of the poem.

5. I heard Nancy say that The turning point in the book is when Thomas tells the young boy, I ought not to help you in your quest. It wouldn't be right.

6. I met a man who said he had a secret recipe for potato chips.

Worked Solutions

1. Her mother asked her, "What time did you drop the dog off at the vet?" (Use quotation marks with a direct quotation.)

2. The newspaper mentioned that we could see "several inches of snow with possible drifts." (Use quotation marks with a direct quote from a newspaper article.)

3. What do you think of that Elvis tune "I Can't Help Falling in Love"? (Use quotation marks for a song title. The question mark is placed outside of the quotation marks because it is not part of the song title; it only indicates that the entire sentence is a question.)

4. I read "The Rime of the Ancient Mariner" and was amazed at the tone of the poem. (Use quotation marks for the title of a poem.)

5. I heard Nancy say that "The turning point in the book is when Thomas tells the young boy, 'I ought not to help you in your quest. It wouldn't be right.'" (The standard quotation marks surround the direct quote from Nancy; single quotation marks surround the line from the book that she quotes directly.)

6. I met a man who said he had a "secret recipe" for potato chips. (Use quotation marks for words given special emphasis.)

Hyphens

Hyphens are single marks used to divide words at the end of a line, when the sentence continues onto the following line of text. Hyphens are also used between individual words that together form compound words. On a typewriter or word processor, a hyphen is a single mark. Dashes, on the other hand, are created with two hyphens (typewriter) or a single, long horizontal line (word processor) (dashes, p. 246).

The following are some basic rules for hyphens:

❏ Hyphens are used when words need to be divided at the end of a line of text and continued on another line. Most word processors insert these hyphens automatically.

❏ Hyphens cannot be used to divide one-syllable words.

> *Incorrect:* th-rough

❏ Words with two or more syllables must be divided between syllables. Consult a dictionary if you are in doubt as to the division of words.

> *Incorrect:* fundame-ntal

> *Correct:* fundamen-tal

❏ When hyphenating words, be sure that at least three letters are left over as a result of the hyphenation. Never hyphenate a word so that only one letter is left alone at the end of the prior line or the beginning of a subsequent line.

❏ If a word already has a built-in hyphen, try to divide the word at the hyphen.

> *Incorrect:* cross-coun-try race

> *Correct:* cross-country race

Hyphens are also used in variety of ordinary words and expressions. Numbers between twenty-one and ninety-nine take a hyphen. Other sequences of numbers, such as telephone numbers and social security numbers usually contain hyphens. Compound nouns and adjectives often take hyphens.

(317) 555-1212	four-cycle	long-winded	out-of-pocket
pitch-dark	Saint-Laurent	twice-told	Winston-Salem

The use of hyphens is generally not standardized. Consult a dictionary for the proper use of hyphens in words and expressions.

Dashes

Dashes are used to interrupt sentence flow and to provide variety to normal sentence structure. Sometimes, the use of a dash suggests an informal tone in sentence structure. Dashes are created with two hyphens on a typewriter or word processor; some word processors have special dash characters which are longer than hyphens.

Dashes are used to set off a sentence element that either radically changes the structure of the main sentence, or expounds upon or digresses from the main sentence.

> He was thinking of ways to extricate himself—how stupid he felt for being in this situation—but his mind drew a blank.
>
> In education there are the three Rs—reading, writing, and arithmetic—that govern the curriculum in our schools.

Example Problems

Explain why the hyphens and dashes are used in the following sentences.

1. The touchdown scored was a seventy-seven yard play.

   Answer: Use hyphens to separate numbers from twenty-one to ninety-nine.

2. Paula thought about a way to get out of this mess—how pitiful she felt!

   Answer: A dash is used for dramatic effect when a sentence's structure changes radically.

Work Problems

For each sentence, add hyphens and dashes as needed.

1. Where are the forty eight hamburgers I ordered?

2. Carolyn paused and thought for a moment is everything here? did we forget anything? what else is missing?

3. He was once called wishy washy.

4.   Twenty five of the forty eight dancers had on the wrong shoes.

5.   The city council voted for several major issues street improvements, new parking spaces, and repairing old sidewalks in quick order.

Worked Solutions

1.   Where are the forty-eight hamburgers I ordered? (Use a hyphen in numbers between twenty-one and ninety-nine.)

2.   Carolyn paused and thought for a moment—is everything here? did we forget anything? what else is missing? (Use a dash when the sentence structure changes radically.)

3.   He was once called wishy-washy. (Use hyphens in accordance with the dictionary spelling of a word.)

4.   Twenty-five of the forty-eight dancers had on the wrong shoes. (Use hyphens in numbers between twenty-one and ninety-nine.)

5.   The city council voted for several major issues—street improvements, new parking spaces, and repairing old sidewalks—in quick order. (A dash is used to separate the phrase **street improvements, new parking spaces, and repairing old sidewalks** because the phrase expounds upon the preceding clause, and represents a radical change in structure from the main sentence.)

Parentheses

Parentheses are always used in pairs to enclose explanatory material, supplemental material, or other material that explains the text of a sentence.

The hotel begun in 1980 (and finished in 1985) was a model for how not to construct a building.

Parentheses also can be used to draw attention to individual listed items.

Aviation maps include indications of (1) height and elevation, (2) the height of objects from the ground, (3) airports, (4) airspace, and (5) recognized airways.

Parentheses also are used in textual references.

California's annual budget is roughly equal to that of Italy (see Table 4.1).

Brackets

Brackets are used in pairs to indicate comments, editorial corrections, or explanations in text.

It has been noted that there are several versions of Shakespeare's quartos [reproduced from extant texts dating from 1600–1616] that seem to show variations in dialogue in his plays.

The use of the Latin [sic] or "thus" in sentences indicates that a passage has some sort of error or questionable fact, but it is being quoted as originally written. The use of **sic** is still used in academic writing and more sophisticated newspapers and magazines.

He said, "I seen [sic] it all."

Brackets are used to indicate a set of parentheses inside a set of parentheses.

I checked the source of the Mark Twain quote, "Training is everything. The peach was once a bitter almond; cauliflower is nothing but cabbage with a college education.— *Pudd'nhead Wilson's Calendar*" (See Mark Twain's *The Tragedy of Pudd'nhead Wilson*. Mark Twain, pseud.; Samuel Langhorne Clemens, American Publishing Company, Hartford, Conn., [1900]).

Example Problems

Explain why each set of parentheses and brackets is used in the following sentences.

1. The first work on the U.S. Capitol building was begun around 1793 (and later continued into the 1950s) by The Architects of the Capitol.

   Answer: The information in the parentheses is additional information, considered a good fact, but does not pertain to the point of the sentence. Such information is considered explanatory material and enclosed in parentheses.

2. The medieval play *Everyman* [taken from an anonymous text ca. 1485] is known as a morality play.

   Answer: The title of the play is italicized and the bracketed information is an editorial addition to the facts about the play.

3. As a class, we had read *Utopia* (by Sir Thomas More [1478–1535]) and enjoyed the comments that the author was making about the social condition he witnessed in sixteenth-century England.

   Answer: In this sentence, we have editorial information and factual information presented together in a single location. Because the dates are in addition to the author's name, the brackets go inside the parentheses. This type of construction is proper and should be handled carefully by a writer.

Work Problems

Insert parentheses and brackets as needed in the following sentences.

1. Thomas Gray 1716–1771 finished his most famous poem, "Elegy Written in a Country Churchyard," in 1751.

2. The baseball game began with a famous rock star singing, "Oh, hey can you see by the dawn's early light."

3. We were told there were several obstacles in the area that we would have to negotiate a rather large ditch, two logs, and a rope ladder.

4. While some dispute the assertions made by William Blake noted British Romantic Era author and illustrator 1757–1827 we cannot deny the power and majesty of his works.

Worked Solutions

1. Thomas Gray (1716–1771) finished his most famous poem, "Elegy Written in a Country Churchyard," in 1751. (Use parentheses to set off the explanatory material, Gray's birth and death dates.)

2. The baseball game began with a famous rock star singing, "Oh, hey [sic] can you see by the dawn's early light." (We put quote marks around the direct quote, but because the rock star misquoted the lyrics of "The Star Spangled Banner," we put a **[sic]** immediately after the error.)

3. We were told there were several obstacles in the area that we would have to negotiate: (1) a rather large ditch, (2) two logs, and (3) a rope ladder. (Use parentheses to enclose numbers in text that indicate an order.)

4. While some dispute the assertions made by William Blake (noted British Romantic Era author and illustrator [1757–1827]), we cannot deny the power and majesty of his works. (Use brackets for parenthetical text when it is enclosed within another set of parentheses.)

Ellipses

Ellipses are a series of three periods indicating that material has been omitted from a quotation. A few words, an entire phrase, or even lengthy text might be included, but not necessarily all the original text.

This is an example of a long quote:

> Thomas Jefferson wrote the Declaration of Independence as a statement of political will and to arouse the peoples of the thirteen colonies: "We hold these Truths to be self-evident, that all Men are created equal, that they are endowed by their Creator with certain unalienable Rights, that among these are Life, Liberty, and the Pursuit of Happiness."

Using ellipses to emphasize the parts of a sentence that are most important shortens and focuses the quotation.

> Thomas Jefferson wrote the Declaration of Independence as a statement of political will and to arouse the peoples of the thirteen colonies: "We hold these Truths to be self-evident, that all Men are created equal . . . with certain unalienable Rights . . . Life, Liberty, and the Pursuit of Happiness."

If the statement runs out at the end of a sentence, use four periods to show the ellipses and the period at the end of the sentence.

> Thomas Jefferson wrote the Declaration of Independence as a statement of political will and to arouse the peoples of the thirteen colonies: "We hold these Truths to be self-evident, that all Men are created equal . . . with certain unalienable Rights . . . Life, Liberty, and the Pursuit of Happiness. . . . Governments are instituted among Men, deriving their just Powers from the Consent of the Governed."

Ellipses are also used to indicate broken or hesitant speech.

> "I . . . I can't go on," David sighed as he collapsed to the ground.

Slashes

Slashes are used to indicate breaks in lines of poetry when the poetry is reproduced in regular text. The slashes indicate the breaks of the poem's lines to show how the poet originally had written the poem. The original and revised versions of a poem, using slashes to indicate the line breaks, follows. The poem is "From In Memoriam A.H.H." by Alfred, Lord Tennyson.

> Thou wilt not leave us in the dust:
>
> Thou madest man, he knows not why,
>
> He thinks he was not made to die;
>
> And thou hast made him: thou art just.
>
> (Lines 9–12)

Using slashes, these lines of poetry can be incorporated into written text. A single space is placed on both sides of the slash.

> Tennyson used the idea of anxiety and hope for man in his poem "From In Memoriam A.H.H." when he wrote, "Thou wilt not leave us in the dust: / Thou madest man, he knows not why, / He thinks he was not made to die; / And thou hast made him: thou art just." (lines 9–12).

The slashes appear with the punctuation intact from the poem.

Slashes can also be used to indicate that one of two terms is applicable. However, overuse of this construction breaks the flow of a sentence and can become cliché.

> The choice we had was either/or; both could not be chosen.

Work Problems

1. Shorten the following quote from Lincoln's "Gettysburg Address" using ellipses.

   "It is rather for us to be here dedicated to the great task remaining before us—that from these honored dead we take increased devotion to that cause for which they gave the last full measure of devotion—that we here highly resolve that these dead shall not have died in vain, that this nation under God shall have a new birth of freedom, and that government of the people, by the people, for the people shall not perish from the earth."

2. Using slashes, incorporate into text the following lines from the poem "Do Not Go Gentle into That Good Night," by Dylan Thomas.

   > Do not go gentle into that good night,
   >
   > Old age should burn and rave at the close of day;
   >
   > Rage, rage against the dying of the light.
   >
   > (Lines 1–3)

Worked Solutions

1. The trick to excerpting a long quote is to select the phrases that are central to the quote's meaning. Answers may vary.

   ". . .we here highly resolve that these dead shall not have died in vain, that this nation under God shall have a new birth of freedom, and that government of the people, by the people, for the people shall not perish from the earth."

2. One possible answer is:

   Thomas' poem reminds us, "Do not go gentle into that good night, / Old age should burn and rave at the close of day; / Rage, rage against the dying of the light." (lines 1-3)

Capitalization

Capital letters are used for the beginning of sentences; proper names of persons, places, or things; peoples and their languages; proper titles; or any specific name for a location. General locations, such as **street, river,** or **direction,** without a specific designation are usually not capitalized. Consult a good dictionary if specific questions exist about the capitalization of a word.

Follow these rules for correct capitalization:

❏ The beginning of a sentence is always capitalized.

❏ Proper names are always capitalized; this includes a person's given name and the names of peoples and their languages.

   Example: Alex, Brittney, Carl Davidson, Germans, German, Poles, Polish, Spaniards, Spanish, Latinos, Latin, Asians, African Americans.

❏ Professional, civil, military, and religious titles are only capitalized when immediately followed by the person's given name.

   Example: A retired professor taught our class today.

   Example: Professor John Lane was scheduled to teach this class.

   Example: The president of the United States in 1972 was Richard Nixon.

   Example: In 1972, President Richard Nixon visited China.

   Example: Two bishops, a cardinal, and three rabbis attended the conference on human rights.

   Example: Many religious leaders, including Bishop O'Malley, Cardinal Lewis, and Rabbi Berkowitz, attended the conference on human rights.

❏ There are two exceptions to this rule. When someone is introduced or addressed by their title, the title is capitalized.

   Example: Ladies and gentleman, here is the General.

   Example: Thank you, General, for your analysis of the situation.

❏ The pronoun *I* and the interjection *O* are always capitalized.

   Example: Do you think I should go?

   Example: I saw the capitol building last night, and O, what a sight!

❑ Religions, holy books, believers, holidays, and words that refer to a specific deity are capitalized.

Example: Christian, Christianity, the Bible, Christmas, God.

Example: Jew, Judaism, Judaic, Yom Kippur, Yahweh.

Example: Islam, Muslim, Koran or Quran, Ramadan, Allah.

Example: Hindu, Hinduism, Bhagavad-Gita, Brahman.

❑ Geographical names are capitalized, including unofficial but commonly accepted nicknames.

Examples: England, United Kingdom, North Carolina, Tar River, Mississippi River, the Eternal City, Lake Erie, El Salvador, Pacific Ocean, Mediterranean Sea, the Twin Cities, Black Sea, Mount St. Helens, Yellowstone National Park, Slippery Rock State Park, Cross Creek Park, Vietnam Veterans Memorial.

❑ Names of organizations, governmental agencies, institutions, and companies are capitalized. Also, abbreviations, acronyms, or shortened versions of words are capitalized.

Examples: AFL-CIO, ACLU, NTSB, FAA, American Red Cross, Boy Scouts of America, Omicron Delta Kappa, National Institutes of Health, Western Carolina University, Cessna, IBM, Xerox, NC, LA, IMHO, NYSE, UN.

❑ Names of trademarked goods are capitalized.

Examples: Adidas, Puma, Coca Cola, Kleenex, Velcro, Ralph Lauren's Chaps.

❑ Days of the week, months of the year, and holidays are capitalized, but the names of seasons are not capitalized.

Examples: Monday, Friday, March, October, Fourth of July, Veterans Day, Thanksgiving, spring, summer, autumn, winter.

❑ Historical documents, events, periods, and movements are capitalized.

Examples: Magna Carta, Declaration of Independence, Boston Massacre, Romantic Era, Impressionism, Cubism.

❑ Personifications, to give a persona to an object, are capitalized.

Example: At the instant he looked up, Death walked into the room and glared at him.

❑ Words that come from proper names are capitalized.

Examples: Americanized, Marxism, Taoist, Machiavellian.

Note: Be consistent in your treatment of certain words or phrases because both versions of certain words are acceptable (French doors and french doors, Roman numerals and roman numerals).

❑ The titles of books, plays, essays, poems, and subtitles are capitalized. The only words not capitalized in a title are the articles and conjunctions. Prepositions are not capitalized unless they are the first or last word of the title.

Example: Moby-Dick by Herman Melville.

Example: "A Defence of Poetry" by Percy Shelley.

Example: "The Red Wheelbarrow" by William Carlos Williams.

❑ In the title of a work, always capitalize words joined by a hyphen.

Example: "The Anti-American Sentiment in Europe"

Example: "How the Arab-Israeli Peace Accords Began"

❑ Capitalize the first word of a quoted source inside the quotation marks.

   Example: He asked me, "Where are the teachers meeting today?"

❑ Indirect quotes are not capitalized.

   Patrick Henry begged his countryman to give him liberty or give him death.

❑ The names of heavenly bodies are capitalized. The words **earth, moon,** and **sun** are not capitalized, except when cited alone and not with other heavenly bodies.

   Examples: Mercury, Venus, Mars, Halley's Comet, Milky Way.

❑ Compass directions when referring to a specific location are always capitalized. General direction is not capitalized.

   Example: He came from a Southern state.

   Example: She represents the West at the tournament.

   Example: He flew in from an easterly direction.

   Example: Raleigh is west of Greenville.

❑ The names of bridges, buildings, monuments, planes, roads, ships, spacecraft, or other man-made objects are capitalized.

   Examples: The Brooklyn Bridge, Interstate 95, The Empire State Building, The *USS Enterprise*, The Washington Monument, The space shuttle *Endeavor*, The Spirit of St. Louis, The Museum of Natural History (italics, p. 262).

❑ A designated title is always capitalized before a proper name. Also, if a person is a Jr. or Sr., these designations are capitalized.

   Examples: Mr. John Williams, Mrs. Ethel Harris, Ms. Wilma Blane, Dr. Marcus Jackson, Drs. Wilson and Martin, Mr. M. W. Ford, Jr., Rev. Jim Wells.

Example Problems

What should be/should not be capitalized in the following sentences?

1. The restaurant in New York has Americanized European food.

    Answer: Capital letters are used for **New York** because it is a geographical name. **Americanized** comes from the proper name America. **European** is a geographical location and it also denotes a people.

2. Janet is the president of the Ladies Auxiliary at her church.

    Answer: **Janet** is capitalized because the name is the first word of a sentence and a proper name. In this sentence, the title **president** is not capitalized because the person's name (Janet) does not come immediately afterward. Her group is capitalized because it is a proper name for an organization.

3. Members of all faiths: Christians, Jews, Muslims, and Hindus gathered on campus for an all-faiths rally.

    Answer: Religious groups and their followers are capitalized.

4. A fellow from the National Transportation Safety Board gave a lecture on the accidents he had investigated.

    Answer: Government agencies are always capitalized.

5. The NTSB investigator said he often works with representatives of local and state governments, as well as with representatives from the FAA.

    Answer: Capital letters are used with government agencies (abbreviations and acronyms, p. 255).

6. We read *Of Mice and Men* for class today.

    Answer: Titles and subtitles of books, plays, essays, and poems are capitalized. The only words not capitalized in a title are the articles and conjunctions; prepositions are not capitalized unless they are the first or last word of the title.

Work Problems

Please correct the capitalization in the following sentences.

1. The novel we read was *to kill a mockingbird*.

2. we visited the sears tower in chicago.

3. I saw a launch of the space shuttle *voyager* in florida.

4. the afl-cio is a major labor organization in the united states.

5. rene wilson is president of the raleigh rotary club.

6. In two weeks we visited germany, belgium, france, and luxembourg.

7. we were able to see mercury and venus on a clear night in the south.

8. she mentioned to us, "I have nowhere to go during the holidays."

9. john had to show off his new nike sneakers.

10. the civil war took at least two weeks to cover in our class.

Worked Solutions

1. The novel we read was ***To Kill a Mockingbird***. (Capitalize and italicize the titles of books.)

2. **We** visited the **S**ears **T**ower in **C**hicago. (Capitalize the first word of a sentence, the name of a man-made structure, and the name of a city.)

3. I saw a launch of the space shuttle ***Voyager*** in **F**lorida. (Capitalize the actual name of a spacecraft and the name of a state.)

4. The **AFL-CIO** is a major labor organization in the **U**nited **S**tates. (Capitalize the first word in a sentence, the name of an organization, and the name of a country.)

5. **R**ene **W**ilson is president of the **R**aleigh **R**otary **C**lub. (Capitalize the first word of a sentence, the proper name of a person, the name of a city, and the name of an organization.)

6. In two weeks, we visited **G**ermany, **B**elgium, **F**rance, and **L**uxembourg. (Capitalize the names of countries.)

7. **W**e were able to see **M**ercury and **V**enus on a clear night in the **S**outh. (Capitalize the first word of a sentence, the names of planets, and specific compass directions when they refer to geographic locations.)

8. **S**he mentioned to us, "I have nowhere to go during the holidays." (Capitalize the first word of a sentence.)

9. **J**ohn had to show off his new **N**ike sneakers. (Capitalize the first word of a sentence, the proper name of a person, and the name of a trademarked product.)

10. **T**he **C**ivil **W**ar took at least two weeks to cover in our class. (Capitalize the first word in a sentence, a historical event, and the name of a specific class.)

Abbreviations and Acronyms

Abbreviations and acronyms are shortened words, or letters that denote the first letter of each word in a titled organization. When an acronym refers to a specific organization, the letters are always capitalized (capitalization, p. 251).

The following rules apply for correct usage of abbreviations and acronyms:

❑ Abbreviated titles should only be shown with the full name of the person. These titles include those used by college faculty, clergy, government officials, and military personnel. If only the last name is used, it is proper to write out that title in full.

Examples: Prof. John Lane, Rev. Samuel Right, Sen. John Glenn, Gov. Jim Hunt, or Governor Hunt.

❑ Some titles, such as doctor, can be written several different ways; choose only one spelling for each person's name. However, if a person has multiple titles, you can list all of them as appropriate.

Incorrect: Dr. Marsha Feelgood, M.D.

Correct: Dr. Marsha Feelgood

Correct: Marsha Feelgood, M.D.

Correct: Professor and President Mary Wilkins of DePauw University

❑ The names of towns, cities, states, counties, countries, continents, days of the week, months of the year, and units of measurement are not abbreviated when they appear in a sentence:

Example: We rode 120 miles from Raleigh to Winston-Salem. Our next stop was miles away in the neighboring state of South Carolina.

❑ Words such as Avenue, Road, Street, Park, and Company should be abbreviated only when they appear in addresses. It is necessary to write out the designations when used alone in sentences:

Example: Highland Drive is near Greenwood Park, located south of Fayetteville.

❑ The words chapter, page, and volume are written out in the text of papers, but can be abbreviated in a bibliography, a works-cited page, and when listed parenthetically in scholarly and scientific texts.

Example: We were concerned because some of the citations listed conflicting chapters, pages, and volumes. (Spell out these terms because they appear in regular text.)

Example: For information about specific types of wood, see maple (p. 32), oak (pp. 41-42), and cherry (p. 55).

❑ When using accepted abbreviations in a sentence, be sure to be consistent with the use of periods. Do not mix punctuated and unpunctuated abbreviations. Consult a dictionary or style manual for proper use if in doubt. Here are some possibilities:

A.D. or AD　　From the Latin meaning *anno Domini,* Year of our Lord

B.C. or BC　　Meaning before Christ

B.C.E. or BCE　　Meaning before the Common Era

C.E. or CE　　Meaning the Common Era

A.M., AM, a.m., or am　　From the Latin meaning *ante meridiem,* before noon

P.M., PM, p.m., or pm　　From the Latin meaning *post meridiem,* after noon

E.S.T. or EST　　Meaning Eastern Standard Time

❑ When using abbreviations for states, it is not necessary to use periods between the letters of the states.

Example: TX for Texas

Example: Washington, DC

Example: U.S. for United States

Example: USA or U.S.A.

❑ The names of some organizations, government agencies, countries, persons, or things that have been accepted as common usage can be abbreviated in everyday writing:

Examples: TV, CD, VCR, DVD, CDC, NCAA, NFL, PC, ABC, IQ, RFK, NORAD

Abbreviations and Acronyms in Writing

If an abbreviation or acronym might be unfamiliar to the reader, write out the meaning of the abbreviation or acronym the first time it is used to avoid confusion.

The Recording Industry Association of America (RIAA) has begun prosecuting those individuals suspected of online music piracy.

OR

The RIAA (Recording Industry Association of America) has begun prosecuting those individuals suspected of online music piracy.

Common Pitfall: Latin Abbreviations

Certain Latin expressions are abbreviated, but not italicized because they have come into common usage, as shown in the following table:

Abbreviation	*Latin Meaning*	*How it Is Used*
cf.	*confer*	compare
e.g. or eg	*exempli gratia*	for example
et al.	*et alii*	and others
etc.	*et cetera*	and so forth
i.e.	*id est*	that is
vs. or v.	*vide supra*	versus

Example Problems

Explain the reasons for the way the abbreviations and acronyms are handled in the following sentences.

1.   Socrates lived in ancient Greece from 470–399 B.C.

     Answer: In this sentence either **B.C.** or **BC** can be used to designate an abbreviation of the time period.

2.   He addressed the letter as follows: C.W. Smith, 501 E. Maple St., Dallas, TX, 71001.

     Answer: Abbreviations can be used to shorten a person's name. In the address portion, **E.** is an accepted abbreviation for East and **St.** is an accepted abbreviation for Street. Also, in addressing a letter for mailing, **TX** is the proper postal abbreviation for Texas. If in doubt about accepted postal abbreviations, consult a good reference book, dictionary, or local post office.

3.   The case was known as *Martin vs. Tate* by the attorneys involved in the litigation.

     Answer: In this sentence, it is acceptable to refer to the case as **Martin vs. Tate** or **Martin v. Tate.** Also, court cases are italicized (italics, p. 262).

4.   The new PC could accept input from a CD-ROM, DVD, and VCR.

     Answer: Common abbreviations and acronyms for everyday items are acceptable in regular text; the computer field is rife with these.

5.   The U.S. Air Force officer mentioned that he had once worked at NORAD.

     Answer: In this sentence, **U.S. Air Force** is an official designation of a group or organization of the federal government. **NORAD** is abbreviated and capitalized because it is an acronym for the North American Air Defense Command (capitalization, p. 251).

Work Problems

Correct any errors in the use of capitalization, abbreviations, and acronyms in the following sentences.

1. The case named Jackson Smith et al as defendants.

2. Is Maine abbreviated ma or me?

3. The train left from Washington, dc at 5:10 pm. Est.

4. We wrote down the citations in vols, chs, and pgs.

5. Prof Sam Norton spoke as the representative from the cdc.

6. Kay flew from Raleigh to Dallas, Texas, and then onto Houston, Corpus Christi, and San Antonio.

7. Caroline took an iq test when she was about to go to work for the irs.

8. The National Institutes of Health nih released a statement on smallpox.

Worked Solutions

1. The case named Jackson Smith et al**.** as defendants. (A period follows the abbreviation for the Latin phrase *et alii,* meaning "and others.")

2. Is Maine abbreviated **MA** or **ME?** (The abbreviation for Maine is **ME. MA** is the abbreviation for Massachusetts. They are both capitalized.)

3. The train left from Washington, **DC** at 5:10 **pm, EST.**

    OR

    5:10 **p.m., E.S.T.** (The abbreviation for District of Columbia is **DC,** and it is capitalized. **EST, E.S.T., pm,** and **p.m.** are all acceptable abbreviations.)

4. We wrote down the citations in **volumes, chapters,** and **pages.** (In writing sentences, it is not acceptable to abbreviate **volumes, chapters,** or **pages.**)

5. Prof**.** Sam Norton spoke as the representative from the **CDC.** (It is acceptable to abbreviate the title professor as **Prof.** because the person's entire name is used. The abbreviation for the name of a government agency is also capitalized.)

6. Kay flew from Raleigh to Dallas, Texas, and then onto Houston, Corpus Christi, and San Antonio. (Correct as is. Do not abbreviate a state name in the context of a sentence.)

7. Caroline took an **IQ** test when she was about to go to work for the **IRS.** (Capitalize abbreviations that are accepted as common usage and abbreviations for government agencies.)

8. The National Institutes of Health **(NIH)** released a statement on smallpox.

    OR

    The **NIH (National Institutes of Health)** released a statement on smallpox. (Capitalize the abbreviation of an organization. Write out the name of an abbreviated organization the first time it is used in a sentence. After the first time, it is acceptable to use only the abbreviation.)

Numerals

There are only a few rules when using numbers in sentences. The key is consistency.

❑ Whole numbers from one through one hundred are typically spelled out when they occur in regular text; numbers larger than one hundred are written with numerals. However, groups of similar numbers in a sentence should be treated identically.

   Example: One in ten users were disappointed.

   Example: Our school has 320 students.

   Example: We estimate that between 99 and 110 users were surveyed.

   Example: Tom has a collection of 42 cassettes, 127 CDs, and 188 DVDs.

❑ When beginning a sentence with a number, either spell it out or rewrite the sentence so that it does not begin with a number.

   Example: Sixty-eight members were present.

   Example: One thousand two hundred seventy-seven town citizens voted in the last election. OR In the last election, 1,277 citizens from our town voted.

❑ Large numbers can be expressed in several ways:

   Examples: 12 million members, 12,000,000 members, OR twelve million members

❑ It is acceptable to use a combination of numbers and words, always remembering to follow the rules expressed earlier in this list.

   Examples: Sixty million dollars, $60 million, $60,000,000

❑ In business and legal writing, numbers often appear written out and as numerals to avoid confusion.

   Examples: The architect's fees are not to exceed three million (3,000,000) dollars for the project. OR The architect's fees are not to exceed three million dollars ($3,000,000) for the project.

Expressing Dates and Times with Numbers

The following list gives examples of numbers used in dates, years, or decades.

   March 17, 2002 or 17 March 2002

   The sixties, the '60s, or the 1960s

   The eighteenth century, *not* the 18th century

   In 1066, or from 1066 to 1087, or from 1066–1087

Note: In some foreign countries, the expression for March 17, 2002 might appear as 17 March 2002 with the date first, followed by the month and the year. It can also be expressed as 17/03/02 or 17/3/02. In American usage, the same date would be 03/17/02, 3/17/02, or 3/17/2002.

Time of day can be expressed as follows:

> 2 p.m., or 2:00 p.m., or two o'clock in the afternoon
> 6:30 a.m., or six thirty in the morning

Note: It is also okay to use the other forms of AM/PM (abbreviations and acronyms, p. 255).

If international or military time is used, there is no need for the a.m. or p.m. designation because time in either convention is expressed using the 24-hour clock.

> 0300 is 3:00 a.m.
> 1400 is 2:00 p.m.
> 2150 is 9:50 p.m.

Other Uses of Numbers

The following list presents examples of other ways numbers can be used.

- ❑ **Addresses**   1234 Maple Lane, 1600 Pennsylvania Avenue
- ❑ **Decimals**   .0925, 0.238, .10, .5
- ❑ **Percentages**   17½%, 17.3 percent, seventeen point three percent
- ❑ **Pages in books**   page 22, page 104
- ❑ **Chapters in books**   chapter 17
- ❑ **Scenes in plays**   Act V, Scene III; Act II, Scene I, Lines 103–109
- ❑ **Degrees**   79 degrees, 79°
- ❑ **Money** $2.35, twenty one dollars and sixty cents
- ❑ **Identification numbers**   Channel 5, Interstate 95, King James II, Area 51

Example Problems

Explain why each number in the following sentences appears written out or as a numeral.

1. It took sixty-seven out of ninety-five members to reach a quorum.

   Answer: Numbers between one and one hundred are typically written out.

2. The important date to remember is October 12, 1492.

   Answer: Separate date numerals with a comma and express the date in numeral form for the day and year.

3. The city paid $12.7 million to build the bridge.

   Answer: Express the cost in dollars in one of several acceptable ways: **$12.7 million** with the dollar sign as the implied monetary amount, **12.7 million dollars, more than twelve million dollars,** or **nearly thirteen million dollars.**

4. The reference is found in Chapter 8 of the book.

    Answer: If you are referring to a specific chapter, capitalize "Chapter." The specific designation can be expressed in numeric form.

5. In the United States, the 1960s are remembered as a time of great social and political turmoil.

    Answer: In this sentence, either construction, **the 1960s** or **the sixties,** can be used.

Work Problems

In the following sentences, correct any errors in the use of numbers, and explain why you made the correction.

1. We headed down Interstate 95 to Florida.

2. The project is slated to cost no more than two million dollars $2,000,000.

3. The address was listed as 1045 Oak Avenue.

4. The afternoon temperature was sixty-eight degrees Fahrenheit or twenty degrees Celsius.

5. The hamburger special was three seventy five.

6. Geoffrey Chaucer was the master of fourteenth-century literature.

7. July one through three, 1863, was the time of the Battle of Gettysburg.

Worked Solutions

1. We headed down Interstate 95 to Florida. (Correct as is. Identification numbers, such as highway numbers, are represented as numerals.)

2. The project is slated to cost no more than two million dollars ($2,000,000). (In legal and business documents, numbers are often presented in written form, followed by a numeral in parentheses.)

3. The address was listed as 1045 Oak Avenue. (Correct as is. Use the digit form for numerals in an address.)

4. The afternoon temperature was **sixty-eight degrees Fahrenheit** or **twenty degrees Celsius.**

    OR

    The afternoon temperature was **68 degrees Fahrenheit** or **20 degrees Celsius.**

    OR

    The afternoon temperature was **68° F** or **20° C.**

    (Use either numerals or word expressions of numerals for temperature.)

5. The hamburger special was **three dollars seventy-five cents.**

OR

The hamburger special was **$3.75.**

(Use either numerals or word expressions to define currency.)

6. Geoffrey Chaucer was the master of **fourteenth**-century literature.

7. July 1–3, 1863, was the time of the Battle of Gettysburg. (Use numerals to indicate specific dates. A dash can be used to include consecutive dates.)

Italics

Words in italics (for example, *italics*) are slightly slanted to make them stand out from regular print. Most word processors have settings to create italic texts. In handwritten papers or tests (such as essay tests), it is permissible to underline words or phrases that ordinarily would be italicized. *Note:* Because this is a printed book, all the examples in this section are in italics instead of underlined.

Italics are used to give words heavy emphasis, indicate the titles of some types of works (such as book titles), and denote foreign words that have not been adapted to common English usage. The following list illustrates some words and phrases that are still italicized because they remain foreign to most English speakers.

mano a mano	*tête-à-tête*	*prix fixe*
je ne sais quoi	*Doppelgänger*	*coup de grâce*
persona non grata	*pro bono*	*verboten*

If a foreign word makes its way into English language common usage, it is no longer italicized. Usually, repeated use of the word and adoption by the mass media or the publishing industry dictates when a word has entered the vocabulary of English-speaking peoples. When in doubt, always consult a dictionary.

There are quite a few words that have become so common in the English language that they have become part of the language, so they are not written in italics.

rodeo	tote	cappuccino	casino	karaoke
khaki	drama	chauffeur	cuisine	coiffure
boutique	soprano	lasso	kayak	igloo
lemming	ski	bazaar	caravan	taffeta
yogurt	tulip	jackal	mattress	algebra

Italics are used for the titles of books, newspapers, magazines, journals, plays, long poems, comic strips, genera, species, software, movies, paintings, sculpture, and longer musical works.

❑ **Books**   *Tom Sawyer*

❑ **Newspapers**   *The New York Times*

❑ **Magazines**   *People*

- ❑ **Journals**   *Journal of the American Medical Association*
- ❑ **Plays**   *Our Town*
- ❑ **Long poems**   *The Iliad* and *The Odyssey*
- ❑ **Comic strips**   *Calvin and Hobbes*
- ❑ **Genera, species**   *Homo sapiens*
- ❑ **Software**   *Microsoft Windows XP*
- ❑ **Movies**   *Saving Private Ryan*
- ❑ **Paintings**   *Mona Lisa*
- ❑ **Sculpture**   *The Thinker*
- ❑ **Long musical works**   *The Messiah*

Italics are not used for major religious works or major historical documents, such as The Bible, The Declaration of Independence, or The Magna Carta.

Italics are used with court cases.

> *Brown vs. Board of Education of Topeka*
> *Roe vs. Wade*

Also, a shortened version of a court case is italicized.

> It is acknowledged that *Brown* was a landmark case in civil rights.

Italics are used to identify satellites, ships, and spacecraft.

> The first satellite sent into orbit was *Sputnik.*
> One of the oldest ships in the U.S. Navy is the *USS Constitution.*
> The space shuttle *Endeavor* made a historic flight orbiting the earth a record 136 times.

Italics are used to indicate algebraic expressions, illustrations, and statistical symbols.

> *x + y = 12*
> *Figure 2*

Italics are used to highlight or to put emphasis on certain words in a sentence. Be sure not to overuse this convention:

> St. Patrick's Cathedral is a *beautiful* building.
> He mentioned in his letter that the *problems* of the local population affected him.

Example Problems

Explain why italics are used in the following sentences.

1. We invited thirty people to our party last night, but more than *eighty* showed up.

   Answer: Answers may vary; however, in this case the word **eighty** was highlighted to emphasize the enormous difference between the number of people who were invited, and the number who showed up.

2. In the following problem, please refer to *Figure 12.*

   Answer: **Figure 12** is italicized because it refers to an illustration.

3. The attorney working on the case of *Miller vs. Macon County* offered his services *pro bono.*

   Answer: Italicize or underline court cases and Latin expressions. The Latin phrase in this instance means "without charge or fee, or done for the public good without compensation."

4. The *Times-Picayune* from New Orleans gave us the information we needed on Mardi Gras.

   Answer: The newspaper title is italicized in this case. However, even though Mardi Gras is a foreign word (French), it has become accepted into the English language and is not italicized. It does need capitalization because it is a celebration or holiday (capitalization, p. 251).

Work Problems

In the following sentences, add capitalization and italics where appropriate.

1. Did you get a copy of USA Today to see the sports section?

2. The detective spoke of an mo or modus operandi for the crime.

3. We reviewed the case of Miller vs. CA 1973 for our ethics class.

4. Our English Literature class read The Second Shepherd's Play in a study of medieval literature.

5. We installed Windows XP on our laptops this week.

Worked Solutions

1. Did you get a copy of *USA Today* to see the sports section? (Italicize or underline the title of a newspaper or magazine.)

2. The detective spoke of an **MO** or *modus operandi* for the crime. (The phrase **MO** is the abbreviated form of the Latin ***modus operandi,*** which means "a way or method of operating." Also, MO is capitalized as an abbreviation. *Note:* The use of the article, **an,** before MO is correct, as the abbreviation is commonly pronounced *em-o.*) (capitalization, p. 251; abbreviations and acronyms, p. 255; articles, p. 41)

3. We reviewed the case of *Miller vs. CA* (1973) for our ethics class. (Court cases are italicized.)

4. Our English Literature class read *The Second Shepherd's Play* in a study of medieval literature. (The titles of plays are always italicized.)

5. We installed *Windows XP* on our laptops this week. (The titles of software programs are italicized.)

Chapter Problems

Problems

Insert punctuation, capital letters, abbreviations, acronyms, numerals, and italics as needed.

1. we were the first to reach 12 luke street washington north carolina

2. Some 1300 us marines and 5500 sailors shipped out last week on the uss abraham lincoln.

3. Othello is a tragedy by william shakespeare 1564–1616.

4. One of the best rock albums is bostons self-titled album boston and my favorite song is More than a Feeling.

5. The supreme court is hearing new arguments in Wallace vs Jaffree 1985 for a new ruling.

6. There were times when we looked for more information at the same time we had managed to gather quite a few articles on the subject.

7. After the cold front moved through the winds started to howl from the north.

8. The vietnam war began for the united states in 1945 and ended on april 30 1975.

9. The student saw his paper and shouted hallelujah

10. I vaguely remember the poem stopping by a wood on a snowy evening by robert frost.

Answers and Solutions

1. We were the first to reach 12 Luke Street, Washington, North Carolina. **We** is the first word of the sentence, so it is capitalized (capitalization, p. 251). In addresses, commas are placed after the street name **12 Luke Street** and the city Washington (commas, p. 229). The number **12** is written as a numeral because it is part of an address (numerals, p. 259). A period ends a declarative sentence (periods, p. 227).

2. Some 1,300 U.S. Marines and 5,500 sailors shipped out last week on the *USS Abraham Lincoln.* The numbers **1,300** and **5,500** are greater than 100, so they are written as numerals; also commas are used to divide the digits of numerals into groups of three (numerals, p. 259). **U.S. Marines** is capitalized because it is the name of an organization; also, periods are used in **U.S.** because it is an abbreviation for **United States** (capitalization, p. 251; abbreviations and acronyms, p. 255). **USS Abraham Lincoln** is a proper name, so each word is capitalized; it is also the name of a ship, so it is italicized (capitalization, p. 251; italics, p. 262).

3. *Othello* is a tragedy by William Shakespeare (1564–1616). **Othello** is the name of a play, so it is italicized (italics, p. 262). William Shakespeare is a proper name, so it is capitalized (capitalization, p. 251). The numbers **1564** and **1616** represent years, so they are written as numerals (numerals, p. 259). The years of Shakespeare's life are supplementary information, so they are placed in parentheses (parentheses, p. 247).

4. One of the best rock albums is Boston's self-titled album *Boston,* and my favorite song is "More than a Feeling." **Boston** is the name of a rock group; it is a proper name, so it is capitalized (capitalization, p. 251). The **self-titled album** belongs to **Boston**, so an apostrophe is added to the name **Boston** to form the possessive **Boston's** (apostrophes, p. 239). A comma is placed before the coordinating conjunction that joins two independent clauses (commas, p. 229). **More than a Feeling** is the title of a song, so it is surrounded with quotation marks (quotation marks, p. 243). Note that the period ending the sentence is placed inside the quotation marks (periods, p. 227).

5. The Supreme Court is hearing new arguments in *Wallace vs. Jaffree* (1985) for a new ruling. The **Supreme Court** is a government organization, so each word in the name is capitalized (capitalization, p. 251). **Wallace vs. Jaffree** is the name of a court case, so it is italicized (italics, p. 262). Also, a period is placed after **vs.** because it is an abbreviation for *vide supra* (abbreviations and acronyms, p. 255).

6. There were times when we looked for more information; at the same time, we had managed to gather quite a few articles on the subject. The phrase **at the same time** is a transitional phrase joining two independent clauses, so a semicolon is placed before the phrase, and a comma is placed after the phrase (semicolons, p. 233; commas, p. 229).

7. After the cold front moved through, the winds started to howl from the North. A comma is placed after the dependent clause, **After the cold from moved through,** because it precedes an independent clause, **the winds started to howl from the North** (commas, p. 229). The word **North** is a compass direction that refers to a specific location, so it is capitalized (capitalization, p. 251).

8. The Vietnam War began for the United States in 1945 and ended on April 30, 1975. Names of wars, countries, and months are capitalized (capitalization, p. 251). In dates, a comma is used to separate the day of the month from the year (commas, p. 229).

9. The student saw his paper and shouted, "Hallelujah!" The word **Hallelujah** is the first word of a direct quote, so it is capitalized (capitalization, p. 251). Quotation marks are placed around direct quotes (quotation marks, p. 243). An exclamation point is used after Halleluiah to indicate the student's excitement at being finished with his paper; note that the exclamation point is placed inside the quotation marks (exclamation points, p. 238).

10. I vaguely remember the poem "Stopping by a Wood on a Snowy Evening" by Robert Frost. Quotation marks are placed around the title of a short poem (quotation marks, p. 243). Robert Frost is a proper name, so it is capitalized; also, in titles, most words other than articles and prepositions are capitalized (capitalization, p. 251).

Supplemental Chapter Problems

Problems

Insert punctuation, capital letters, abbreviations, acronyms, numerals, italics, or underlining as needed.

1. the state attorneys general filed the lawsuit against the 123 company

2. the hon mike foster presided over the court

3. we read the metamorphosis by franz kafka for our world literature class at the university of alabama

4. neato was an expression i hadn't heard since the sixties

5. the references were found in shel silversteins a light in the attic on pages 84 and 94

6. tabitha was so lovely and had that je ne sais quoi about her

7. we can assume that 1587 people who came to the concert were pleased

8. from what i hear the july 4th celebration is great fun and happens on thursday this year

9. pc magazine had an article about some of the old software programs being used windows 3.1 and windows 95

10. what did you mean

11. she left germany in 1979

12. i found a reference in the world book encyclopedia patton, george s

13. no we dont have any messages for you

14. purple green and gold are the colors we see all the time when were in louisiana during mardi gras season

15. we parked the new well polished cessna 172 at the airport ramp at the same time a large dc 3 landed and we watched it taxi close to us

16. the game is scheduled to begin at 900 pm

17. although piers plowman 1372–1389 was written in the 14th century we are not sure of the exact dates or who wrote it

18. the meeting was scheduled for san diego in may 2003

19. the kittens mother was the jones cat

20. the supreme court decided meyer v holley et al on January 22 2003

21. a new game started at 605 pm pst

22. the class i took was on spanish and portuguese cooking

23. the headline in people magazine was when good celebrities go bad

24. cnn had the best internet web page for us and world news

25. jeffs editor okd the whole manuscript

Answers

1. The State Attorneys General filed the lawsuit against the 123 Company. (capitalization, p. 251)

2. The Hon. Mike Foster presided over the court. (periods, p. 227; capitalization, p. 251)

3. We read "The Metamorphosis" by Franz Kafka for our World Literature class at the University of Alabama. (quotation marks, p. 243; capitalization, p. 251)

4. "Neato" was an expression I hadn't heard since the sixties. (quotation marks, p. 243; capitalization, p. 251; numerals, p. 259)

5. The references were found in Shel Silverstein's *A Light in the Attic* on pages 84 and 94. (capitalization, p. 251; italics, p. 262; numerals, p. 259)

6. Tabitha was so lovely and had that *je ne sais quoi* about her. (capitalization, p. 251; italics, p. 262)

7. We can assume that 1,587 people who came to the concert were pleased. (numerals, p. 259)

8. From what I hear, the July 4th celebration is great fun and happens on Thursday this year. (commas, p. 229; numerals, p. 259; capitalization, p. 251)

9. *PC Magazine* had an article about some of the old software programs being used: *Windows 3.1* and *Windows 95*. (capitalization, p. 251; italics, p. 262)

10. What did you mean? (question marks, p. 238)

11. She left Germany in 1979. (capitalization, p. 251; numerals, p. 259)

12. I found a reference in the *World Book Encyclopedia:* "Patton, George S." (capitalization, p. 251; italics, p. 262; commas, p. 229)

13. No, we don't have any messages for you. (commas, p. 229; apostrophes, p. 239)

14. Purple, green, and gold are the colors we see all the time when we're in Louisiana during Mardi Gras season. (commas, p. 229; capitalization, p. 251)

15. We parked the new, well-polished Cessna 172 at the airport ramp; at the same time, a large DC-3 landed, and we watched it taxi close to us. (commas, p. 229; capitalization, p. 251; semicolons, p. 233)

16. The game is scheduled to begin at 9:00 pm. (colons, p. 236; abbreviations and acronyms, p. 255)

17. Although *Piers Plowman* (1372–1389?) was written in the fourteenth century, we are not sure of the exact dates or who wrote it. (numerals, p. 259; italics, p. 262; question marks, p. 238)

18. The meeting was scheduled for San Diego in May 2003. (capitalization, p. 251; numerals, p. 259)

19. The kitten's mother was the Jones' cat. (apostrophes, p. 239; capitalization, p. 251)

20. The Supreme Court decided *Meyer v. Holley, et al.* on January 22, 2003. (capitalization, p. 251; italics, p. 262; abbreviations and acronyms, p. 255; numerals, p. 259)

21. A new game started at 6:05 p.m., P.S.T. (numerals, p. 259; abbreviations and acronyms, p. 255; commas, p. 229)

22. The class I took was on Spanish and Portuguese cooking. (capitalization, p. 251)

23. The headline in *People Magazine* was "When Good Celebrities Go Bad." (capitalization, p. 251; italics, p. 262; quotation marks, p. 243)

24. CNN had the best Internet Web page for U.S. and world news. (capitalization, p. 251)

25. Jeff's editor OK'd the whole manuscript. (capitalization, p. 251; apostrophes, p. 239)

Customized Full-Length Exam

Find the plural form of the following nouns.

1-1. Tooth

Answer: Teeth

If you answered correctly, go to problem 1-2.
If you answered incorrectly, review plural nouns, p. 36.

1-2. Medium

Answer: Media

If you answered correctly, go to problem 1-3.
If you answered incorrectly, review plural nouns, p. 36.

1-3. Roof

Answer: Roofs

If you answered correctly, go to problem 1-4.
If you answered incorrectly, review plural nouns, p. 36.

1-4. Box

Answer: Boxes

If you answered correctly, go to problem 1-5.
If you answered incorrectly, review plural nouns, p. 36.

1-5. Buzz

Answer: Buzzes

If you answered correctly, go to problem 1-6.
If you answered incorrectly, review plural nouns, p. 36.

1-6. Bunch

Answer: Bunches

If you answered correctly, go to problem 1-7.
If you answered incorrectly, review plural nouns, p. 36.

1-7. Stimulus

Answer: Stimuli

If you answered correctly, go to problem 1-8.
If you answered incorrectly, review plural nouns, p. 36.

1-8. Cab

Answer: Cabs

If you answered correctly, go to problem 1-9.
If you answered incorrectly, review plural nouns, p. 36.

1-9. Brother

Answer: Brothers, brethren

If you answered correctly, go to problem 1-10.
If you answered incorrectly, review plural nouns, p. 36.

1-10. Television

Answer: Televisions

If you answered correctly, go to problem 1-11.
If you answered incorrectly, review plural nouns, p. 36.

In the following sentences, form the possessive case for each.

1-11. _____ (Bill) and _____ (Jeff) cars were repaired by the same garage.

Answer: Bill's and Jeff's cars were repaired by the same garage.

If you answered correctly, go to problem 1-12.
If you answered incorrectly, review showing possession with nouns, p. 38.

1-12. _____ (Eunice) new apartment was quite large.

Answer: Eunice's new apartment was quite large.

If you answered correctly, go to problem 1-13.
If you answered incorrectly, review showing possession with nouns, p. 38.

1-13. The _____ (solicitor general) briefcase was left in the courtroom.

Answer: The solicitor general's briefcase was left in the courtroom.

If you answered correctly, go to problem 1-14.
If you answered incorrectly, review showing possession with nouns, p. 38.

1-14. The _____ (Jones) dog chased a car down the street.

Answer: The Jones's dog chased a car down the street.

If you answered correctly, go to problem 1-15.
If you answered incorrectly, review showing possession with nouns, p. 38.

1-15. My _____ (sister-in-law) flight was delayed this morning.

Answer: My sister-in-law's flight was delayed this morning.

If you answered correctly, go to problem 1-16.
If you answered incorrectly, review showing possession with nouns, p. 38.

1-16. I thought I saw _____ (Elaine) novel in the breakroom.

Answer: I thought I saw Elaine's novel in the breakroom.

If you answered correctly, go to problem 1-17.
If you answered incorrectly, review showing possession with nouns, p. 38.

1-17. The _____ (Horowitz) boat is docked in New Bern.

Answer: The Horowitz's boat is docked in New Bern.

If you answered correctly, go to problem 1-18.
If you answered incorrectly, review showing possession with nouns, p. 38.

1-18. My _____ (mother) and _____ (father) house is white with green shutters.

Answer: My mother and father's house is white with green shutters.

If you answered correctly, go to problem 1-19.
If you answered incorrectly, review showing possession with nouns, p. 38.

1-19. We bought _____ (Delores), _____ (Vicki), and _____ (Leigh) new computers at bargain prices.

Answer: We bought Delores's, Vicki's, and Leigh's new computers at bargain prices.

If you answered correctly, go to problem 1-20.
If you answered incorrectly, review showing possession with nouns, p. 38.

1-20. They had _____ (Barbara) retirement party at the Chinese restaurant.

Answer: They had Barbara's retirement party at the Chinese restaurant.

If you answered correctly, go to problem 1-21.
If you answered incorrectly, review showing possession with nouns, p. 38.

Insert **a, an, the,** or no article in the following problems.

1-21. Donna took _____ computer upstairs to install it in _____ lab.

Answer: Donna took the/a computer upstairs to install it in the/a lab.

If you answered correctly, go to problem 1-22.
If you answered incorrectly, review articles, p. 41.

1-22. He worked at _____ same hospital that I did.

Answer: He worked at the same hospital that I did.

If you answered correctly, go to problem 1-23.
If you answered incorrectly, review articles, p. 41.

1-23. My teacher assigned us _____ homework.

Answer: My teacher assigned us (no article) homework.

If you answered correctly, go to problem 1-24.
If you answered incorrectly, review articles, p. 41.

1-24. _____ police officer stopped _____ motorist for speeding.

Answer: The/A police officer stopped the/a motorist for speeding.

If you answered correctly, go to problem 1-25.
If you answered incorrectly, review articles, p. 41.

1-25. Kurt received _____ prestigious alumni award for community service.

Answer: Kurt received a prestigious alumni award for community service.

If you answered correctly, go to problem 2-1.
If you answered incorrectly, review articles, p. 41.

Select the correct pronoun option.

2-1. Brent saw Jill and I/me at the café.

Answer: Me

If you answered correctly, go to problem 2-3.
If you answered incorrectly, go to problem 2-2.

2-2. Michael and he/him are going to help we/us.

Answer: He, us

If you answered correctly, go to problem 2-3.
If you answered incorrectly, review personal pronouns, p. 51.

2-3. The class who/whom/whose/which/that you took is no longer offered.

Answer: That or which

If you answered correctly, go to problem 2-5.
If you answered incorrectly, go to problem 2-4.

2-4. The professor who/whom/whose you like has retired.

Answer: Whom

If you answered correctly, go to problem 2-5.
If you answered incorrectly, review relative pronouns, p. 57.

2-5. I like this/these plan that you developed.

Answer: This

If you answered correctly, go to problem 2-7.
If you answered incorrectly, go to problem 2-6.

Insert the correct pronoun.

2-6. You can save these seats, but _____ are already taken.

Answer: Those

If you answered correctly, go to problem 2-7.
If you answered incorrectly, review demonstrative pronouns, p. 60.

2-7. They were assigned the project. Because the project is _____, not _____, we should not tell them what to do.

Answer: Theirs, ours

If you answered correctly, go to problem 2-9.
If you answered incorrectly, go to problem 2-8.

2-8. They can do what they want with their profits, but I will invest _____ in the company.

Answer: Mine

If you answered correctly, go to problem 2-9.
If you answered incorrectly, review possessive pronouns, p. 63.

2-9. He cut _____ shaving this morning.

Answer: Himself

If you answered correctly, go to problem 2-11.
If you answered incorrectly, go to problem 2-10.

Select the correct option.

2-10. Margaret and I/me/myself are preparing the holiday dinner.

Answer: I

If you answered correctly, go to problem 2-11.
If you answered incorrectly, review reflexive and intensive pronouns, p. 65.

Insert the correct form of the verb *to be*.

2-11. Everyone _____ talking about the president's speech.

Answer: Is

If you answered correctly, go to problem 2-13.
If you answered incorrectly, go to problem 2-12.

2-12. Few _____ daring enough to climb Mount Everest, and many _____ injured in the attempt.

Answer: Are, are

If you answered correctly, go to problem 2-13.
If you answered incorrectly, review indefinite pronouns, p. 67.

Insert the missing word.

2-13. _____ are you cooking for dinner?

Answer: What

If you answered correctly, go to problem 3-1.
If you answered incorrectly, go to problem 2-14.

2-14. _____ are you inviting to the reception?

Answer: Whom

If you answered correctly, go to problem 3-1.
If you answered incorrectly, review interrogative pronouns, p. 70.

Identify the direct object in the following sentences.

3-1. I am packing my clothes for the trip.

Answer: Clothes

If you answered correctly, go to problem 3-3.
If you answered incorrectly, go to problem 3-2.

3-2. Misha cleaned up the mess we had made.

Answer: Mess

If you answered correctly, go to problem 3-3.
If you answered incorrectly, review transitive and intransitive verbs: direct objects, p. 79.

Identify the direct object and the indirect object in the following sentences.

3-3. Has anyone told Dr. Khoury the good news?

Answer: Direct object = news, indirect object = Dr. Khoury

If you answered correctly, go to problem 3-5.
If you answered incorrectly, go to problem 3-4.

3-4. I gave Lara my purple shirt.

Answer: Direct object = shirt, indirect object = Lara

If you answered correctly, go to problem 3-5.
If you answered incorrectly, review indirect objects, p. 81.

Supply the correct form of the verb indicated.

3-5. I wanted to watch *Citizen Kane,* but Marco said he (see) it already.

Answer: Had seen

If you answered correctly, go to problem 3-7.
If you answered incorrectly, go to problem 3-6.

3-6. Every morning she (go) to the gym to work out.

Answer: Goes

If you answered correctly, go to problem 3-7.
If you answered incorrectly, review verb tenses, p. 84.

Change the following sentences from active to passive.

3-7. Ibrahim is helping Carlos.

Answer: Carlos is being helped by Ibrahim.

If you answered correctly, go to problem 3-9.
If you answered incorrectly, go to problem 3-8.

3-8. The junior class decorated the gym.

Answer: The gym was decorated by the junior class.

If you answered correctly, go to problem 3-9.
If you answered incorrectly, review voice, p. 107.

Supply the correct form of the verb indicated.

3-9. If I (be) a little taller, I could reach that shelf.

Answer: Were

If you answered correctly, go to problem 3-11.
If you answered incorrectly, go to problem 3-10.

3-10. The judge required that the witness (respond) to the question.

Answer: Respond

If you answered correctly, go to problem 3-11.
If you answered incorrectly, review mood, p. 111.

Identify the verb in the following sentences.

3-11. He picked his coat up from the floor.

Answer: Picked up

If you answered correctly, go to problem 3-13.
If you answered incorrectly, go to problem 3-12.

3-12. Put on your sweater.

Answer: Put on

If you answered correctly, go to problem 3-13.
If you answered incorrectly, review phrasal verbs, p. 113.

Choose the correct option.

3-13. I could/might not hear anything he said.

Answer: Could

If you answered correctly, go to problem 3-15.
If you answered incorrectly, go to problem 3-14.

3-14. If I were you, I may/would not let this opportunity get away.

Answer: Would

If you answered correctly, go to problem 3-15.
If you answered incorrectly, review modal auxiliaries, p. 116.

Supply the correct form of the verb indicated.

3-15. His mother warned him about _____ (stay) out late.

Answer: Staying

If you answered correctly, go to problem 3-17.
If you answered incorrectly, go to problem 3-16.

3-16. _____ (finish) all my homework is sometimes difficult.

Answer: Finishing

If you answered correctly, go to problem 3-17.
If you answered incorrectly, review gerunds, p. 120.

3-17. She forgot _____ (add) the sugar to the recipe.

Answer: To add

If you answered correctly, go to problem 3-19.
If you answered incorrectly, go to problem 3-18.

3-18. Tyra asked Brent _____ (go) to the dance.

Answer: To go

If you answered correctly, go to problem 3-19.
If you answered incorrectly, review infinitives, p. 122.

3-19. A _____ (frame) photograph hung on the wall.

Answer: Framed

If you answered correctly, go to problem 4-1.
If you answered incorrectly, go to problem 3-20.

3-20. _____ (see) you there made me very happy.

Answer: Seeing

If you answered correctly, go to problem 4-1.
If you answered incorrectly, review participles, p. 124.

Supply the missing word or words.

4-1. Carrie enjoys hiking, skiing, _____ running.

Answer: And

If you answered correctly, go to problem 4-3.
If you answered incorrectly, go to problem 4-2.

4-2. I want to go out, _____ I have to finish my homework.

Answer: But

If you answered correctly, go to problem 4-4.
If you answered incorrectly, review coordinating conjunctions, p. 135.

4-3. We can _____ eat leftovers _____ go out for a pizza.

Answer: Either, or

If you answered correctly, go to problem 4-5.
If you answered incorrectly, go to problem 4-4.

4-4. This vehicle drives _____ on snow _____ on sand.

Answer: Not only, but also (or not/but)

If you answered correctly, go to problem 4-5.
If you answered incorrectly, review correlative conjunctions, p. 137.

Which sentence has no errors?

4-5. A. Florida is humid because, it rains a lot.

B. Florida is humid, because it rains a lot.

C. Florida is humid because it rains a lot.

Answer: C

If you answered correctly, go to problem 4-7.
If you answered incorrectly, go to problem 4-6.

Supply the missing word.

4-6. I enjoy art class _____ I like to be creative.

Answer: Because

If you answered correctly, go to problem 4-7.
If you answered incorrectly, review subordinating conjunctions, p. 138.

Which sentence has no errors?

4-7. A. The CEO was unavailable; therefore, the vice president handled the decision.

B. The CEO was unavailable therefore the vice president handled the decision.

C. The CEO was unavailable therefore; the vice president handled the decision.

Answer: A

If you answered correctly, go to problem 5-1.
If you answered incorrectly, go to problem 4-8.

Which sentence has no errors?

4-8. A. We went for a swim; afterward we heard there were sharks nearby.

B. We went for a swim afterward we heard there were sharks nearby.

C. We went for a swim; afterward, we heard there were sharks nearby.

Answer: C

If you answered correctly, go to problem 5-1.
If you answered incorrectly, review conjunctive adverbs, p. 143.

Find the prepositions in the following sentences.

5-1.   A person cannot live on 10 dollars per day in Europe.

Answer: A person cannot live <u>on</u> 10 dollars per day <u>in</u> Europe.

If you answered correctly, go to problem 5-2.
If you answered incorrectly, review prepositional phrases, p. 154.

5-2.   Letter writing is not easy for many of us.

Answer: Letter writing is not easy <u>for</u> many <u>of</u> us.

If you answered correctly, go to problem 5-3.
If you answered incorrectly, review prepositions, p. 151.

5-3.   If you go to the dance, you will have fun.

Answer: If you go <u>to</u> the dance, you will have fun.

If you answered correctly, go to problem 5-4.
If you answered incorrectly, review prepositions, p. 151.

5-4.   The hurricane swept across the area with tremendous force.

Answer: The hurricane swept <u>across</u> the area <u>with</u> tremendous force.

If you answered correctly, go to problem 5-5.
If you answered incorrectly, review prepositions, p. 151.

5-5.   Most of us find the meetings uneventful.

Answer: Most <u>of</u> us find the meetings uneventful.

If you answered correctly, go to problem 5-6.
If you answered incorrectly, review prepositions, p. 151.

5-6.   The doctor gave her encouragement throughout the night.

Answer: The doctor gave her encouragement <u>throughout</u> the night.

If you answered correctly, go to problem 5-7.
If you answered incorrectly, review prepositions, p. 151.

5-7.   We could not go without the necessary encouragement.

Answer: We could not go <u>without</u> the necessary encouragement.

If you answered correctly, go to problem 5-8.
If you answered incorrectly, review prepositions, p. 151.

Find the prepositional phrases in the following sentences.

5-8.   Should you get there on time, in spite of leaving late, save me a seat.

Answer: Should you get there <u>on time,</u> <u>in spite of</u> leaving late, save me a seat.

If you answered correctly, go to problem 5-9.
If you answered incorrectly, review prepositional phrases, p. 154.

5-9. We drove to Florida by way of Mississippi and Arkansas.

Answer: We drove <u>to Florida by way of Mississippi and Arkansas</u>.

If you answered correctly, go to problem 5-10.
If you answered incorrectly, review prepositional phrases, p. 154.

5-10. In addition to the candles, please light the oil lanterns.

Answer: <u>In addition to the candles</u>, please light the oil lanterns.

If you answered correctly, go to problem 5-11.
If you answered incorrectly, review prepositional phrases, p. 154.

5-11. Tom wasn't watching and almost stepped in front of a car.

Answer: Tom wasn't watching and almost stepped <u>in front of a car</u>.

If you answered correctly, go to problem 5-12.
If you answered incorrectly, review prepositional phrases, p. 154.

5-12. From here to the house, we heard the children read the same book over and over.

Answer: <u>From here to the house</u>, we heard the children read the same book over and over.

If you answered correctly, go to problem 5-13.
If you answered incorrectly, review prepositional phrases, p. 154.

5-13. We picked up the passengers at the airport.

Answer: We picked up the passengers <u>at the airport</u>.

If you answered correctly, go to problem 5-14.
If you answered incorrectly, review prepositional phrases, p. 154.

5-14. He was found guilty by reason of insanity.

Answer: He was found guilty <u>by reason of insanity</u>.

If you answered correctly, go to problem 5-15.
If you answered incorrectly, review prepositional phrases, p. 154.

5-15. Despite all our best efforts, the party was called off on account of darkness.

Answer: Despite all our best efforts, the party was called off <u>on account of darkness</u>.

If you answered correctly, go to problem 5-16.
If you answered incorrectly, review prepositional phrases, p. 154.

5-16. We left a gift by the front door.

Answer: We left a gift <u>by the front door</u>.

If you answered correctly, go to problem 5-17.
If you answered incorrectly, review prepositional phrases, p. 154.

5-17. Except for all the old computers, the classroom was bare.

Answer: <u>Except for all the old computers</u>, the classroom was bare.

If you answered correctly, go to problem 5-18.
If you answered incorrectly, review prepositional phrases, p. 154.

5-18. The bus waited around the corner from the restaurant.

Answer: The bus waited <u>around the corner</u> <u>from the restaurant</u>.

If you answered correctly, go to problem 5-19.
If you answered incorrectly, review prepositional phrases, p. 154.

5-19. Because we arrived early, the program director had us wait outside in the tent.

Answer: <u>Because we arrived early</u>, the program director had us wait outside <u>in the tent</u>.

If you answered correctly, go to problem 5-20.
If you answered incorrectly, review prepositional phrases, p. 154.

5-20. Down by the river, fishermen plied their trade among the docks.

Answer: <u>Down by the river</u>, fishermen plied their trade <u>among the docks</u>.

If you answered correctly, go to problem 5-21.
If you answered incorrectly, review prepositional phrases, p. 154.

5-21. The case was rescheduled in view of the judge having been called out of town.

Answer: The case was rescheduled <u>in view of the judge</u> having been called <u>out of town</u>.

If you answered correctly, go to problem 5-22.
If you answered incorrectly, review prepositional phrases, p. 154.

5-22. I went into and out of the house several times.

Answer: I went <u>into and out of the house</u> several times.

If you answered correctly, go to problem 5-23.
If you answered incorrectly, review prepositional phrases, p. 154.

5-23. There was an omission from the record.

Answer: There was an omission <u>from the record</u>.

If you answered correctly, go to problem 5-24.
If you answered incorrectly, review prepositional phrases, p. 154.

5-24. We planted a palm tree in the backyard.

Answer: We planted a palm tree <u>in the backyard</u>.

If you answered correctly, go to problem 6-1.
If you answered incorrectly, review prepositional phrases, p. 154.

Find the adjectives in the following sentences.

6-1. It was the 15th rewrite of the paper.

Answer: It was the <u>15th</u> rewrite of the paper.

If you answered correctly, go to problem 6-2.
If you answered incorrectly, review adjectives, p. 161.

6-2. There was an idyllic and serene quality around the lake.

Answer: There was an <u>idyllic and serene</u> quality around the lake.

If you answered correctly, go to problem 6-3.
If you answered incorrectly, review adjectives, p. 161.

6-3. We listened to the lyrical verses of a renowned poet.

Answer: We listened to the <u>lyrical</u> verses of a <u>renowned</u> poet.

If you answered correctly, go to problem 6-4.
If you answered incorrectly, review adjectives, p. 161.

6-4. The audience's response was neither positive nor negative.

Answer: The audience's response was neither <u>positive nor negative</u>.

If you answered correctly, go to problem 6-5.
If you answered incorrectly, review adjectives, p. 161.

6-5. The computer was built with off-the-shelf parts.

Answer: The computer was built with <u>off-the-shelf</u> parts.

If you answered correctly, go to problem 6-6.
If you answered incorrectly, review adjectives, p. 161.

Find the comparatives and superlatives, emphasis words, intensifying adverbs, and unnecessary adverbs, and note each, in the following sentences.

6-6. Sam is a much/more/most better tennis player than Dave.

Answer: Sam is a <u>much</u> better tennis player than Dave. (positive)

If you answered correctly, go to problem 6-7.
If you answered incorrectly, review the section on comparatives and superlatives, p. 170.

6-7. Eric is the much/more/most talented tennis player on the team.

Answer: Eric is the most talented tennis player on the team. (superlative)

If you answered correctly, go to problem 6-8.
If you answered incorrectly, review the section on comparatives and superlatives, p. 170.

6-8.   Joe is much/more/most talented than Sam.

Answer: Joe is more talented than Sam. (comparison)

If you answered correctly, go to problem 6-9.
If you answered incorrectly, review the section on comparatives and superlatives, p. 170.

6-9.   The car's paint scheme is beautiful/more beautiful/most beautiful than a car right from the showroom.

Answer: The car's paint scheme is more beautiful than a car right from the showroom.

If you answered correctly, go to problem 6-10.
If you answered incorrectly, review the section on comparatives and superlatives, p. 170.

6-10.   Really, the results of the survey were somewhat surprising.

Answer: The results of the survey were surprising. (unnecessary words — *really* and *somewhat*)

If you answered correctly, go to problem 6-11.
If you answered incorrectly, review the section on unnecessary adverbs, p. 166.

6-11. We found the documents were basically free from defects.

Answer: We found the documents free from defects. (eliminate *were basically*)

If you answered correctly, go to problem 6-12.
If you answered incorrectly, review the section on unnecessary adverbs, p. 166.

6-12. Ed threw the ball _____ precisely.

Answer: Your answers may vary: very, most, extremely, highly.

If you answered correctly, go to problem 6-13.
If you answered incorrectly, review the section on intensifying adverbs, p. 166.

6-13. It was an almost very perfect day to be outside.

Answer: It was an almost perfect day to be outside.

If you answered correctly, go to problem 6-14.
If you answered incorrectly, review the section on unnecessary adverbs, p. 166.

6-14. Ellen moved rather _____ (hurry) and _____ (quiet) through the store to be home on time for her party.

Answer: Ellen moved rather hurriedly and quietly through the store to be home on time for her party.

If you answered correctly, go to problem 6-15.
If you answered incorrectly, review the section on adverbs, p. 163.

6-15. The _____ ship was docked near the downtown bridge.

    Answer: Your answers may vary: large, huge, colossal, small, old, new, modern.

If you answered correctly, go to problem 6-16.
If you answered incorrectly, review the section on adjectives, p. 161.

Find the adverbs in the following sentences.

6-16. The cat crept up to the tree noiselessly and cunningly.

    Answer: The cat crept up to the tree <u>noiselessly</u> and <u>cunningly</u>.

If you answered correctly, go to problem 6-17.
If you answered incorrectly, review adverbs, p. 163.

6-17. The program was generated locally.

    Answer: The program was generated <u>locally</u>.

If you answered correctly, go to problem 6-18.
If you answered incorrectly, review adverbs, p. 163.

6-18. Luckily, Meg had her first choice of schools.

    Answer: <u>Luckily</u>, Meg had her first choice of schools.

If you answered correctly, go to problem 6-19.
If you answered incorrectly, review adverbs, p. 163.

6-19. The teacher said the sentence was grammatically correct.

    Answer: The teacher said the sentence was <u>grammatically</u> correct.

If you answered correctly, go to problem 6-20.
If you answered incorrectly, review adverbs, p. 163.

6-20. Her dad's advice sounded strong.

    Answer: Her dad's advice sounded <u>strong</u>.

If you answered correctly, go to problem 6-21.
If you answered incorrectly, review adverbs, p. 163.

Find the adjective or adverbial phrases in the following sentences and indicate each.

6-21. They came in from the storm.

    Answer: They came <u>in from the storm</u>. (Adjective phrase)

If you answered correctly, go to problem 6-22.
If you answered incorrectly, review the section on adjective and adverbial phrases, p. 168.

6-22. Even though our team was losing, we remained for the game's end.

Answer: <u>Even though our team was losing</u>, we remained for the game's end. (Adverbial phrase)

If you answered correctly, go to problem 6-23.
If you answered incorrectly, review adjective and adverbial phrases, p. 168.

6-23. We cheered until we were hoarse.

Answer: We cheered <u>until we were hoarse</u>. (Adverbial phrase)

If you answered correctly, go to problem 6-24.
If you answered incorrectly, review adjective and adverbial phrases, p. 168.

6-24. Our enthusiasm was for naught.

Answer: Our enthusiasm was <u>for naught</u>. (Adjective phrase)

If you answered correctly, go to problem 6-25.
If you answered incorrectly, review adjective and adverbial phrases, p. 168.

6-25. We went to the game with the best intentions.

Answer: We went <u>to the game</u> <u>with the best intentions</u>. (Adjective phrase, adjective phrase)

If you answered correctly, go to problem 6-26.
If you answered incorrectly, review adjective and adverbial phrases, p. 168.

In the following sentences, find the correct comparatives and superlatives.

6-26. The solution proved to be great/greater/greatest than the problem.

Answer: The solution proved to be greater than the problem.

If you answered correctly, go to problem 6-27.
If you answered incorrectly, review comparatives and superlatives, p. 170.

6-27. The answer I gave was the intelligent/more intelligent/most intelligent I could give.

Answer: The answer I gave was the most intelligent I could give.

If you answered correctly, go to problem 6-28.
If you answered incorrectly, review comparatives and superlatives, p. 170.

6-28. The teacher's response was a little/less/the least than desired.

Answer: The teacher's response was a little less than desired.

If you answered correctly, go to problem 6-29.
If you answered incorrectly, review comparatives and superlatives, p. 170.

6-29. She complimented me on how well/better/the best I solved the problem.

Answer: She complimented me on how well I solved the problem.

If you answered correctly, go to problem 6-30.
If you answered incorrectly, review comparatives and superlatives, p. 170.

6-30. As a result, I did good/better/the best than the class.

Answer: As a result, I did better than the class.

If you answered correctly, go to problem 6-31.
If you answered incorrectly, review comparatives and superlatives, p. 170.

Correct the dangling and misplaced modifiers in the following sentences.

6-31. The truck hit a pothole driving down the street.

Answer: While driving down the street, the truck hit a pothole.

If you answered correctly, go to problem 6-32.
If you answered incorrectly, review dangling and misplaced modifiers, p. 209.

6-32. He didn't hear the phone ringing in the shower.

Answer: He didn't hear the phone ringing because he was in the shower.

If you answered correctly, go to problem 6-33.
If you answered incorrectly, review dangling and misplaced modifiers, p. 209.

6-33. Upon leaving the stadium, the lights went out.

Answer: When we left the stadium, the lights went out.

If you answered correctly, go to problem 6-34.
If you answered incorrectly, review dangling and misplaced modifiers, p. 209.

6-34. Holding the leash, the dog escaped and ran away.

Answer: While I was holding the leash, the dog escaped and ran away.

If you answered correctly, go to problem 6-35.
If you answered incorrectly, review dangling and misplaced modifiers, p. 209.

6-35. Falling asleep in class, the test proved to be too much for Katie.

Answer: When she fell asleep in class, the test proved to be too much for Katie.

If you answered correctly, go to problem 7-1.
If you answered incorrectly, review dangling and misplaced modifiers, p. 209.

Identify the complete subject in the following sentences.

7-1. Eating fruits and vegetables is good for your health.

Answer: Eating fruits and vegetables

If you answered correctly, go to problem 7-3.
If you answered incorrectly, go to problem 7-2.

7-2. The dogs want to chase the ball.

Answer: The dogs

If you answered correctly, go to problem 7-3.
If you answered incorrectly, review subjects, p. 184.

Identify the predicate in the following sentences.

7-3. Deirdre works at the fabric store.

Answer: Works at the fabric store

If you answered correctly, go to problem 7-5.
If you answered incorrectly, go to problem 7-4.

7-4. My new sweatshirt is too small.

Answer: Is too small

If you answered correctly, go to problem 7-5.
If you answered incorrectly, review predicates, p. 188.

Identify the indirect object in the following sentence.

7-5. I offered Cheryl my help.

Answer: Cheryl

If you answered correctly, go to problem 7-7.
If you answered incorrectly, go to problem 7-6.

Identify the direct object in the following sentence.

7-6. We made salad for the barbecue.

Answer: Salad

If you answered correctly, go to problem 7-7.
If you answered incorrectly, review objects, p. 190.

Identify the noun phrase in the following sentence.

7-7. I asked Stuart to fix my old black-and-white television set.

Answer: My old black-and-white television set

If you answered correctly, go to problem 7-9.
If you answered incorrectly, go to problem 7-8.

Identify the participial phrase in the following sentence.

7-8. My sister's room has a ceiling painted with stars.

Answer: Painted with stars

If you answered correctly, go to problem 7-9
If you answered incorrectly, review phrases, p. 192.

Identify the relative clause in the following sentence.

7-9. The part that you ordered is out of stock.

Answer: That you ordered

If you answered correctly, go to problem 7-11.
If you answered incorrectly, go to problem 7-10.

Identify the independent clause in the following sentence.

7-10. I was late because the bus never came.

Answer: Because the bus never came

If you answered correctly, go to problem 7-11
If you answered incorrectly, review clauses, p. 195.

Is the following sentence compound or complex?

7-11. He did not believe me, even though I had warned him.

Answer: Complex

If you answered correctly, go to problem 7-13.
If you answered incorrectly, go to problem 7-12.

7-12. I finished my work, so I got to go home early.

Answer: Compound

If you answered correctly, go to problem 7-13
If you answered incorrectly, review sentence types: compound and complex, p. 200.

Is the following sentence declarative or imperative?

7-13. Tomorrow will be clear but cold.

Answer: Declarative

If you answered correctly, go to problem 17-15.
If you answered incorrectly, go to problem 7-14.

Change the following sentence to a question.

7-14. Jay knows how to water ski.

Answer: Does Jay know how to water ski?

If you answered correctly, go to problem 7-15.
If you answered incorrectly, review sentence types: declarative, imperative, and interrogative moods, p. 202.

Change the following sentence from active to passive.

7-15. Denise ordered all the supplies.

Answer: All the supplies were ordered by Denise.

If you answered correctly, go to problem 7-17.
If you answered incorrectly, go to problem 7-16.

Change the following sentence from passive to active.

7-16. The pandas were loaned by the government of China.

Answer: The government of China loaned the pandas.

If you answered correctly, go to problem 7-17.
If you answered incorrectly, review sentence types: passive and active voice, p. 204.

Which sentence contains no errors?

7-17. A. The weather was gloomy it rained all day.

   B. The weather was gloomy, and it rained all day.

   C. The weather was gloomy, it rained all day.

Answer: B

If you answered correctly, go to problem 7-18.
If you answered incorrectly, review punctuating clauses within sentences, p. 200.

7-18. A. The book, that I loaned you, belongs to my sister.

   B. The book that I loaned you, belongs to my sister.

   C. The book that I loaned you belongs to my sister.

Answer: C

If you answered correctly, go to problem 8-1.
If you answered incorrectly, review common sentence problems, p. 219.

Correct any errors in the following sentences.

8-1. dr ted mavis was in durham north carolina to give a lecture at duke university about the latest cancer research.

Answer: Dr. Ted Mavis (or Ted Mavis, M.D.) was in Durham, North Carolina, to give a lecture at Duke University about the latest cancer research.

If you answered correctly, go to problem 8-2.
If you answered incorrectly, review capitalization, p. 251.

8-2. Dr. Christina Wendt, M.D. opens her office at 8:30 am every morning.

Answer: Dr. Christina Wendt (or Christina Wendt, M.D.) opens her office at 8:30 a.m. every morning.

If you answered correctly, go to problem 8-3.
If you answered incorrectly, review abbreviations and acronyms, p. 255.

8-3. Michael performs in musical comedies dramatic movies and magic shows.

Answer: Michael performs in musical comedies, dramatic movies, and magic shows.

If you answered correctly, go to problem 8-4.
If you answered incorrectly, review commas, p. 229.

8-4. I moved into the house at 3614 Creole Street in Lafayette Louisiana on June 12 1998.

Answer: I moved into the house at 3614 Creole Street in Lafayette, Louisiana, on June 12, 1998.

If you answered correctly, go to problem 8-5.
If you answered incorrectly, review commas, p. 229.

8-5. Heidi the woman I work with gave me great advice.

Answer: Heidi, the woman I work with, gave me great advice.

If you answered correctly, go to problem 8-6.
If you answered incorrectly, review commas, p. 229.

8-6. Working togther as a team Alex and Janet were able to finish the project on time.

Answer: Working together as a team, Alex and Janet were able to finish the project on time.

If you answered correctly, go to problem 8-7.
If you answered incorrectly, review commas, p. 229.

8-7. You are going to the movie with us tonight aren't you?

Answer: You are going to the movie with us tonight, aren't you?

If you answered correctly, go to problem 8-8.
If you answered incorrectly, review commas, p. 229.

8-8. The House of the Seven Gables is a well known novel by Nathaniel Hawthorne.

Answer: *The House of the Seven Gables* is a well-known novel by Nathaniel Hawthorne.

If you answered correctly, go to problem 8-9.
If you answered incorrectly, review italics, p. 262.

8-9. The defense lawyer in the case of Reynolds vs. Megacorp has done a great deal of work pro bono.

Answer: The defense lawyer in the case of *Reynolds vs. Megacorp* has done a great deal of work *pro bono*.

If you answered correctly, go to problem 8-10.
If you answered incorrectly, review italics, p. 262.

8-10. Here is my advice about motorcycles always drive defensively, and always wear a helmet.

Answer: Here is my advice about motorcycles: Always drive defensively, and always wear a helmet.

If you answered correctly, go to problem 8-11.
If you answered incorrectly, review colons, p. 236.

8-11. My sister-in-law car is a blue Saturn Ion.

Answer: My sister-in-law's car is a blue Saturn Ion.

If you answered correctly, go to problem 8-12.
If you answered incorrectly, review apostrophes, p. 239.

8-12. My mom and dad car is older than I am.

Answer: My mom and dad's car is older than I am.

If you answered correctly, go to problem 8-13.
If you answered incorrectly, review apostrophes, p. 239.

8-13. The artists works were displayed this weekend at a new gallery on Montague Street.

Answer: The artists' works were displayed this weekend at a new gallery on Montague Street.

If you answered correctly, go to problem 8-14.
If you answered incorrectly, review apostrophes, p. 239.

8-14. Its our class turn to take a field trip to the museum and enjoy all its paintings.

Answer: It's our class's turn to take a field trip to the museum and enjoy all its paintings.

If you answered correctly, go to problem 8-15.
If you answered incorrectly, review apostrophes, p. 239.

8-15. The Cask of Amontillado is one of my favorite short stories by Edgar Allan Poe.

Answer: "The Cask of Amontillado" is one of my favorite short stories by Edgar Allan Poe.

If you answered correctly, go to problem 8-16.
If you answered incorrectly, review quotation marks, p. 243.

8-16. That is one of the best movies I've ever seen, she said with a smile.

Answer: "That is one of the best movies I've ever seen," she said with a smile.

If you answered correctly, go to problem 8-17.
If you answered incorrectly, review quotation marks, p. 243.

8-17. Did you ask me a question? she replied in a haughty tone.

Answer: "Did you ask me a question?" she replied in a haughty tone.

If you answered correctly, go to problem 8-18.
If you answered incorrectly, review quotations, p. 243.

8-18. In her speech about the poem The Love Song of J. Alfred Prufrock, Mary said, The reader is presented with a series of metaphors that suggest the narrator's desperate loneliness. Perhaps the best example is the narrator's lament: I should have been a pair of ragged claws scuttling across the floors of silent seas.

Answer: In her speech about the poem "The Love Song of J. Alfred Prufrock," Mary said, "The reader is presented with a series of metaphors that suggest the narrator's desperate loneliness. Perhaps the best example is the narrator's lament: 'I should have been a pair of ragged claws scuttling across the floors of silent seas.'"

If you answered correctly, go to problem 8-19.
If you answered incorrectly, review quotation marks, p. 243.

Correct any problems with numbers and numerals.

8-19. Please give me 3 more minutes to complete the test.

Answer: Please give me three more minutes to complete the test.

If you answered correctly, go to problem 8-20.
If you answered incorrectly, review numerals, p. 259.

8-20. My change jar has 55 quarters, 121 dimes, 67 nickels, and 147 pennies.

Answer: Correct as written.

If you answered incorrectly, review numerals, p. 259.

Appendix A
Glossary

Abbreviation   A shortened version of a word or phrase that is recognizable to most English speaking peoples, for example, *Mr.* for *Mister*, *lb.* for *pound*, *Dr.* for *Doctor*, and so on. Other examples include *BSA* for the *Boys Scouts of America*, *GSA* for the *Girl Scouts of America*, *CIA* for the *Central Intelligence Agency*, *FBI* for the *Federal Bureau of Investigation*, etc.

Absolute phrase   A phrase that includes a noun, a participle, and any words modifying them. Absolute phrases modify the entire sentence, adding information that would not otherwise be known.

Acronym   A word formed from the first letters (or the first few letters) of a series of words. For example, *radar* comes from *ra*dio *d*etecting *a*nd *r*anging; VOR comes from *v*ery high frequency *o*mnidirectional *r*ange finding.

Active   A variety of **voice,** applied to verbs and sentences. In active voice, the subject does the action of the verb. *Example:* Sam *held* the ladder. See also **passive.**

Adjective   A word that modifies a noun or pronoun.

Adverb   A word that modifies a verb, adjective, or other adverb.

Agreement   The requirement that a verb indicate the number and person of its subject, or the requirement that a pronoun indicate the number, person, and gender of the noun it replaces.

Antecedent   The noun or noun phrase that a pronoun replaces.

Appositive   A noun or noun phrase that closely follows another noun and explains, describes, or renames that noun.

Arabic numeral   An actual number, not the word representing that number. For example, *1, 2, 3,* and so on (as opposed to *one, two, three,* and so on).

Articles   *A* or *an* indicate a noun or pronoun in sentences. Nouns that begin with a consonant usually take *a* as an article: a house, a horse, a truck, and so on. Nouns that begin with a vowel or vowel sound (like the *h* in hour) take *an* as their article: an apple, an eel, an hour, an instrument, an order, an umbrella, and so on.

Auxiliary verb   A short verb (usually a form of *to be, to do,* or *to have*) that appears along with the main verb in many verb tense forms, negative verb forms, and verbs inverted to ask questions. Examples: I *do* not think so; they *are* leaving soon. Also called a helping verb.

Capitalization   The use of capital letters and the rules that apply to capital letters in writing or printing.

Case   The form a pronoun takes depending on its grammatical function in the sentence. Case is **nominative** or **objective.**

Clause   A closely related group of words that has both a subject and a verb.

Collective noun   A noun that refers to a specific group of persons, places, or things.

Comma splice   A sentence consisting of at least two independent clauses joined with only a comma (a common sentence error).

Common noun   A nonspecific noun that refers to a general idea and not a specific person, place, or thing. These nouns are not capitalized.

Comparative degree   Compares two related persons, places, or things; used with adjectives and adverbs to compare two nouns.

Complement   A word or phrase that follows a verb and explains, describes, or renames the subject or object of the verb.

Complex sentence   A sentence containing one independent clause and at least one dependent clause

Compound sentence   A sentence containing two independent clauses joined by a coordinating conjunction and a comma, or by a semicolon alone.

Compound-complex sentence   A sentence containing at least two independent clauses plus at least one dependent clause

Conditional   see **"if" clause.**

Conjunction   A word that links or connects other groups of words in a sentence. See **conjunctive adverb, coordinating conjunction, correlative conjunction,** and **subordinating conjunction.**

Conjunctive adverb   A type of conjunction; that is, an adverb that connects independent clauses (*afterwards, besides, therefore*).

Coordinating conjunction   A word that connects words or groups of words of the same grammatical type, such as nouns, clauses, or adjectives (*and, but, or, nor, for, yet, so*).

Correlative conjunction   Conjunctions that are similar to coordinating conjunctions, but consist of two parts. (*either . . . or, such . . . as, not only . . . but also*)

Dangling participle   A participial phrase that is separated from the noun it should modify. Dangling participles often appear at the beginning of a sentence, but do not modify the subject of the sentence.

Demonstrative pronoun   A pronoun pointing out specific things (*this, that, these, those*).

Dependent clause   A clause that depends upon an independent clause to complete its meaning. A dependent clause cannot stand alone as a complete thought.

Direct object   The receiver of the action of a **transitive** verb. Direct objects may be nouns, pronouns, or noun/pronoun phrases. The direct object tells who or what received the action of the verb. *Example:* I bought *candy* (what did I buy? *candy*).

Expletive   A word that has a grammatical function in a sentence but has no meaning of its own. Examples: **do** (when used for questions or negatives); **it** (when used in the construction "It is . . . "); **there** (when used in the construction "There is/are . . . ").

Gerund   A **verbal** that acts as a noun. Gerunds look like the **present participle** form of the verb (base form plus **–ing**). *Example: Running* is good exercise.

"If" clause   A clause introduced by the word *if*, expressing a condition that must be fulfilled before another action can take place. Also called a **conditional.**

imperative   A variety of verb **mood** expressing commands or orders. The implied subject of an imperative verb is always *you*, singular or plural. For example: *Stand* over here; *choose* an answer; *be* quiet. See also **subjunctive** and **indicative.**

Indefinite pronoun   A pronoun that does not refer to any specific antecedent. Indefinite pronouns refer to general or unspecified persons or things (*anyone, everybody, some, many, others,* and so on).

Independent clause   A clause that expresses a complete thought. Because it expresses a complete thought, an independent clause can stand alone as a sentence.

Indicative   A variety of verb **mood.** Indicative is the normal mood of most English verbs, simply stating that an action is so. See also **subjunctive** and **imperative.**

Indirect object   The object of a verb that tells to whom or for whom the action of the verb is done. Indirect objects always appear with **direct objects.** An indirect object is usually a person or other living creature. *Example:* I gave *Lee* a rose. Lee = indirect object (to whom did I give it? to *Lee*); rose = direct object.

Infinitive   A **verbal** that acts as a noun. The infinitive is the particle **to** followed by the base form of the verb. *Example:* You need *to listen* closely.

Intensive pronoun   A pronoun form used for emphasis. The forms are the same as **reflexive pronouns** (*myself, herself, themselves,* and so forth.).

Interrogative   The form of a verb or sentence indicating a question.

Interrogative pronoun   A pronoun introducing a question (*which, what, who, whom*).

Intransitive   A variety of **verb,** one that does not need an object to receive the action of the verb. *Examples:* the sun *shone*, the bell *rang*. See also **transitive.**

Italics   A slanted font *(italics)* that is used in printing to denote items that would be underlined in handwritten or typewritten materials; used to highlight proper names, titles of printed materials, or foreign non-Anglicized words. The phrase comes from an Italian first edition of Virgil's works published in 1501.

Linking verb   An intransitive verb that links the subject to a **subject complement** (such as a **predicate adjective** or **predicate noun**). Forms of the verb *to be* are the best known linking verbs. *Examples:* I *am* happy; the flowers *smell* sweet; the sky *looks* blue.

Misplaced modifier   A well-intentioned modifier that misses the word it was intended to modify in a sentence.

Modal auxiliary   One of a small group of auxiliary verbs which indicate ability, possibility, permission, or obligation (*would, could, should, will, can, shall, might, may, must*).

Modifier   Any word or phrase that describes or limits another word or group of words.

Mood   The quality of a verb expressing how the action of the verb should be thought of. Mood may be **indicative, subjunctive,** or **imperative.**

Negative   A word that expresses contradiction or denial (*no, not, never*). Also, a form of a verb expressing contradiction, generally using the word **not.**

Nominative   The case a pronoun takes when it is the subject of a verb.

Nonrestrictive clause   A clause that gives information that is nonessential or could be omitted without compromising the meaning of a sentence.

Noun   A person, place, or thing. Also, an activity, collection, concept, condition, event, group, or quality. Nouns have both tangible elements and intangible elements.

Noun clause   A clause that acts as a noun (a subject or object) within a sentence. A common example is the "that" clause that follows certain verbs of communication, thought, or emotion.

Noun phrase   A phrase consisting of a noun or pronoun and any words modifying it (such as adjectives, prepositional phrases, participial phrases, and so on).

Numeral   A figure, letter, word, or group of words used to express a number, as in Arabic numerals or numbers, and Roman numerals or numbers.

Object   Something that receives the action of a verb. See **direct object** and **indirect object.**

Object complement   A word or phrase that follows the object of a verb and explains, describes, or renames the object.

Objective   The case a pronoun takes when it is the object of a verb.

Parallelism   A rule of style which says that parts of a sentence that have the same grammatical function or weight should have the same grammatical form.

Participial phrase   A phrase introduced by a participle; participial phrases always modify nouns.

Participle   A **verbal** which acts as an adjective. Participles look like the **present participle** form of the verb (**–ing**) or the **past participle** form of the verb (**-ed** or irregular forms).

Particle   A short word that forms part of a **phrasal verb** or an **infinitive.** In phrasal verbs, particles look exactly like **prepositions** (*to, by, for, on, off,* and so on) but do not have the same meaning or function that prepositions normally do. In an infinitive, the word *to* is a particle.

Passive   A variety of **voice**, applied to verbs and sentences. In passive voice, the subject receives of the action of the verb. *Example:* The ladder *was held* by Sam. See also **active.**

Past participle   For regular verbs, the base form of the verb plus **–ed.** English also has many irregular past participle verb forms. Used in **perfect** verb tenses and also as an adjective (see **participle**).

Perfect   A variety of verb **tense**, used to indicate an action that occurred prior to another action, or a prior action which continues to affect the present situation.

Person   Forms of pronouns or verbs that indicate the relationship to the speaker. Types are first person (the speaker), second person (the person spoken to), and third person (others). These forms can be singular or plural.

	Singular	*Plural*
First person	I	We
Second person	You	You
Third person	He, She, It	They

Personal pronoun   A pronoun that takes the place of nouns referring to people (*I, we, she, they*) or things (*it, they*).

Phrasal verb   A verb that requires more than one word to express its meaning. Phrasal verbs consist of a **verb** and at least one **particle.** *Examples: put on, take off, turn up, come across.*

Phrasal verbs are either separable (the direct object can come between the verb and the particle) or inseparable (the direct object must follow the verb and particle).

Phrase   A closely related group of words that lacks either a subject or a verb. In sentences, phrases act as grammatical units, such as subjects, objects, or modifiers. See also **clause.**

Possessive   The form of a noun or pronoun indicating ownership. Possessive nouns are usually indicated by adding apostrophe+s to the end of the word. Possessive pronouns are indicated by a change in form (mine, hers, theirs). Possessive pronouns also have an adjective form (my, her, their).

Predicate   In a sentence, the verb and any objects, modifiers, or complements associated with it. In a sentence, anything other than the subject is part of the predicate.

Predicate adjective   In a sentence, an adjective following a **linking verb.** The predicate adjective always describes the subject of the sentence. Also called a **subject complement.**

Predicate noun   In a sentence, a noun following a **linking verb.** The predicate noun always renames or explains the subject of the sentence. Also called a **subject complement.**

Predicate prepositional phrase   In a sentence, a prepositional phrase that follows the verb "to be." The predicate prepositional phrase always modifies the subject of the sentence, usually by telling where the subject is.

Preposition   A word or phrase that is used with a noun or pronoun in a sentence.

Prepositional phrase   A phrase that includes a preposition, the noun or pronoun object of the preposition, and any adjectives modifying that object.

Present participle   The base form of a verb plus –ing (singing, flying, hoping). Used in **progressive** verb tenses and also as an adjective (see **participle**).

Progressive   A variety of verb tense, used to indicate an action that is currently in progress or actively taking place. Uses the **present participle** form of the verb.

Pronoun   A word that takes the place of a noun or noun phrase.

Proper noun   A noun that names a specific person, place, thing, particular event, or group. Proper nouns are always capitalized.

Punctuation   The use of certain symbols or marks and the rules that apply to those symbols or marks in writing and printing.

Reciprocal pronoun   A pronoun that indicates mutual action by the subjects of the verb. (each other, one another)

Reflexive pronoun   A pronoun used when the object of a verb in a sentence is the same as its subject.

Relative clause   A dependent clause that refers back to a noun or pronoun.

Relative pronoun   A pronoun that begins a relative clause.

Restrictive clause   A clause that defines or limits a noun or pronoun; commas are not generally used in the clause.

Roman numerals   Roman letters used to represent numerals, for example, I, II, III, IV, V, VI, VII, VIII, IX, X, XI, XII, XIII, L, C, M, and so on.

Run-on sentence   A sentence consisting of at least two independent clauses joined together without proper punctuation or conjunctions (a common sentence error).

Sentence   A subject and predicate that expresses a complete thought.

Sentence fragment   A phrase or dependent clause that is incorrectly used as a complete sentence (a common sentence error). A sentence fragment does not express a complete thought.

Simple   A variety of verb **tense** that is not **perfect** or **progressive.** There are three simple verb tenses: past, present, and future.

Subject   The noun, pronoun, or noun/pronoun phrase that governs the action of the verb in a sentence. In **active** sentences, the subject does the action of the verb. In **passive** sentences, the subject actually receives the action of the verb.

Subject complement   A noun, pronoun, or adjective that follows a **linking verb** (usually a form of the verb *to be*) and describes or explains the subject of the verb. Also called a **predicate noun** or **predicate adjective.**

Subjunctive   A variety of verb **mood** indicating desired, demanded, or hypothetical situations, or situations that are contrary to fact.

Subordinate clause   A clause that depends on an independent clause for its meaning; it cannot stand alone as a complete thought. Also called a **dependent clause.**

Subordinating conjunction   A conjunction that connects **subordinate clauses** to **independent clauses.**

Superlative degree   Adjectives or adverbs used to compare three or more persons, places, or things.

Tense   The function of a verb that expresses when an action takes place (past, present, or future). Tenses may be **simple, perfect,** or **progressive.**

Transitive   A variety of **verb** that needs an object to receive the action of the verb. Examples: The cat *bit* me; I *broke* the plate. See also **intransitive.**

Verb   A word that expresses action, state of being, or condition. In a sentence, every verb must have a subject (a noun or pronoun). Verbs express **tense, mood,** and **voice.**

Verbal   A word form derived from a verb. Verbals do not act as verbs. Instead, they act as nouns or adjectives. **Gerunds, infinitives,** and **participles** are verbals.

Voice   The function of a verb that expresses whether the subject is doing the action of the verb or receiving the action of the verb. Voice is either **active** or **passive.**

"Wh- words"   A group of words that frequently introduce questions *(who, whom, whose, what, which, where, why, when).* The word *how* is included in this category even though it does not begin with *wh.*

Appendix B
Abbreviations

List of State Abbreviations

AL	Alabama	MT	Montana
AK	Alaska	NE	Nebraska
AZ	Arizona	NV	Nevada
AR	Arkansas	NH	New Hampshire
CA	California	NJ	New Jersey
CO	Colorado	NM	New Mexico
CT	Connecticut	NY	New York
DE	Delaware	NC	North Carolina
DC	District of Columbia	ND	North Dakota
FL	Florida	OH	Ohio
GA	Georgia	OK	Oklahoma
GU	Guam	OR	Oregon
HI	Hawaii	PA	Pennsylvania
ID	Idaho	PR	Puerto Rico
IL	Illinois	RI	Rhode Island
IN	Indiana	SC	South Carolina
IA	Iowa	SD	South Dakota
KS	Kansas	TN	Tennessee
KY	Kentucky	TX	Texas
LA	Louisiana	UT	Utah
ME	Maine	VT	Vermont
MD	Maryland	VI	Virgin Islands
MA	Massachusetts	WA	Washington
MI	Michigan	WV	West Virginia
MN	Minnesota	WI	Wisconsin
MS	Mississippi	WY	Wyoming
MO	Missouri		

Other Common Abbreviations

abr.	abridged version
Acad.	academy
anon.	anonymous
app.	appendix
Apr.	April
Assn.	Association
Assoc.	Association
Aug.	August
biog.	biography, biographer, biographical
bk., bks.	book, books
bull.	bulletin
c.	circa, Latin meaning "about, nearly or around," for example: c. 1940
cf.	compare
ch., chs.	chapter, chapters
Coll.	College, Collection
comp.	compiler, compiled by
Cong. Rec.	Congressional Record
cont.	contents, continued
d.	division
DAB	*Dictionary of American Biography*
Dec.	December
dept.	department
dir.	director
diss.	dissertation
DNB	*Dictionary of National Biography*
ed., eds.	editor, editors
enl.	enlarged
et al.	Latin for "and others"
etc.	et cetera, Latin for "and so forth"
Feb.	February
fig.	figure
fwd.	foreword, foreword by

gen. ed.	general edition
govt.	government
GPO	Government Printing Office
HR	House of Representatives, Human Resources
illus.	illustration, illustrated by, illustrator
Inc.	incorporated or including, included
Inst.	Institute, Institution
intl.	international
Jan.	January
jour.	journal
l., ll.	line or lines (from a play or poem)
mag.	magazine
Mar.	March
ms., mss.	manuscript, manuscripts
n., nn.	note or notes
natl.	national
n.d.	no date
no., nos.	number or numbers
Nov.	November
n.p.	no place or no publisher
n. pag.	no pagination
Oct.	October
P	Press
p., pp.	page or pages
pref.	preface or preface by
pseud.	pseudonym
pt., pts.	part or parts
rept.	report or reported by
rev.	revised, revision, review, reviewed by
rpt.	reprint, reprinted
sec., secs.	section, sections
Sept.	September
ser.	series
sic	Latin for "thus," so meaning "as is written"

Soc.	Society
trans.	Supplement
trans.	translated by, translation
U	University
UP	University Press
vol., vols.	volume or volumes

Index